Whiteness

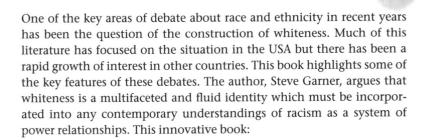

One of the key areas of debate about race and ethnicity in recent years has been the question of the construction of whiteness. Much of this literature has focused on the situation in the USA but there has been a rapid growth of interest in other countries. This book highlights some of the key features of these debates. The author, Steve Garner, argues that whiteness is a multifaceted and fluid identity which must be incorporated into any contemporary understandings of racism as a system of power relationships. This innovative book:

- provides a critical review of key themes for the multidisciplinary literature on whiteness;
- utilises a balanced combination of theory, existing empirical data and new fieldwork to demonstrate how political identities are being expressed with the idea of whiteness holding them together;
- presents ways in which whiteness has been conceptualised in the past and at present;
- presents examples of marginal Whites, nation-building and white minorities.

Whiteness is an essential purchase for students of Sociology, History, Politics and Cultural Studies studying topics relating to Race and Ethnicity and Whiteness Studies.

Steve Garner is Senior Lecturer in Sociology at the University of the West of England, Bristol. He has published on racism, immigration, whiteness and colonialism.

Whiteness

An introduction

Steve Garner

Routledge
Taylor & Francis Group

LONDON AND NEW YORK

First published 2007
by Routledge
2 Park Square, Milton Park, Abingdon, Oxon OX14 4RN

Simultaneously published in the USA and Canada
by Routledge
270 Madison Ave, New York, NY 10016

Routledge is an imprint of the Taylor & Francis Group, an informa business

Typeset in Stone Serif by
RefineCatch Limited, Bungay, Suffolk
Printed and bound in Great Britain by
The Cromwell Press, Trowbridge, Wiltshire

British Library Cataloguing in Publication Data
A catalogue record for this book is available from the British Library

Library of Congress Cataloging in Publication Data
Garner, Steve, 1963–
    Whiteness : an introduction / Steve Garner.
        p. cm.
    ISBN 978-0-415-40363-4 (hardcover)—ISBN 978-0-415-40364-1
(papercover)
    1. Whites – Race identity.   2. Racism.   3. Race discrimination.
I. Title.
    HT1575.G37 2007
    305.8 – dc23   2007002177

ISBN10: 0–415–40363–4 (hbk)
ISBN10: 0–415–40364–2 (pbk)
ISBN10: 0–203–94559–x (ebk)

ISBN13: 978–0–415–40363–4 (hbk)
ISBN13: 978–0–415–40364–1 (pbk)
ISBN13: 978–0–203–94559–9 (ebk)

Contents

Acknowledgements

My fascination with whiteness as a state of being has a long genealogy, going back to experiences in England and the USA in the 1980s, France and Ireland in the 1990s and the early twenty-first century. Working seriously on whiteness as a conceptual tool, however, can be traced back to my interest in the extraordinary experiences of Ireland and the Irish that is still expressing itself in my publications. The background work to my book *Racism in the Irish Experience* (RIE), done in the period 1998–2003, raised a lot of the questions, without providing many answers, and I realised that it could not satisfactorily contain these. I gave a paper at a conference in March 2004, which later became *The Uses of Whiteness*, and began to feed, to a certain extent, into a project on identity, home and community funded by the ESRC. So acknowledgements must go, first, to the people mentioned in the acknowledgements page of RIE, and then to the ESRC, and especially the Programme Director Margie Wetherell, for all her constructive criticism and support. My work never really gets going without a series of dialogues, so the roll of honour must start with my colleague Simon Clarke, whose engagement with the theme has helped me clarify enormously. Thanks also to people who have discussed the idea of whiteness with me, whether they are sceptics or believers, or even dropped me an email on the subject (in alphabetical order): Ama de Graft Aikins, Lisa Anderson-Levy, Les Back, James Barrett, Woody Doane, Charles Gallagher, Yasmin Gunaratnam, Mike Hill, Paul Hoggett, Derek Hook, Caroline Howarth, David James, Cecily Jones, Eric Kaufman, David Lambert, Karyn McKinney, Karim Murji, Alice Pettigrew, Chris Quispel, Diane Reay, David Roediger, Ben Rogaly, Bev Skeggs, Becky Taylor, Ann Twinam, Katherine Tyler, and Paul Watt. If I have missed you off the list I apologise profusely.

Three cohorts of students on my undergraduate module on racism at Bristol-UWE have also contributed to this work, in various ways.

Of course, no-one writes an introductory text without standing on the proverbial shoulders of giants, who are, in this case, *inter alia*: James Baldwin, W.E.B. Du Bois, Toni Morrison, bell hooks, Cheryl Harris, David Roediger, John Hartigan, Ruth Frankenberg, Charles Mills, and Richard Dyer.

At Routledge, I was fortunate to have very competent and supportive colleagues, Gerhard Boomgarden and Constance Sutherland, then Ann Carter.

As ever, my family bear the brunt of writing activity, and I thank them for their love and support.

Introduction

The political stakes of using whiteness

What is 'whiteness' exactly, and what is the point of using it as a separate problematic in the social sciences? Isn't this exactly the kind of American cultural imposition that Bourdieu and Wacquant (1998) rail against? How could American debates have relevance in Britain, Latin America, Australia, for example? The first thing to establish is that whiteness has no stable consensual meaning, and has been conceptualised in a number of different yet not mutually exclusive forms. As much as anything, it is a lens through which particular aspects of social relationships can be apprehended.

When, in early 2004, I began the task of grappling with whiteness as it had been deployed by academics in the USA, I did so with two assumptions. The first was that whatever was specific about one country's historical experience and the ways that the fiction of 'race' are managed collectively, it could not be specific to another's. The meanings attached to 'race' are always time- and place-specific, part of each national racial regime. Whiteness is no exception. The second was that whatever I was studying had to be part of the endeavour to contribute to anti-racist scholarship, by emphasising the social relationships referred to as racism. Since then, after conducting qualitative research, and through reading through and talking around issues that using whiteness throws up, I have realised that when we talk about this topic we do so from points of knowledge and experience in which such assumptions are not the norm. In this book, I want to emphasise that these two assumptions have guided me so far and I have no reason to replace them. In fact, I am pushed to stress, first, that the best way to understand whiteness is to think both relationally and comparatively, and second, that if what we are doing is not a contribution to anti-racist scholarship then we should stop doing it immediately.

There are two main problems that this position generates. First of all, not everyone yet agrees as to how best to combat racism. This would be true even if the academic study of whiteness did not exist. As it does, the debate about whether using whiteness actually contributes anything will go on. Sara Ahmed's (2004) influential article, for example, declares whiteness as non-performative (i.e. unable to actually be anti-racist given the structural racism that surrounds production of texts on whiteness). Howard (2004) criticises the use of racist ideas within the whiteness paradigm, and Eric Kaufman (2006b) calls the whiteness paradigm a 'blunt instrument', and likens it to a training bicycle with stabilisers in the developmental sequence of studies of ethnicity. Clearly, these critiques require responses, which shall be attempted on the back of the arguments presented here, and expressed in the final chapter. Moreover, many social scientists are squeamish about using the term 'whiteness'. Wendy Shaw notes that '. . . research on whiteness has tended to suffer from guilt by discursive association with the bulk of *Whiteness Studies*' (2006: 854).

This guilt derives, first, from the perceived dangers involved in giving credence to racists who think that 'white' really is a 'race', with an essential cultural core and collective destiny. Second, there is the conceptual problem of the limits of whiteness. How do we know what we are studying is 'whiteness' and not something else? Don't we already have enough conceptual arms in the arsenal (racialisation, dominant ethnicities, etc.) without further complicating things by contriving another? These questions haunt the writing of this book, and I am by no means a whiteness 'booster'. Like any other analytical tool, the whiteness problematic has particular limits and advantages, but is not a groundbreaking panacea. I make no claims for its application outside the field of the social sciences, and have no wish to use it as an excuse to focus solely on the ways white people do things per se. In this book, I present an argument, based on my reading of the texts, as to what the limits and advantages might be. I concede from the outset that someone else might have produced a different text from the one that follows; however, this is an introductory text aiming to highlight work, raise further questions and encourage engagement: it is not an overarching super-theory nor even a definitive answer.

My relational and comparative argument is that:

1   'White' is a marked racialised identity whose precise meanings derive from national racial regimes.
2   Whiteness as an identity exists only in so far as other racialised identities, such as blackness, Asianness, etc., exist.
3   Whiteness has been conceptualised over the century or so since it was first used, as terror, systemic supremacy, absence/invisibility, norms, cultural capital, and contingent hierarchies (Garner 2006).

4   Whiteness is also a problematic, or an analytical *perspective*: that is, a way of formulating questions about social relations.
5   The invocation of white identities may suspend other social divisions and link people who share whiteness to dominant social locations, even though the actors are themselves in positions of relative powerlessness.

That argument is presented in three sections of the book. Chapters 1–4 deal with the ways in which whiteness has been theorised and applied to social relationships so far. Since the predominant academic production of work on whiteness has emanated from the USA, it is, I think, normal to see it as the cradle of such theory and thus to give it adequate coverage. However, the essence of the book involves invoking comparative perspectives, both historical and geographical, so chapters 5–7 look at some case studies of the significance of whiteness in other contexts. I attempt here to make some connections enabled by using whiteness as a tool. Chapters 8–9 draw more on empirical fieldwork done in the UK since the early 1990s and particularly the beginning of the twenty-first century. Here I apologise to readers keen to work with the concept in the contexts of Australia, New Zealand, Canada and South Africa, for example. There is a little on Australia and nothing here on the other three countries.[1] My knowledge is based primarily on the UK, the USA, Ireland, the anglophone Caribbean, and Latin America. My strategy consists of highlighting the key areas, pointing the reader towards the in-depth reading to follow up on these arguments, and trying to give a flavour of the variety of approaches and ways to use whiteness as a tool for social scientists engaged in the analysis of racism.

Indeed, throughout the argument I will be stressing the necessity of keeping focused on the unique set of power relations that constitute racism, rather than slipping into an identity-focused paradigm (Field 2001). Steve Bruce (2000) contends that a fundamentalist in religious terms is a person who places absolute primacy on the foundational text(s). I have to confess that if such a definition is extended, I am a fundamentalist on the issue of whiteness. The initial impetus for theorising whiteness was an anti-racist recasting of the world through a critique of existing power relations by African-Americans (see chapter 1), and one of my arguments is that analysing whiteness is only effective when deployed to accomplish this end.

There is some discussion of whiteness as a way of re-centring the academic gaze onto white males and creating a subdiscipline for academic advancement (Ahmed 2004, Andersen 2003). This type of outcome is one of the pitfalls of not reading the founding texts, produced from the multiple perspectives subsumed by the term 'African-American', and the questions they raise about social location and the wider structures of oppression. Put bluntly, if you are a white academic or student reading Du Bois, Baldwin, Wells, hooks, Hughes, Ellison, etc., you are forced to identify yourself within their narratives. Even though you might place yourself ethically on the side of the oppressed in this process, in relation to the structures that place parameters on collective development, progress and freedoms, you are inescapably granted advantages (regardless of gender, age or class) that you would not enjoy if you were not racialised as white. It is not only a question of being one thing rather than another, but that the social locations make sense only relative to each other, and within a broader social structure. As Mills (1997: 11) asserts, in relation to his concept of the 'Racial Contract': 'All whites are beneficiaries of the Contract, though some whites are not signatories to it'.

To draw a loose parallel, if you are a non-union employee in an industry where the union negotiates more advantageous conditions, you will still benefit from those after a deal has been made, whether or not you campaigned, wanted (or even voted) for them in a ballot.

This realisation can be traumatic for those white people who see themselves as not racist, even liberal, or whatever other adjective you wish to use. Research that we shall look at more closely (Phoenix 1996, Farough 2004, McKinney 2005) suggests that white people frequently construct themselves as raceless individuals, unfettered by the kinds of collective identifications that they view other people as having. The distinction between white/individual and non-white/communal represents a way of understanding the world that has developed since Enlightenment thinkers instated the rational European individual at the top of the hierarchy as the universal man (Eze 1997). Moreover, of the three discursive repertoires in which Ruth Frankenberg's (1994: 188) interviewees respond – 'essentialist racism, color and power evasion, and race cognisance' – evasion seems the most pervasive, generated as it is in the 'production of a white self innocent of racism' (ibid.).

What is important for us is to understand that one of the constitutive elements of white identities in late modernity is to simultaneously see and not see difference. While many whites consider themselves free individuals who have selected the path to take and chosen not to be prejudiced against Others, they still frequently see those Others as racialised (rather than as individuals), trapped in prejudice (maybe historical), and unable to make the step up from the world of communally-defined rights and wrongs to the level playing field of contemporary colour-blind western democracies. Indeed, seeing 'race' at all is often imagined as being racist in itself. Like gender ('Surely women are now equal to men?'), and class ('Surely that is a divisive old-fashioned way of looking at the world?'), 'race' often is viewed as something that doesn't matter any more, especially if the interlocutor has some black or Asian friends or acquaintances. 'We don't think of her/him as one of them, (s)he's one of us.'

Thinking about whiteness as a *system* of privilege is a huge source of anxiety for individuals who consider themselves white. The often venomous media coverage of 'whiteness studies' in America testifies to the profound defensiveness that shifting the gaze onto white privilege engenders. The message is clear: scrutiny of the dominant rather than minority racialised group is invalid. One commentator expresses his understanding thus: 'The essence of the discipline can be summed up in two words: Hating Whitey'.[2] This representation of the thrust of whiteness studies wilfully displaces the argument from the complexity of group relations to the focus on responses to racism. Studying whiteness links the realm of individual prejudices with the systemic patterns of discrimination that began before we were born *and whose impact is still felt today*. The conclusion for the liberal individual is that she cannot overcome the collective institutionalised structures of oppression, and has a stake in not wanting to. Of course there are stakes in not wanting to, which I address below, but this is merely a brief introduction to try and make the nub of the problem apparent.

A further reason for deploying whiteness as a lens is that it strips a normative privileged identity of its cloak of invisibility. John Hartigan provides a concise definition of whiteness, 'as a concept honed by academics and activists' in the introduction to his cultural analysis of white people (Hartigan 2005: 1). 'Whiteness', he argues, 'asserts the obvious and overlooked fact that whites are racially interested and motivated. Whiteness both names and critiques hegemonic beliefs and practices that designate white people as "normal" and racially "unmarked". '

Indeed, for decades, the gaze of white academia has been trained on those defined as Other, whether using the terminology of 'race' or ethnicity. The researcher would go and gather data about and/or from communities and individuals representative of what came to be labelled 'minorities'. The dominant post-war 'race relations' paradigm (Miles 1993, Jacobson 1998) constructed racialised communities which it then placed in antagonistic relationships. A number of studies of minorities began to constitute the corpus. It was not until the late 1970s that a serious attempt was made to theorise the relationship between the state, the dominant majority and the minorities in the UK (Hall *et al.* 1978) and this was not exactly followed up by a stampede of researchers.[3]

Indeed in Britain it has only been since the mid 1990s that ethnographers and sociologists have gone into the field intent on problematising white people as agents in racialisation (Hoggett *et al.* 1996, Back 1996, Phoenix 1996). It was in this period also that one of the key cultural studies texts in the field, Richard Dyer's *White* (1997), was published. The objective was to mark white as a racialised identity like any other. Yet crucially, and this is the point that makes everything else in this book comprehensible, *unlike any other*, because it is the dominant, normalised location. All deviance in societies dominated by white people is measured as distance from selected white norms of a given society. Those norms are usually class-based, gender-biased and ageist, they may or may not be secular or Christian to varying degrees, but the key point is that these norms dictate the criteria by which the behaviour of people who are not racialised as white are understood and evaluated. What we are trying to do when we use whiteness as a conceptual tool is insert an intellectual crowbar between whiteness as 'looking white', and whiteness as the performance of culture and the enactment of power, then pull the crowbar down.

Yet what we see when we decouple, or dis-articulate, these two constitutive elements of 'race' – bodies and culture – differs from one place to another and from one period to another. This is elementary social science: social structures and significance cannot be envisaged or comprehended as either frozen in time or universal. Indeed, in working here on a topic potentially as ideologically bloated as whiteness, one way to focus is by carefully examining context for its precise tempo-spatial relevance. I hope therefore to acknowledge Pierre Bourdieu and Loïc Wacquant's claim (1998: 109) that: 'Cultural imperialism rests on the power to universalize particularisms related to a specific historical tradition by making them (mis)understood as universally true'.[4] They are writing primarily about the imposition of multiculturalism in its American sense, as well as the black–white binary, on other nations' structures for attaching meaning to the social. Yet the critique is more widely pertinent than this. The obvious thing to say is that the US model of blackness and whiteness is not applicable *in toto* to other contexts, but how and why is more interesting. So if you come to this text with the idea that any attempt to use whiteness in other contexts is potentially dangerous, I encourage you to bear with me.

What strikes me most about using whiteness to understand aspects of social relationships is how it might impact on the emancipatory possibilities of white social identities. There are a number of positions on this question, ranging from the 'race traitors', who seek to abolish whiteness, to those who want instead to inscribe an oppositional radical whiteness,[5] and all points in between. If you think using the whiteness problematic is a waste of energy in the fight against racism, you will not be on this spectrum at all. Yet if you have read this far, you might still be interested in where we are going with this.

While 'abolishing whiteness' has a pleasing ring to it, it seems more like wishful thinking than a programme. Oppositional whiteness, on the other hand, plays dangerously with the racialised identity that has generated if not channelled oppression for centuries. Part of the argument put forward in this book is driven by the need to dismantle the idea that 'white' is a monolithic identity, and make it apparent that the privilege accrued is actually masking far more harmful inequalities affecting the vast majority of white people, through the disproportionate control of resources by tiny minorities. However much you can disaggregate the populations covered by the location 'white' into classes, genders, regions, religions, and political identifications, the structure of discrimination means that the option of identifying as white in particular social and political contexts remains open and rewarding. Thinking of yourself as 'white', as the whiteness problematic forces you to do, means you are trying to understand how you as an individual are ensnared in the social relationship of oppressed and oppressor, where the very fact that white is a social identity implies that 'black', 'Asian', 'Latino', 'Indigenous', 'Pakeha' – or whatever the categories are called in your racial regime at this time – are also conjured into being. Logically, the abolition of whiteness means the abolition of blackness and Asianness and so forth. White anti-racists are caught between the urge to assert the equality of 'races', and the necessity of deconstructing it under conditions that do not allow the actors to let go of their racialised identities with the same consequences. This is clearly non-performative in Sara Ahmed's terms, but it is an objective whose attainment necessitates passing through stages of apparently counter-productive work. First, this involves acknowledging that whiteness is a source of terror, realising that white people are part of the privileged structure regardless of what their personal opinions may be and wherever they lie in the social hierarchy. Second, it means drawing attention to whiteness in a way that suggests it is a real *social* identity. This approach inevitably gives rise to a number of pitfalls, which I indicate in the sections below:

FIVE PITFALLS OF USING WHITENESS AS A PARADIGM

Pitfall 1: Reification

The term 'reifying', drawn from Marx, means turning something that is an effect of ideology, rather than a real thing, into an object itself. Reification occurs when an abstract concept (e.g. one created to describe a relationship) is treated as a concrete thing. Georg Lukács (1971: 83) contends that: 'Its basis is that *a relation between people* takes on the character of a thing and thus acquires a "phantom objectivity", an autonomy that seems so strictly rational and all-embracing as to conceal every trace of its fundamental nature: the relation between people' (my emphasis).

The first pitfall of analysing whiteness is thus to reify it. In other words, by studying the racial identity, 'white', which has been constructed historically as an exploitative set of power relations – and only in relation to Others – it may appear to be a homogenous group recognised as having biological and cultural links across time and space. The 'white race' per se, as a transnational homogenous bloc, is not mentioned until the mid nineteenth century, although white had been used to describe groups of people in the New World for a couple of hundred years before that. Even then, racialised subdivisions began to form part of the picture, in the writings of Gobineau, Knox, and later Chamberlain.[6] So, instead of treating whiteness as a social relationship, or process, or any other viewpoint characterising social science, whiteness becomes an object in itself. The idea of reification can also be described using the vocabulary of essentialism, wherein biological essences are seen as constituting the core of a group's identity. From this perspective, there are elements of whiteness to do with the social as well as the biological, which are transmitted inter-generationally. The error of reification bestows legitimacy on groups proclaiming either white supremacy or white victimhood (as a result of multicultural policies argued to have tilted the balance of power away from the indigenous white population) or both simultaneously.

Pitfall 2: Whiteness is merely fluid and contingent

The counter pitfall to number one is that of conceptualising 'whiteness' as the opposite of essentialised. In approaches developed from postmodernism, social identities are seen primarily as hybrid, contingent and fluid, almost to the point of representing a choice. 'Race' is just one trope like others. The element of cultural choice is emphasised to the exclusion of the material (or structural) parameters on people's agency, to give the idea of people opting in and out of racial identification. Here 'race' as a social identity becomes so de-essentialised that the approach undermines its relevance by over-emphasising context and fluidity. The solidity of specific configurations and power relationships thus melts into the air of hybridity, devoid of an understanding about how asymmetrical the choices and relationships between them are (Dei 1999, 2000). If white is simply one of a range of identity products open to a consumer, like which ringtone to download, it becomes difficult to explain the enduring patterns of diminished life chances for those not racialised as white, if this question even remains on the agenda.

Pitfall 3: The level playing field

Whiteness invokes power relations. It will be argued throughout that whiteness represents normality, dominance, and control. While the enterprise of marking it as a racialised identity should involve the same rigour as that applied to other racialised identities, it is paramount to remember that white is *not* like any other racialised identity. This is not to argue that white privilege is experienced and distributed evenly, just as the effects of racism are not experienced identically or evenly by its victims.

The various racialised identities do not lie on a level playing field. Lynching was not a cultural practice replicated by African-Americans. Hispanic Americans do not organise campaigns and sign covenants to keep White Americans out of their residential areas in urban settings. Gypsy-Travellers do not take property developers to court when the latter attempt to build on land adjoining their sites. To lose sight of this imbalance allows identity politics based on white victimhood to be given credence. A constant refrain in what might be described as the 'backlash' against multiculturalism and racial equality that has been identified in fieldwork and public discourse since the 1980s (Hewitt 2005) is that the balance of justice has tipped away from the indigenous white population towards minorities. It is not clear from statistical analyses of poverty, educational achievement, health, etc., that minor- ities have made absolute rather than relative progress. Programmes such as affirmative action are cited as unfair impositions on white male employment, while the variety of efforts made by public authorities to reduce verbal abuse is constructed as authoritarian control over people's freedom of expression: the dreaded 'political correctness'. The problem for social scientists interested in the racialisation of white identities is how to represent these discursive claims and figure out what the conditions of their production are, without endorsing them as uncontested reality. Karyn McKinney (2005), for example, demonstrates how the white undergraduates she works with understand their racial positions as disadvantaged because of affirmative action programmes and due to social taboos on language. Addressing racialised difference may manifest itself in what is referred to in the USA as 'color blind' racism (Bonilla-Silva 2003), in which the period of racial discrimination is viewed as historical and complete.

Awareness or acknowledgement of wider structural racism is absent, and the model is one in which all 'races' compete for resources on a level playing field. However, the contemporary situation is viewed not as of disproportionate power being held by a small minority of white people, but of all the breaks being given to everyone else. The loss of economic and cultural status can thus be displaced onto 'people of colour' who are constructed as taking unfair advantage of loopholes, and the shackles binding white people.

Pitfall 4: 'Recentring'

One problem that emerges is that the focus of research can shift to the details of white identities. I argue that the foci of studies in whiteness should always be racism and racialisation. How do these relationships become embodied in real people in real places at specific times? If analysis becomes solely the dissection of fine distinctions between various groups of white people, then we are moving away from this ethos towards studies of class, gender, sexuality per se. They are fine, but are not directly of concern to us in an introduction to whiteness. Jesse Daniels (1997), for example, shows how white men and women are racialised (and sexualised) in far-right propaganda in America, yet she does so by using a comparative method, showing how the process also impacts on representations of African- and Jewish-Americans. Her study is about whiteness explicitly projected as a dominant and cherished identity, but shows how the discourses of power relate to racism, class, gender, sexuality and nation. One of the points to be made in the following chapters is that whiteness has two simultaneous borders: one between white and Other and the second separating grades of whiteness. Over-emphasis on the latter is problematic. In zooming in on the distinctions at that end, the overarching frame goes out of focus.

Pitfall 5: Assuming that analysing whiteness is an anti-racist procedure per se

This could in some ways be seen as a synthesis of the first four. Clearly, if we assume that merely by trying to mark whiteness as a racialised location we are producing anti-racist scholarship, then there is plenty of leeway for error. The assumptions underlying our research questions, our methods, focus and the dissemination of our work are all areas where the outcomes may unintentionally bolster, rather than challenge, the racialised status quo. Moreover, most of us work and study in institutional contexts where white people wield the most decision-making power and hold the highest-paid jobs.

One of the many challenges arising from this work is to try and pick up the thread and find ways to make this type of work have an impact.

Having flagged these issues at an early stage we will encounter some of them in the first section on theories.

The structure of the book

In the chapters that follow I am going to suggest that the ways in which whiteness has been theorised reflect the multidisciplinary tensions of the work done on it. This is hardly a surprising conclusion, given that academics from cultural studies, literary criticism, law, history, philosophy and political sciences have accompanied sociologists, ethnologists and anthropologists in this enterprise. This all means that when someone asks me 'what is the definition of whiteness?' I find it impossible to answer directly. You may as well ask 'what is the definition of love?' or of 'sadness'. I have indicated that whiteness is a theoretical approach as much as anything else, in which it is presumed that practices and discourses engaged in reflect white dominance in a given society. They do this by bolstering the idea that white people (regardless of sex, age, class, etc.) have particular collective claims on the nation which are and should be prioritised by the state over those of other groups. These claims can only make sense if the centuries-long ideological labour establishing the idea that white people are superior in terms of civilisation is acknowledged. A person racialised as white can be ideologically exiled from this privilege, or may pursue values seen as antagonistic, or adhere to a minority religion, or are from a different country, for example (e.g. Travellers/Gypsies, 'white trash', Jews, various migrant groups such as the Irish in Britain). The function that whiteness as a social identity performs is to temporarily dissolve other social differences – sex, age, class, region and nation – into a delusion that the people labelled white have more in common with each other than they do with anyone else, purely because of what they are not – black, Asian, asylum seeker, etc. After looking at a lot of texts on whiteness produced in the USA, my conclusion was that whiteness is not one thing in particular but simultaneously a problematic – a set of conceptual frameworks – and a collection of rival perspectives about the effects of power. I decided to group the mainstream approaches deployed into five themes (Garner 2006), which, with revisions, provide the structure for the first section of this book, chapters 1–4. These are: terror/supremacy, invisibility-absence/visibility-content, norms and values, cultural capital and contingent hierarchies. It will become apparent in the second and third part (chapters 5–7 and 8–9, respectively) that elsewhere in the world, other issues are addressed more than those exercising our American colleagues over the past two decades. Whatever the focus, however, the dissolving of other lines of difference remains a recurrent feature in the functioning of these mechanisms. In a way, the capacity of whiteness to shut down other avenues of difference that count a lot in people's lives is similar to the power of nationalism. Indeed, the point at which a discourse of whiteness in our own fieldwork[7] became most acute was where nation was invoked as the property (in terms of space, money, culture and the ability to say what is normal and what is not) of particular people vis-à-vis others: ownership, as we know, is a primary source of power.

1 Whiteness as terror and supremacy

I think that one fantasy of whiteness is that the threatening Other is always a terrorist. This projection enables many white people to imagine there is no representation of whiteness as terror, as terrorizing.

(bell hooks 1992: 174)

On 22 July 2005, armed British police held down and shot a man several times in an underground train at Stockwell station, South London. He had been chased into the station by detectives searching for suspects involved in the attempted bombings in London that had taken place the previous day. The police were looking for Hussain Osman, who was arrested later in Italy. Jean-Charles de Menezes was a Brazilian electrician, with a pale brown complexion and dark short curly hair. The officers' racial misrecognition of Menezes thus resulted in his death. Regardless of where you stand on the play-off between civil liberties and public security (the incident happened a fortnight after the 7/7 bombings that had killed 52 people and injured hundreds in London) it is surely uncontroversial to posit that had Menezes been a blue-eyed blond he would not have been mistaken for a terrorist. The point of this is to demonstrate that being or not being white can be a matter of life and death, and that those on the white side of the equation generally make the decisions that mean this is so. It is the word 'always' in bell hooks's formulation that transforms suspicion into systemic practice.

The earliest reflexive writing on white identities originated in black America, then being adopted by radical elements within the dominant culture. The corpus can be traced back through Ida Wells-Barnett[8] at the end of the nineteenth century, W.E.B Du Bois (1996 [1903], 1999 [1920], 1998[1935]), at the beginning of the twentieth century, through Langston Hughes (1947), Richard Wright (1992 [1940], 1957), Ralph Ellison (1952), James Baldwin (1955, 1984, 1985a, b, c), all the way to Toni

Morrison (1987, 1993), bell hooks (1992, 2000) and Charles Mills (1997, 1998), whose work we shall look at more closely at the end of this chapter. David Roediger's survey of black perspectives (1999) and George Yancy's modern edited collection of philosophical essays (2004) serve to emphasise the genealogy of, and vernacular setting for, the trope of whiteness as 'terror' identified both by early and contemporary writers. One could emerge from an initial reading of the material convinced that the whiteness studies paradigm is so specific to America's largely bipolar racial arena that it is simply an exotic outpost of academia with little to bring to anyone else's self-knowledge, or applicable to the way collective identities are formed and sustained elsewhere.

The power talked of here is of unchecked and untrammelled authority to exert its will; the power to invent and change the rules and transgress them with impunity; and the power to define the 'Other', and to kill him or her with impunity. The arbitrary imposition of life and death is one end of the spectrum of power relations that whiteness enacts, across the parts of the world where white people are preponderant in positions of power. From Ida Wells's anti-lynching crusade, through Malcom X's comment that 'We didn't land on Plymouth Rock: that rock landed on us', to Carmichael and Hamilton's pioneering and striking claims about the way structural racism functions as a compound of class and 'race' (1967), the recurrent theme is of African-Americans developing an ethnographic gaze of which the subject is the way power is wielded by White America and how it impacts painfully on them.

The critique pieced together over the centuries, however, is not a one-dimensional identification of behaviours with oppression. While much of this is understandably focused on slavery, rape, and murder, there is more to it. There is an explicit linking of capitalism with the specifics of whiteness: indeed the exchange of people for money, labour for money and the idolatry of things thus purchased emerges as a point where core African-American values diverge from European ones.[9] Patricia Hill-Collins quotes one of John Gwaltney's respondents:

> One very important difference between white people and black people is that white people think you are your work . . . Now a black person has more sense than that because he knows that what I am doing doesn't have anything to do with what I want to do or what I do when I am doing for myself. Now black people think that my work is just what I have to do to get what I want.
>
> (Gwaltney 1980: 174, in Hill-Collins 1990: 48)

Carmichael and Hamilton go further than the distinction between careers and instrumental labour carried on in the spaces that structural discrimination allows, arguing that the costs of capitalism include child mortality and poverty that disproportionately impacts on them:

> When white terrorists bomb a black church and kill black children, that is an act of individual racism, widely deplored by most segments of society. But when in that same city – Birmingham, Alabama – 500 black babies die each year because of the lack of proper food, clothing, shelter and proper medical facilities, and thousands more are destroyed or maimed physically, emotionally and intellectually because of conditions of poverty and discrimination in the black community, that is a function of institutional racism.
>
> (1967: 6)

The cross-cutting and compounding effects of 'race' and class discrimination have exercised thinkers such as Cox (1948) and Robinson (1982), working from within the Marxist tradition, and have inspired a critique from Mills (2003b), and we will pay closer attention to the latter's work in the second half of this chapter.

STRUCTURES OF DOMINATION

Beyond the history of slavery, lynching, the Klan (Trelease 1971), Jim Crow and segregation specific to the USA lie more widely recognisable social formations, such as the use of deadly force in the case of Menezes above or any of a number of people killed by security forces. Morrison (1987) and bell hooks (2000, 1992) stress the terror and domination of whites as the primary values seen from a black perspective in terms of the power of naming, defining, decision making and the use of symbolic and physical violence. Indeed, I have stressed this structural element because of the need to establish that all the micro-level interactions that are identified and analysed in the fieldwork, which we will spend a portion of this book looking at in the other chapters, are fully intelligible only when the macro-level power relations within which they occur are specified. These macro-level relations include those involving international capital, the movement of labour, military and industrial technology, the allocation of funds and resources throughout and between national societies. Going into these in detail would mean writing a book-about-everything, which is clearly not within the grasp of this project. Instead, as a starting point, I want to give some examples of what could be considered terror-inducing relationships using material generated in the American context, and add a couple of my own. The impact of decision-making processes on people who are not white can then be seen at a number of levels, constituting, at its most acute, a question of life and death.

Loans for housing, and residential segregation

Most people who own their homes need to borrow money to buy them, and the most obvious source for obtaining a loan is a financial institution. George Lipsitz (1995, 1998) analyses the ways in which the authorisation of loans for the purchase of housing were raced. Even if the sample was controlled for class (i.e. white working-class compared to black working-class applicants) then more money was made available, for longer and under better conditions, to white applicants than to black ones. In a similar vein, the study by the Institute on Race and Poverty on housing in Long Island, New York[10] concluded that between 1999 and 2000, the rates at which conventional home loan applications were denied rose by more than 20 per cent for both African-Americans and Latinos. In 2000, Latinos in Nassau-Suffolk (a county in Long Island) earning more than $91,800 (around £47,500/€70,000) were more likely to be turned down for conventional home loans than were Whites earning less than $38,250 (£20,000/€29,400). This kind of practice explains why patterns of racialised residential segregation are observable in cities across the USA.

Clearly this has a major impact in determining who gets to live where. In the USA, the most expensive housing is generally found in suburban areas, and the failure to obtain loans means that black and Hispanic Americans remain primarily in cheaper neighbourhoods where they can afford to buy. Moreover, the practice of 'Restrictive covenants, explicit or implicit threats of violence, and generally adverse social conditions kept blacks out of white areas' (Cutler *et al.* 1999: 496). When placed alongside other segregationist practices such as redlining, this results in the development of areas that black and other minority people cannot easily access (Gotham 2000). They are therefore over-concentrated in other areas. These methods should be seen as collective segregationist action. Moreover, Lipsitz (1995) points to the functioning of the Federal Housing Authority (FHA), set up in 1934, which lent virtually exclusively to white families in the post-war period. He points to the organisation's area reports and appraiser's manuals as maps of discriminatory practice. The combination of these structural patterns with the deterrent factor facing the first black families to move into an area means that there are tangible material and ideological factors at work, granting privilege to white Americans and impeding the mobility of African-Americans, and other minorities (Massey and Denton 1994).

All of this serves to undermine one of the ideological edifices on which capitalism, and racism in its contemporary forms, are constructed: the rule of individual responsibility. This means, you get what you deserve, both for hard work and for idleness. Yet, obviously if you are a Hispanic earning US$90k and not getting loans that are offered to white people earning US$38k, as in the Nassau-Suffolk County example, there is obviously a breakdown in the logic of that system. This is not to say that the latter do not work hard for their incomes, but most importantly, that there is not a level playing field. In the pre- and post-war periods, unionised labour was dominated by unions operating colour bars, and therefore transferring benefits of industry disproportionately to white male workers. The FHA channelled more money and loans into white counties, which then developed white suburbs, obtained government funding for services and often sought independent status. Massey and Denton (1994) note that although black people also moved to the suburbs, this process was uneven. In the 1960–1977 period, 0.5 million African-Americans and 4 million white Americans moved to the suburbs from inner-city areas. Of the latter, 86 per cent were living in highly segregated areas (with a maximum of 1 per cent African-Americans) by 1993.

So there is no simple relationship between income, ambition and social mobility. If you literally cannot move out of the 'ghetto', because you have less chance of accessing the type of employment that leads to loans being granted, and even then, less access to the loans on top of that due to the financial organisations' lending practices, then how do you get to live outside it? There are observable socially-constructed mechanisms for restricting the movement of non-white people, which develop from the practices of white decision makers. In these mechanisms, all white people, regardless of class and gender, are ostensibly granted an a priori advantage over everyone else, even if it consists primarily in *not* encountering as many obstacles. That is still a serious set of privileges. How can we link this notion of 'white privilege' to broader issues that do not necessarily have an overwhelmingly economic basis?

The discourse on segregation and urban renewal is far too large to digest here (Gotham 2000, Massey and Denton 1994, Lipsitz 1995, 1998). I shall instead point towards three trends identified by Lipsitz (1995) that are indirect results of the decline of former industrial areas and new development:

- First, urban renewal impinged disproportionately on areas where

minorities live, i.e. industrial belts of larger cities that used to provide relatively cheap housing for workers in those industries. This
renewal displaced communities and destroyed more buildings than
were constructed

- Second, renewal through business development in these areas
  means larger taxes (to pay for redevelopment) levied on a smaller
  number of households.
- Third, there is an environmental aspect, in that there is a greater
  amount of waste dumping in those predominantly minority areas,
  yet lower penalties for infringing rules by dumpers than exist in
  white areas.

The spatial considerations of larger cities in business cores are to do with
protection of capital, and new high-return housing units that appeal to
the middle classes, often in gated communities. Mike Davis (1992)
argues that in Los Angeles, for example, downtown space has been
reorganised to suit business interests, and the urban poor are both
policed away and are free to move around in increasingly smaller areas.

So this map of social ripples shows that decision making on one
issue has a series of ramifications that hinder people from being as
geographically and socially mobile as they would like, worsening their
living conditions by making it more likely that the area they live in will
be downgraded, pay higher local taxes and all the associated things such
as the heightened probability of crime, poorer-performing schools, etc.,
thus limiting their life chances. My argument then is twofold. First, that
the arbitrary use of power in order to set in place a set of structural
parameters that bear on a given group of people constitutes a form of
terror. Simply because fewer people beat other people with sticks than
was the case in the past does not mean that this is not a form of violence,
but instead a form of mundane low-intensity terrorism. The second is
that in this ongoing scenario, white people emerge as beneficiaries, even
if they do not support such a system or benefit much from it in other
areas. There is no such thing as a neutral white person in this process
because it is a *social* process, that is, an individual cannot remove him or
herself from it, solely by wishing it away or changing behaviour as an
individual. Regardless of class and gender, *inter alia*, being white per se is
a relatively free ride, and the privileges in terms of options can be seen
in the forthcoming chapters, where some of the complexity attached
to experiencing whiteness from differing points on the class and gender hierarchy will emerge. Meanwhile, I would like to return to the
thread of terror as a property of whiteness and suggest a second set of
connections.

Invisible men and women?

Racism is not only a material but an ideological reality. There are numerous 'ifs' and 'buts' occluded in that little sentence, but for the moment let us take it at face value. James Baldwin, writing of the impact of racism on his life, refers to the cumulative effect of 'the millions of details twenty-four hours of every day which spell out to you that you are a worthless human being' (1985b: 404).

A central tenet, and I would argue a constitutive element of any system of discrimination, is that the dominant group considers the dominated on a collective level, as worth less than itself. In most parts of the developed world this involves white people racialising others as less civilised, less appropriate for membership of or access to their nation, neighbourhood, etc., although of course in other places, where the dominant group is not white, a similar dynamic may exist.[11]

The basis for the American relations is that of imperialism and slavery, and can be summarised in Frantz Fanon's (1967) argument that white Europeans *made him a negro*, in other words, the identity of a black person is derived from the construction of a white identity, based on a number of assumptions about human agency. These include exaggerated claims about civilisation and barbarity. From the outset in North America, black people were declared property rather than persons. Their lives were therefore worth less. They could be killed and raped with relative impunity. What they said and did was seen as evidence of inferiority. Even after the Civil War, fought in part over the issue of free labour, debates over the establishment of the new order involved many arguments that black Americans were not morally or culturally ready for democracy (the franchise, etc.) while foreign white immigrants were not generally subject to this discourse. Du Bois (1998 [1935]: 282) cites President Andrew Johnson in a March 1866 debate, as asking of the freed slaves: 'Can it reasonably be supposed that they possess the requisite qualifications to entitle them to all the privileges and equalities of citizens of the United States?' He went on to argue that granting of the franchise to the freedmen would be unfair to 'large numbers of intelligent, worthy and patriotic foreigners' (ibid.) who knew American democracy better than the 'Negro' and had to wait five years to qualify for citizenship.

The practice of lynching at one extreme, and of judicial history at the other, were premised on the idea that only Whites could give accurate evidence and that guilt was presumed for Blacks.[12] Indeed, the dominant white gaze on black people conflates them into an undifferentiated mass: men as threats to white employment and womanhood, and women as threats to male virtue. In the context of the institutions of slavery, post-war Jim Crow, and all the legacy of learned superiority, these practices became normal, unquestionable assumptions on which everything else was based: what Pierre Bourdieu (1977) calls a *'doxa'*. What I am going to suggest is that while no-one could claim that the situation in the late twentieth and early twenty-first century in terms of vigilante attacks on and intimidation of African-Americans is comparable to that of a century before,[13] the core ideas underlying those actions can still be easily activated.

This can be seen in two cases where white perpetrators of murder blamed their crimes on fictitious black men. The first is explored by D. Marvin Jones (1997) in his study of how 'race' as a social practice evacuates individuality from those objectified and reduces them to a list of imputed bio-cultural characteristics. It is the Charles Stuart case in Boston. In October 1989, Stuart and his brother murdered his pregnant wife. They then wounded Stuart in order to throw the police off the scent. The pair then blamed the murder on a black man in jogging pants with a raspy voice. The area of Boston where the murder was committed, Mission Hill, then witnessed a very intensive police operation in which many black men were questioned. The surrounding media and political discourse involved talk of restoring the death penalty, etc. Stuart's brother finally confessed that the scheme was a set-up to claim life insurance. The readiness with which Stuart's narrative was believed, despite a lack of evidence, and with which the police suspect (local man Willie Bennett) was believed to be guilty, demonstrates continuity with the previous century's practices. Stuart eventually committed suicide and Boston's black community reacted angrily to the scrutiny to which it had been unfairly subjected. Jones argues that assumptions of black criminality thus form the basis of white responses to black subjects at particular moments, when 'race' constitutes a line dividing innocence from guilt. White people are willing to accept a script of black violence and guilt because this is how they expect black men to act.

A similar case was that of Susan Smith in South Carolina in 1994. Smith drowned her two infant sons and told police they had been kidnapped by a black man wearing a knitted hat. Again, local black men were soon questioned, although, as in Stuart's case, it is usual practice to first eliminate the spouses from a murder enquiry about the death of a family member. These situations reflect broader issues of media and police responses to crime, which serve to bolster and provide the framework in which events are understood. Moreover, neither Stuart nor Smith have been constructed in media discourse as shameful to their 'race'. Nor do white Bostonians or white South Carolingians necessarily feel collectively ashamed about these crimes. Indeed, the attention given to the victims far outweighs comparable attention for black victims of shootings in Boston or of children murdered. American society shares the base line of suspecting black men as capable of anything, whereas the sexualised practice of lynching (Harris 1999) encapsulates the fall into savagery visited on, rather than enacted by, African-Americans. Toni Morrison's character Sethe in *Beloved* (1987: 198–199) also suggests that the question of savagery is a projection:

> Whitepeople believed that whatever the manners, under every dark skin was a jungle. Swift unnavigable waters, swinging screaming baboons, sleeping snakes, red gums ready for their sweet white blood . . . But it wasn't the jungle blacks brought with them to this place from the other (livable) place. It was the jungle whitefolks planted in them . . . It spread . . . until it invaded the whites who had made it . . . Made them bloody, silly, worse than even they wanted to be, so scared were they of the jungle they had made. The screaming baboon lived under their own white skin; the red gums were their own.

Using the Rodney King case, Janine Jones (2004) maintains that white Americans can sympathise but not empathise with African-Americans, both because the latter are seen as behaving according to different and less civilised rules, and since white Americans lack motivation to find a 'mappable experience' to help them understand. Thus by not seeing one's own collective historical implication, it can be projected instead onto the collective guilt of the victims. Ellison's 'invisible man' is invisible only as a human being: he is visible as a representation of fear, crime, sex and danger conjured from the centuries of white violence and terror visited upon non-whites: a distorting mirror in which the dominant see themselves deformed.

Where this becomes even more serious is when we consider the next stage of the legal process: the judicial treatment of the perpetrators of homicide. It is clearly easy to blame black men for murders they do not commit. Even when they do commit murder, the path they take through the legal system is a race-specific one. In terms of the death penalty, for example, the statistics show a pattern of differential treatment for black and white murderers, particularly where the victim is white. A 1998 report compiled by the Death Penalty Information Center (Dieter 1998) concludes that:

> The new studies revealed through this report add to an overwhelming body of evidence that race plays a decisive role in the question of

who lives and dies by execution in this country. Race influences which cases are chosen for capital prosecution and which prosecutors are allowed to make those decisions. Likewise, race affects the makeup of the juries which determine the sentence. Racial effects have been shown not just in isolated instances, but in virtually every state for which disparities have been estimated and over an extensive period of time.

A rough grasp of the issue can be achieved through using figures compiled by the DPIC from the NAACP/CLP reports (2006) in tandem with those from the Bureau of Justice (Fox and Zawitz 2004).[14] Combining these datasets allows us to suggest the ratio of criminals actually executed for murders and the probability of them being executed. Clearly there are elements of the criminal justice system that are not captured in this (such as the prosecution of cases, interrogation, representation at trial, juries, judges, appeals, etc.); however, the figures suggest stark distinctions between the likelihood of the murderer of a black or a white victim being executed, and the relative probabilities of a white murderer of a black victim, and the black murderer of a white victim being executed.

We might then argue that one mechanism for the way in which whiteness functions is the conferral of an otherness made visible only through collective characterisation. An individual is merely the reflection of a larger trend anchored in behaviour deemed normal, or at least common for that group. So black males are here transformed into what Jean Baudrillard (1984) terms 'simulacra', which means multiple identical images with no original. The 'hyper-reality' (ibid.) thus constituted comprises the opposite of whiteness, which consists of a set of individuals. This phenomenon is recognised in 'confessional' and activist literature on whiteness (McIntosh 1988, Kendall 2006) as well as critical

Table 1 Death Penalty Statistics for perpetrators and victims in Black/White and White/Black homicides

'Race' of murderer (m) / victim (v)	Total (1976–2004)	No. of executions (1976–2006)	Rate of executions per murder	Probability of execution
White (m) of Black (v)	10,925	14	0.13%	13 in 1000
Black (m) of White (v)	28,503	213	0.75%	75 in 1000

Source: author's calculations based on figures from NAACP/CLP (2006) and Bureau of Justice (Fox and Zawitz 2004).

race theory such as D. Marvin Jones (1997), and fiction by Ellison and Wright. Bigger Thomas, the central character in Wright's *Native Son* (1992 [1940]), accidentally suffocates the daughter of the middle-class white family he works for because he knows that being caught alone with her will have serious consequences for him. Moreover, he then hurriedly burns her body because he understands that the action will be understood as homicide rather than manslaughter: the pathological black male murder of vulnerable white woman. The collective seeing of whiteness as sovereign individuality is only possible through the concomitant collective practice of not-seeing non-Whites except as abstractions.

The question of not-seeing leads us to the next section, addressing the conceptualisation of whiteness, this time as *systemic*. Two contributions seeking to theorise whiteness as a system or structure of power relations will now be introduced: the work of Charles Mills on 'white supremacy' and 'racial exploitation', and Cheryl Harris on 'whiteness as property'.

WHITENESS AS SYSTEMS AND PROPERTY

'White supremacy'

Charles Mills has been working on approaches to racism from within the discipline of philosophy since the 1990s. In a series of key publications (Mills 1997, 1998, 2003a, b, 2004) he has sketched the contours of an understanding of whiteness as systemic. His departure point is the failure of philosophy to even address racism. A set of interlocking assumptions produce the discipline's 'eurocentric' standpoint (2004: 27): the taking of white experience as representative (the focus on 'ideal theory'); the idea that class is the primary social division; and the refusal to engage with social justice as it pertains to racism, despite the centrality of the legacy of Plato in philosophy. Overall he identifies 'a debilitating whiteness in mainstream political philosophy in terms of its critical assumptions, the issues that it has typically taken up, and the mapping of what it has deemed to be appropriate and important subject matter' (ibid.: 30).

Mills's attempt to define a 'more accurate global socio-political paradigm' (ibid.: 26) involves delineating a structure he calls 'white supremacy' rather than 'white privilege', as the former 'implies the existence of a system that not only privileges whites but is run by whites for white benefit' (ibid.: 31). Moreover, the legacy of previous clearly supremacist structures in US history is thus highlighted in the present, constituting 'no less than a fundamental paradigm shift' (2003a: 40). This necessity of asserting continuity with the past is acknowledged also in Harris's work (below).

Mills asserts that there are six dimensions of white supremacy:

1   Juridico-political: the state and the legal system.
2   Economics: access to and accumulation of wealth.
3   Cultural: 'nonwhite' peoples' contributions are either appropriated or minimised so that Europeans become the only people capable of culture.
4   Cognitive-evaluative: where white supremacy becomes 'character-istic and pervasive patterns of not-seeing and not-knowing' (ibid.: 46), so that the generalisation of white racialised experience becomes normalised.
5   Somatic: relating to the body's appearance and judgements made about it.
6   Metaphysical: 'People of color have always recognised that racial subordination is predicated on regarding them as less than fully human, as subpersons rather than persons. A social theory whose implicit ontology fails to register this reality is getting things wrong at a foundational level . . .' (ibid.: 48).

White supremacy is thus constructed as 'objective, systemic, multi-dimensional' and 'constitutive of a certain reality' (ibid.). What is striking is Mills's emphasis on the collective acts of wilful not-seeing, of the evasions entailed in the violence of assimilating the 'nonwhite non-nation' to the white nation (2004: 27). The systemic exertion of power and reaping of benefits can be sustained only if whiteness requires its practitioners *not to see* the benefits as accruing from structural advantages, but as manifestations of individual failings. At best, it sees racism as something that disadvantages some groups, rather than simulta-neously advantaging others. It is to the mechanics of this advantaging process that we shall now turn.

'Racial exploitation'

Starting from the premise that Marx's class exploitation is systemic and *normal* in that it requires no extra measures, Mills (2004) goes on to assert that 'race' has 'relative autonomy' and therefore racism is a system of oppression in itself (we might add 'for itself' in particular cases and forms). However, while class exploitation is primarily based on wages, the racialised subordinate population (R2) is either excluded from work altogether or recruited by members of the dominant group (R1) under different conditions from other workers. In the colonial system, non-whites are coerced to work, while white workers in the metropolis are compelled by the market to work. Mills maintains that: 'This is not a minor but a major and qualitative difference' (2004: 39). Moreover, the R2s are not part of the group to which democratic norms apply. The normative social justice claims are therefore not available to them as a matter of course, which means that following Rogers Smith (1999) 'racism is not an anomaly in the global system but a norm in its own right' (ibid.). This insight has been presented in the sociology of racism for many years, but in the context of political philosophy it represents a breakthrough, containing as it does an implicit rebuttal of colourblind liberal and socialist positions. Mills goes on to identify areas other than wages as arenas of exploitation, and the state as an actor in them:

> not merely in writing the laws and fostering the moral economy that makes racial exploitation normatively and juridically accept-able, but in creating opportunities for the R1s that are not exten-ded to the R2s, and in making transfer payments on a racially differentiated basis.
>
> (2004: 41–42)

Indeed, from the examples Mills gives (ibid.: 44–45), what emerges is 'not a matter of a single transaction but . . . a multiply interacting set with repercussions continually compounding and feeding back in a destruc-tive way' (ibid.: 46). There is thus a form of exploitation analogous to, but not reducible to, class exploitation. So the importance of Mills's interventions is to underscore the systemic aspect of whiteness and sug-gest that it benefits white people regardless of whether they want to benefit. His *Racial Contract* explicitly states that:

> The Racial Contract is that set of formal or informal agreements or meta-agreements . . . between the members of one subset of humans, henceforth designated by . . . 'racial' . . . criteria . . . as 'white' . . . to categorise the remaining subset of humans as 'non-white' and of a different and inferior moral status (. . .) in any case the Contract is always the differential privileging of the whites as a group, the exploitation of their bodies, land and resources, and the denial of equal socioeconomic opportunities to them. All whites are beneficiaries of the Contract, though some whites are not signatories to it.
>
> (1997: 11)

Moreover, he suggests that there is a rational side to it (i.e. it is linked to interest perceived as racial), the terms of which have been demonstrated economically (Lipsitz 1995, 1998, Oliver and Shapiro 1997, Massey and Denton 1988). Yet as Du Bois intimated, not all wages are economic, and there appear to be psychological bonuses available, as 'one can only be white in relation to nonwhites' (Mills 2004: 52). In these works, Mills thus evokes whiteness as a multi-dimensional systemic phenomenon that has emerged from a specific history. Among its mechanisms is racial exploitation, here conceptualised as distinct from class exploitation.

Whiteness as property

Indeed, Mills echoes some of the themes of Cheryl Harris's earlier groundbreaking work, 'Whiteness as Property' (1993), which we shall now address. Her framework is the socio-legal *enracinement* of white supremacy in terms of the validation of White European norms of ownership of people and land. The development of white supremacy is outlined as a system of economic and social domination secured by its anchoring in law. Harris argues that whiteness as property survived the civil rights era, to resurface in the form of successful legal challenges to affirmative action programmes. She ends by explaining how affirmative action can best be conceptualised as combining both reparative and distributive justice, thus avoiding the impasse of individuals competing for employment, university places, etc. Space here does not permit an exploration of all the richness of Harris's thesis,[15] so I will concentrate on three strands; property in bodies; property in land; and property in expectations, as well as the issues arising from these configurations that help us understand how whiteness works.

Property in bodies

The shift in status for European- and African-descended elements of the workforce in seventeenth-century America is the starting point for the process that ended with black bodies being the property of Whites. The early decades of settlement involved white indentured labour working alongside enslaved labour (Jordan 1968). The correspondence of the 'free' labourer to the 'Christian' and 'white' categories, along with that of the 'Heathen', 'black' and 'slave' ones, was not absolute until the latter half of that century (indeed so many slaves converted that the code of Christian/Heathen was scrapped in favour of white/black). This, argues Harris, was a deliberate strategy to make black people *as a class* subordinate to whites. The first slave codes did not appear until the 1660s (Harris

1993: 1718). It was at this point that the term 'negro' (with a lower case 'n') emerged.

The free status of some former slaves and their descendants, and the ambivalence over whether they were persons or property, is shown in the way that the size of constituencies for the House of Representatives were computed, with slaves worth 'three-fifths of all other persons' (ibid.: 1720). By the end of the seventeenth century white corresponded with 'free' labourer. While not all Blacks were un-free, no Whites were slaves. For the poor white workers of the South, whiteness had become

> a line of protection and demarcation from the potential threat of commodification, and it determined the allocation of the benefits and burdens of this form of property. White identity and whiteness were sources of privilege and protection, their absence meant being the object of property.
>
> (ibid.: 1721)

This safety net provided by whiteness is the context for Du Bois's 'public and psychological wage' (1998 [1935]: 700), in that however far white people could fall in economic terms, they could never end up as property.

This discrepancy in status became naturalised, a badge of inferiority rather than the result of a social system. This naturalisation is apparent in the 1896 Plessy judgement. The plaintiff was appealing for compensation for having been removed from a 'whites only' carriage on a train. The court ruled both that segregation per se was not discrimination, and that moreover, no harm could be inflicted on Plessy's reputation by consigning him to the 'Coloured' section of the train because he was not entitled to claim whiteness. This was despite the fact that socially, he 'passed' as white. Harris maintains that the courts' logic of understanding 'race' was not the objective one that they claimed:

> The legal definition of race was the 'objective' test propounded by racist theorists of the day who described race to be immutable, scientific, biologically determined – an unsullied fact of the blood rather than a volatile and violently imposed regime of racial hierarchy.
>
> (Harris 1993: 1739)

In fact the concept of the 'one drop rule' of descent required knowledge of genealogy that could not always be proven, and was based on two contestable ideas: first, that 'race' is purely biological and has no social component; and second, that whiteness can be polluted in a way that blackness cannot. If a white plaintiff were treated as not white, then he or she would have grounds for complaint because of the status difference between groups qua groups. However, a black plaintiff had no claim for damaged reputation because his/her reputation for whiteness was based on a social lie. So what the court did was assume that the naturalised status quo resided in the dominance of white over black (the rationale for why Plessy could not sit in the whites only carriage). Yet it ignored the social implications of that status quo (i.e. what Plessy lost in terms of economic and social opportunities by being considered Black rather than White).

Property in land

On the issue of Europeans' relations with Native Americans, Harris's key point is the formulation of land rights. Land settled by Native Americans for centuries was taken and redistributed among white Americans. The facilitating structure for this was the way in which property was conceptualised in solely European terms, as the right of an individual to acquire and dispose of. Native Americans did not own land in this way, rather they saw themselves as collective stewards of the land, managing it for the following generations. So if the courts only recognised European property-holding ideas, then only Europeans could actually own property. 'This fact infused whiteness with significance and value because it was solely through being white that property could be acquired and secured under law. Only whites possessed whiteness, a highly valued and exclusive form of property' (Harris 1993: 1725).

Indeed, property-ownership has been identified as one of the key elements of civilisation justifying the sixteenth-century colonisation of Ireland (Garner 2003), for example. Part of the practice of defining Native Americans as savages involved them being cast as communal wanderers who did not make the land productive. There are strong resonances here with the case of the Australian Aboriginal peoples' land struggles with the authorities (Moreton-Robinson 2005a, b, Pearson 2003). The concept of *terra nullius* (uninhabited land) had been deployed in the settlement of Australia, despite the presence of Aboriginal groups, a legal strategy that privileged the European concept of property-ownership. After the 1992 Mabo 2 ruling, in which Torres Strait Islanders successfully proved that they had 'owned' the land even by European standards of proof, two much-criticised High Court decisions delivered in 2002 – Mirriuwung Gajerrong and Yorta Yorta[16] – have interpreted land ownership rules in a way that has so far prevented a repeat of Mabo 2.

Even if ownership can be proven, the very basis upon which a group claims land back can be rejected, as with the 1978 Mashpee case, which Harris uses to underscore the role of whiteness in the powerful function of definition. The case was an attempt by this Massachusetts tribe to recover land conveyed to non-Indians without the requisite Federal government approval. The basis of their claim had to be that they constituted a tribe *at the time of conveyancing*. Over the years, the Mashpee had mixed with runaway slaves, other tribes and Europeans. For the trial judge, this meant they had lost their tribal essence, yet for the Mashpee, it was relationship to land and shared culture that defined them rather than racial purity (Harris 1993: 1764–1765). Their practices of absorption led to them being considered 'un-tribelike' in law: 'The Mashpee were not "passing" ', comments Harris, 'but were legally determined to have "passed" – no longer to have distinct identity' (ibid.: 1765). Yet the Mashpees' twin survival strategies, of mobility and mixing, have to be understood in a context where they suffered threats from disease and competition for resources, as well as pressure to Christianise, which the majority did. So presenting these strategic choices as legally *giving up* their Mashpee identity is also an effect of power, not a neutral reflection of a situation. In addition to demonstrating the awesome power of definition to determine people's life chances (the land contested was very valuable), the case also shows that one additional and increasingly important element of whiteness as property is its 'rejection of the ongoing presence of the past' (ibid.: 1761), which impacts most noticeably on the post-civil rights era cases that Harris turns to at the end of her article.

Property in expectations

Harris indicates that property is not restricted to the tangible, but can also come in the shape of expectations, e.g. those deriving from a belief in individual rights based on membership of the white 'race'. In three notable cases in the 1970s and 1980s (*Bakke*, 1978; *Croson*, 1989; and *Wygant*, 1986), she identifies the unifying element of the court's rejection of the past as having any impact on the current racialised status quo. In *Bakke*, the plaintiff's claim to have a place in a University of California medical school class, where 12 per cent of the places were reserved for minorities, is based on white individuals' claim on 100 per cent of the places (as in the past) due to centuries of oppression. Moreover, only GPA and MCAT scores were used in court to prove merit, when there are other criteria used to determine an applicant's suitability for a place. The ruling prevented the University of California from maintaining its minorities programme, while leaving in place the 5 per cent of the places reserved for the Dean's discretion (ibid.: 1773), and the de facto age discrimination in medical school recruitment. In this case, the 'innocent white' individual is faced with the burden of compensating for past discrimination, and the court overruled the compensatory dimension of the University's programme.

Similarly, a white businessman brought the *Croson* case (1989) against the City of Richmond because he lost a contract to a black business under the City's programme that was aimed at placing 30 per cent of its spend with minority firms, in a city with a 50 per cent black population. The fact that the City was still actually spending only 0.67 per cent of its budget on business with minority firms was rejected by the judge as being irrelevant. The Court ruled that no basis for affirmative action existed. Harris points out that the issue is one of treating the cases as one-off instances of individual unfairness, when the broader picture is one of widespread and systemic historic discrimination that makes white the most privileged identity: 'Treating white identity as no different from any other group identity, when, at its core, whiteness is based on racial subordination ratifies existing white privilege by making it the referential baseline' (ibid.: 1775).

The last of the three cases, *Wygant*, was brought by senior white teaching staff employed by the City of Jackson, MI. These teachers had been laid off by the City in a retrenchment programme contrary to the usual procedure in which the newest staff are the first to go. This is because a prior union deal had safeguarded the jobs of black junior teachers. The City's policy of making senior staff redundant was overturned by the courts. Harris argues that their seniority was based on obtaining jobs in a period and as part of a system in which there was no competition (i.e. on a racially discriminatory basis).

The error in each of these cases, argues Harris, is to conflate two types of claim: 'distributive' (fairness) and 'compensatory' (overcoming the past). In the context for the law's construction of rights as individual rather than collective, this confusion leads to the case being interpreted as one of the claim and counter-claim of minority person *v.* innocent white. The salient issue is *prior advantage gained through a discriminatory system.*

Harris posits a solution to this problem, arguing for the separation of 'whiteness as property' from 'whiteness as identity'. The idea of distributive justice focuses on introducing fairness into an unfair pattern of distribution that has a historical dimension, thus not focusing 'primarily on guilt and innocence, but rather on entitlement and fairness' (ibid.: 1783).

Conclusion

'Whiteness as property' then has altered in nature over time, but 'retains its core characteristic – the legal legitimation of expectations of power and control that enshrine the status quo as a neutral baseline, while masking the maintenance of white privilege and domination' (ibid.: 1791).

Harris's thesis revolves around this discontinuity between past and present. She relentlessly draws out the idea of ongoing social inequality whose result is that the law at once makes 'whiteness' as an objective fact, although in reality it is 'an ideological proposition imposed through subordination' (ibid.: 1730), and makes of blackness and Native Americanness, *inter alia*, devalued identities. So, even if for many white people in contemporary America, whiteness is little more than a 'consolation prize', it still prevents its bearer from becoming something else, from falling into a status to which penalties are intrinsic. The kind of property protected in affirmative action counter-claims is that of maintaining white people's unquestioned privileged access to resources and reduction of obstacles facing them in the labour and education markets, among others: 'In protecting the property interest in whiteness, property is assumed to be no more than the right to prohibit infringement on settled expectations, ignoring countervailing equitable claims that are predicated on a right to inclusion' (ibid.: 1791).

Taken together, Harris and Mills's contributions set an agenda for analysing whiteness away from both the micro-level and the liberal paradigms of individual rights, placing the emphasis instead on the reproduction, adaptability and institutionalised nature of discrimination in which white identity grants privileges even for the furthest down the hierarchy. These radical and striking understandings of whiteness as a system not only critique the institutional basis of social justice, but challenge activists and researchers to think beyond the immediacy of individual relations into the realm of the structural parameters contouring our actions and cultures.

The core of the writing on whiteness derives from the specific history of the USA: from slavery, Reconstruction, Civil Rights, black feminism's challenge to the mainstream. So we have so far established that in the USA, decision making concentrated in the hands of dominant groups of white people through institutions founded on inequality, serves to frame the hierarchical patterns of segregation in which resources are still unequally parcelled out, and life chances enhanced or reduced. British historian John Belchem, referring to Peter Kolchin (2002), argues that whiteness has come to be presented as omnipresent, unchanging, and 'real', formulations that 'risk losing sight of contextual variations and thereby undermining the very understanding of race and whiteness as socially constructed' (Belchem 2005: 146). While I disagree with this as a general statement – indeed there is as much work covered in this book that is specific to time and place as there is that neglects spatio-temporal specificity – the critique is broadly pertinent. I want to stress that in saying that whiteness potentially equals terror at all times, the argument is not that this is the *only* dimension of whiteness, nor that it is 'unchanging': far from it. This type of debate illustrates the problem of either universalising the American experience or not looking beyond it. American academia's domination of whiteness is reflected in this book, but it should be problematised. What about elsewhere? We clearly need a structure through which to try and make sense of the patterns developed in this corpus, which contends that whiteness can often equal terror. All the other ways in which whiteness can be theorised are dependent on this: it is the thread holding the various dimensions together.

What is useful in understanding whiteness through the prism of terror and supremacy is that it is 'organic', in Gramsci's sense of the term, which means it is a conceptualisation primarily as a form of power *experienced* by people who suffer directly from its exercise. The understandings are informed by but not reducible to personal and collective experience. In this way we can see how the power wielded at a macro-level – the global politics of colonialism and neo-colonialism, the power to define, disregard and destroy – is worked out on the lives of individuals. An effect of this power is to temporarily suspend all other sources of identity and place the white 'we' in unity against the Other, regardless of its disunities and differential access to resources. The international order in which particular states pursue the right to invade others is based on the post-war order in which the USA became dominant and Europe less so. Yet when discussions of whiteness take place, they often do so as if none of the vast *global* backdrop of war, trade imbalance, consumption imbalance, debt and its prolongation is relevant to what goes on at the micro-level.

To resume the caveat begun in the Introduction, it is only worth looking at white identities and their relation to power if it is part of sociology of racism. The starting point of this exercise is recognising that whiteness can mean terror for those who are not white: the possibility of writing rules to suit white people, changing them when they do not have the desired effect, and being able to benefit so much from structural inequalities that non-whites die younger, are less likely to realise potential and grow up in an environment where the overriding ethos is one where they are devalued merely for existing. Any discussion of the intricacies of white internal boundaries, which will be a central theme in what follows, must always occur with the shadow of social death hanging over those who do not fit into the category 'white'.

2 Whiteness as a kind of absence

I have framed this chapter to incorporate two paradoxical but not mutually exclusive ways of conceptualising whiteness. There is a set of arguments that suggest that whiteness is invisible because its normalisation guides scrutiny away from it, and another set arguing that the exercise of power makes it, on the contrary, extremely visible. The latter have been introduced in the previous chapter. Here, I am going to offer a reading in which both are true, at the same time, but the visibility or invisibility of the white subject is contingent: hence whiteness as *a kind of absence* that is *produced* by social relationships. We shall first look at how whiteness can be invisible and unmarked, before taking the alternative view, in which whiteness is heavily marked, to the point where it saturates the field. The last section will develop these ideas, showing how one person's invisibility is another's visibility.

WHITENESS AS INVISIBILITY

Richard Dyer's central point in his study of whiteness, film and photography (1997), is that white is the framing position: a dominant and normative space against which difference is measured. In other words, white is the point from which judgements are made, about normality and abnormality, beauty and ugliness, civilisation and barbarity. Because of the dominance of Western European thought and military and technological power over the last five centuries in its global projects of colonialism and neo-colonialism, whiteness has come to be *represented* as humanness, normality and universality: 'whites are not of a certain race, they are just the human race' (1997: 3). If white is human, then all else requires qualification: everything else is deviant. So, to clarify, the argument is not that whiteness is actually invisible. A better word would be 'unmarked'. Whiteness for the majority of 'white' people is so unmarked that in their eyes, it does not actually function as a *racial* or ethnic identity, at least outside of particular contexts when they might perceive themselves to be in a minority. Whiteness is rendered invisible under the weight of accumulated privileges.

Dyer's book focuses on the visual, and he is talking primarily about film. He builds on work he did in the late 1980s on the ways in which whiteness is represented in a variety of film genres (Dyer 1988).[17] So what we glean from Dyer is that whiteness sustains itself by appearing not to be there.

The power relations of white over black, men over women, and class over class, are fused in presentations of whiteness so that they become a statement of the natural order. White is simply what it is to be human. Here we touch on a well-rehearsed theme: the capacity of power to make itself appear natural and unquestionable. This capacity lies at the root of power's representations of itself in terms of 'race', class and gender. This is just the way it is, and resistance is both futile and unnatural. Cresswell (1996: 19–20), following Bourdieu, suggests that the first efforts of dominated groups are to transform this type of oppressive ideological strategy from *doxa* (common-sense limits) to orthodoxy (a choice of one path over others, and the awareness of alternatives). In other words, resistance aims to reduce the field of what is taken for granted and increase the field of what cannot be.

In a much-referred-to article, Peggy McIntosh (1988)[18] attempts to draw parallels between the privileges inherent in being male and those inherent in being white, and how they impinge on everyday life. The better-known section of this original paper is the part dealing with white privilege, in which she characterises it as

> an invisible package of unearned assets that I can count on cashing in each day, but about which I was 'meant' to remain oblivious. White privilege is like an invisible weightless knapsack of special provisions, maps, passports, codebooks, visas, clothes, tools, and blank checks.
>
> (1988: 1)

Here McIntosh presents a list of privileges underscoring how whiteness can be unmarked. She explains the rationale:

> As a white person, I realized I had been taught about racism as something that puts others at a disadvantage, but had been taught not to see one of its corollary aspects, white privilege, which puts me at an advantage. I think whites are carefully taught not to recognize

white privilege, as males are taught not to recognize male privilege. So I have begun in an untutored way to ask what it is like to have white privilege.

The list contains things that McIntosh feels she can do that colleagues who are not white cannot. They involve unnoticed, unharassed, 'un-othered' movement through public space; being treated as an individual rather than as a representative of a group; and finding her experiences and needs catered for as normal.

McIntosh's reflexivity allows for the focus to be placed on what accrues to white people rather than what disadvantages face Others. One of the themes to come out of fieldwork with white people is their general unease at thinking of themselves as white per se. Just as identifying class inequalities makes people defensive about their achievements (always deserved) vis-à-vis Others' less successful lives, then addressing whiteness evokes a similar response: making people defensive about their social location. The reluctantly performed ideological labour entailed in white people seeing themselves as raced (and, logically, as race-making) raises painful questions about its producers' place in the world. Indeed, even when McIntosh's list of privileges is used in the classroom as an object of discussion, McKinney (2005) reports that the structural elements do not get picked up, the students preferring to emphasise things that make a more immediate impression, like 'flesh-coloured' bandages that are not the same colour as some people's flesh.

The discomfort of white subjects with seeing themselves as raced, a process that disrupts the normality in which the white gaze can roam freely on the Other, emerges clearly from two pieces of empirical field-work by Ann Phoenix (1996) and Karyn McKinney (2005), which we shall look at now.[19]

Ann Phoenix's interviews demonstrate how young white people in London enjoy the luxury of not having to think about racialised identity. This equates to the freedom to idealise egalitarianism, and assert that colour is unimportant in judgements of personal worth. At the same time, the respondents essentialise blackness, which is experienced as a threatening presence in particular spaces. They are thus forced to confront the contradiction expressed by on the one hand, identifying themselves with non-racial identities, while recognising 'that being white signifies a social location, and as such, has a history and interconnections with other colours' (Phoenix 1996: 192). This ideological impasse (whites are individuals, Others are parts of groups) is encapsulated in the idea of 'sovereign individuality' floated by Steven Farough (2004: 244).[20] This consists of always viewing the white subject as a non-racial universal individual, while the Other is primarily a raced member of a collective. Here, Dyer's point about invisibility resurfaces. Treating whiteness as a non-racialised identity conceals racialised power relations and the ideas and practices that sustain them. bell hooks, for example, talks of feeling marginalised by white middle-class girls at Stanford who did not understand that their experiences, social comfort and access to resources were not shared. Among other things, their pranks (messing up her room, emptying her talc and perfume, and dirtying her clothes) cost hooks time and money she didn't have (hooks 2000: 27).

Indeed, Phoenix (1996: 196) concludes that 'silence about "whiteness" implicitly serves to maintain the status quo of power relations between black people and white people . . .'. In this narrative of sovereign individuals we hear confirmation of the arguments formulated in the previous chapter. The white murderers, Charles Stuart and Susan Smith, are dealt with in media coverage as errant *individuals* (and, in Smith's case, partly as a victim herself), while sections of the African-American communities in their areas were collectively pathologised as violent and criminal after they had turned the police hunt onto them. The response of the police and media was based on the postulate that any one of these black men could have killed/kidnapped the woman/children because it is in the nature of black men to do things like this. However, it is not *in the nature* of white people to do these things, although some may do. The distinction is fine but far-reaching: once we talk about nature we think about the incapacity for change, and we have retreated from orthodoxy to *doxa* (Cresswell 1996).

Ruth Frankenberg's (1994) study of white women in California demonstrates a particular understanding of 'race' as only being activated by the presence of Others. Her interviewees express varying degrees of unawareness of their own whiteness until they have epiphanies in specific contexts, such as coming to large urban areas for the first time. Their childhoods and adolescence in white or largely white communities are not understood as being anything to do with 'race'. These experiences mirror those of some of Bridget Byrne's interviewees like 'Sally' (Byrne 2006: 42–54) who talk about life-changing friendships with non-white people, or rural childhoods devoid of 'race' and adult experiences of cosmopolitan London where they understand themselves as being raced as they confront bodies and spaces that disturb their expectations (ibid.: 95–102). These women do not see 'race' as necessarily an important part of their identities in some contexts, and indeed prefer to talk about gender (ibid.: 72–74). Such avoidances and hierarchies of oppression are also referred to explicitly by Gail Griffin (1998).

Karyn McKinney's experiences of teaching an undergraduate course on 'race' and ethnicity in which she focuses on whiteness (McKinney 2005) demonstrate a variety of recurrent themes.[21] One of the most striking is the resentment and anger exhibited by the students who confront their whiteness as a raced identity often for the first time. The general failure to come to terms with the privilege bestowed is expressed in terms of denial. This takes two main forms. The first is to argue that racism is either exaggerated or a question of individual prejudices that the author of the diary does not share. This constitutes what McKinney calls the 'golden rule' of treating everyone as an individual rather than as a member of a group, thus echoing Phoenix and Farough's findings. This colour-blindness (Bonilla-Silva 2003); entailing the idea that even seeing or talking about 'race' is itself racist, anchors a whole post-civil rights political ideology that Winant (2001) calls a 'racial project'.

The second discursive strategy is to reconfigure whiteness as actually detrimental, rather than beneficial, to their life chances. So at the other extreme of the parameters of the idea of whiteness as unmarked is the possibility that it has become marked and transformed into a liability. There are two points to be made here. The first is that such discourse has a very specific American focus: affirmative action. The second is that while affirmative action may be absent from the European landscape, the notion of white Europeans as an emerging unprotected minority is certainly present. Indeed, what Paul Gilroy might include under 'post-colonial melancholia' (2004) is working- and lower middle-class white Europeans' construction of themselves as losing out in a new set of social hierarchies in which the indigenous find themselves unfairly sidelined vis-à-vis minorities. The 'whiteness-as-a-liability' line is indeed being reproduced in the UK, and attention will be paid to that in chapter 9. McKinney's findings[22] show that white students are concerned about quotas and affirmative action, which they perceive has impacted on their entry into university, on their obtaining grants, the size of the grants, on relatives' jobs and promotion prospects. They are confused by the 'rules' regarding the circumstances under which 'race' can be addressed and using what language. The young people here view the slate as having been wiped more or less clean by the reforms of the civil rights era, and see minorities as now on a level playing field with them. Yet in their eyes, quotas mean they are unfairly discriminated against as white people. Indeed, as Harris (1993) maintains, affirmative action is constructed as reverse discrimination, with individual white subjects being held accountable for collective and historic practices. The failure of past patterns of structural disadvantage to be included in the equation that necessitates the establishment of affirmative action in the first place is frequent in these students' accounts. Similarly, the working-class men interviewed by Weis and Fine in Buffalo are critical of affirmative action for having generated white unemployment. 'White male critique', they argue, 'revolves around a sense of being pushed out of an economic marketplace that they see as *formerly functioning fairly*' (Weis and Fine 1996: 502, my emphasis).

This journey, however, from invisible and unmarked racial identity to new visible disadvantaged minority can be understood as a discursive manoeuvre that deflects attention from whiteness as a privilege-holding social location, either to another geographical location or historical period. The subjects created in the narrative of white disadvantage also define themselves through the marking of moral/racial boundaries, which we shall examine in the following chapter.

It has been argued that whiteness is a position from which other identities are constructed as deviant. The invisibility of whiteness therefore stems from never having to define itself explicitly. It is seen as the human and universal position requiring no qualification. So on one level, the entire social science enterprise of studying whiteness is, as Dyer argues, to make white people 'see their particularity', to make whiteness 'strange' (1997: 10). This capacity to be universal and disembodied cannot be separated from the capacity to be an individual rather than the member of a group, to be the liberal and liberated Enlightenment subject. From this position, white people deploy strategies of not seeing 'race', which is paradoxically based on the assumption that only other people are raced. When white sees itself in the mirror, there are usually particular conditions: encounters with unfamiliarity, exposure to raced Others that makes the white subject reflect on his/her whiteness (McKinney 2006). At a further level there is the recognition that white (like male and middle or upper class) is a privilege-bearing position, albeit with varying and contingent privileges attached to it. Understanding how this works, not just to disadvantage people who are not white, but to benefit those who are, requires thinking beyond individual opinions and into the realm of institutionalised, patterned and structural inequality, as we started to do in chapter 1.

Whiteness visible

Much scholarly writing about whiteness and empirical work with white people suggests there is a lack of awareness about 'race', and indifference to the unremarkable nature of being white (Frankenberg 1994). Helen (charles) (1992) even wonders whether white people actually realise they are white. Karyn McKinney presents a large number of accounts by her students that describe white people coming to realise they are raced. This can take a number of forms and have relatively positive or negative outcomes. The epiphanies experienced by Frankenberg's interviewees are found also in McKinney's. These influential 'turning points' for the undergraduates often came when they competed for college places. Their understanding of affirmative action virtually always involves a qualified white person losing out to an unqualified 'person of colour',[23] and of scholarships going principally to minorities. Students express a range of antipathy towards quotas with 'Jerry' even stating that he would be better off black (2005: 163), a sentiment echoed by Rick, who thinks 'being white in this world is getting harder with each passing second' (ibid.: 177).

However, writing from other social locations has long argued that whiteness is excessively visible. As we saw in chapter 1, whiteness has been critiqued as an expression of particular power relations since the end of the nineteenth century. Toni Morrison (1993), for example, in her analysis of early American literature, maintains that it is blackness rather than whiteness that has been rendered invisible. By this she does not mean only that depictions of black characters are rare, but that what constitutes black characters is also more about the white author than about the ostensible subject. Black characterisation is comprised of a projection of fear and guilt, so that the overriding weaknesses of the black characters are constructed as parts of white America's struggle to successfully tame nature, while unsuccessfully, in Morrison's terms, struggling to be human. Both these projects involve exploitation: of enslaved Africans, migrant labour and natural resources, as well as the forced removal of Native Americans from their land. Indeed, she sees whiteness (defined as civilisation, technology and force) defining itself against nature (savagery, primitiveness and weakness) characterised by otherness in the New World. She argues that a dominant theme in early American literature was 'the highly problematic construction of the American as a new white man' (Morrison 1993: 39). This worked by defining Europeans against a physical and figurative background of barbarity to better highlight their civilised status. Of the new man thus created, she writes: 'The site of his transformation is within rawness: he is backgrounded by savagery' (ibid.: 44).

It is therefore important in the relational construction of whiteness and its Others (inextricable from each other in terms of process) that the external boundaries come to reflect savagery. This is also true of ideological attempts to distinguish between more and less civilised white Americans in the late nineteenth and early twentieth centuries, as Rafter (1988: 21) argues, even reprising the wilderness theme – in which the least civilised are depicted as inhabiting forests and are described using animal and insect metaphors. The project of seeing otherness entails the projection of anxieties, and thus what it means to be white can be partly grasped from how the Other is seen. The eponymous narrator in Ralph Ellison's *Invisible Man* captures this process when he states:

> I am invisible, understand, simply because people refuse to see me. Like the bodiless heads you see sometimes in circus sideshows, it is as though I have been surrounded by mirrors of hard, distorting glass.
>
> When they approach me they see only my surroundings, themselves, or figments of their imagination – indeed, everything and anything except me.
>
> (Ellison 1952: 1)

We saw in the previous chapter how the reflexive process of 'backgrounding against savagery' can be read into other contemporary situations, such as the responses to homicide and the workings of the legal system. Indeed, from this perspective, the 'invisibility' alluded to is a form of hidden content whose privileged location reveals itself in the act of narration. Whiteness may well be invisible to those categorising themselves as 'white' until an epiphany triggers greater reflection about racism and the social location of the white interlocutor. This is evident in the almost confessional narratives of white anti-racist feminists such as Mab Segrest (1994), Marilyn Frye (1983, 1992), Stephanie Wildman (1997), Gail Griffin (1998) and Frances Kendall (2006) through to Karyn McKinney's (2005) undergraduates. However, and this is an important 'however', it does not hurt to remind ourselves that whiteness has always been visible from the perspective of people of colour. Indeed, early deployment of the gaze on white people was rooted in African-American experiences of needing working knowledge of what was in the minds of those they interacted with. The accomplishment of this twin set of understandings was termed 'double consciousness' by Du Bois in *The Souls of Black Folk*: 'this sense of always looking at oneself through the eyes of others, of measuring one's soul by the tape of a world that looks on in amused contempt and pity' (1996 [1903]: 5).

Indeed, this reflexive, and, for Du Bois, semi-schizophrenic, gaze can be conferred with a genealogy represented in projects such as those of Roediger (1999) and updated by Yancy (2004), along with more in-depth treatment given to it by hooks (1992).

Quite apart from the terror of arbitrary violence of all sorts, which has been dealt with in the previous chapter, we must address a different problem here. White people experience a number of mundane transactions (e.g. shopping, travelling across borders, banking) as unproblematic, not realising that this is the case because of their whiteness, while others, bearing the burden of suspicion, encounter extra checks, questions, surveillance, policing and worse outcomes. We shall examine the contemporary European phenomenon of conflating people of colour with a variety of statuses into one amorphous threat in chapters 8 and 9. Here we might reflect on the everyday experiences of people being followed around as they shop, being asked to show identity papers and being refused access to services in cases where white people are not. This restricted movement can also escalate into lethal violence. Individual cases are lengthily documented elsewhere, but we might identify as exemplary the June 1982 killing of Vincent Chin, in Detroit. Two men attacked Chin, a Chinese-American, because of the Japanese car industry's impact on local employment.[24] One of the reasons for which it is illustrative is that the men were acquitted of murder and instead given manslaughter charges of three years' probation plus fines. Chin's murder is just one of a long list of arbitrary killings following in the tradition of lynching, but I have selected it to demonstrate that blackness is not the only Other generated by whiteness. There are parallels in the way Chinese immigrants were victims of extra-judicial killings in nineteenth-century California (by white gold-diggers, and by the citizens of Los Angeles, for example, who hung 17 Chinese youths during riots in 1871 because one was suspected of shooting a white man), not permitted to give evidence, not granted citizenship, and had to pay an extra tax in order to immigrate, etc.[25] The LA riots of 1992 and the aftermath of Hurricane Katrina in August 2005 are rich topics for reflection on the power relations still infecting America's domestic policies. For people incensed by the acquittal of the police officers caught on film beating Rodney King in early 1990s California, left to their own devices for days in flooded out New Orleans, or turned back by law enforcement at the bridge out of the city as they fled to neighbouring Gretna,[26] whiteness and blackness (almost inextricable from class) appeared to be the organising principles of justice. It is hard to think about those two massive events in recent American history as other than raced, and as moments in which whiteness became momentarily as visible to white Americans as it is to others all the time.

A kind of absence, a kind of presence

How then can we make sense of these ostensibly contradictory analyses: of whiteness as unmarked and whiteness as the supreme over-determining factor? The question of 'invisibility' seems to be determined primarily by the perspective from which whiteness is *experienced*, i.e. there is nothing 'invisible' about whiteness for African-, Asian- or Hispanic-Americans. I am not convinced that 'absence' in this case is synonymous with 'lack of content'. Like Robert Paynter (2001: 135), I interpret whiteness as a 'filled, rather than empty category'. Invisibility seems a more accurate term, in that it denotes ostensible absence but actual presence. So I am going to bring the two apparent opposites visibility and invisibility together by suggesting that movement through different types of space might reveal a pattern that enables the paradox to be retained and the apparent contradiction resolved.

My starting point is that whiteness is the fulcrum of power relations in the field of racism. Without it, the other constructions fall away, both historically and in the present. The organising principle of 'race', whether you think of it as a biological and/or cultural reality, or as a social construction, was developed by actors working *from* a social location. There is agency here: the construction of 'race' in the modern world has been achieved by people working within structural parameters and utilising available cultural repertoires. And the position from which the idea of 'race' as we understand it in the twenty-first century (going back to the sixteenth century, through the Enlightenment, scientific racism, social Darwinism, colonialism and Nazism) was propagated, was that of white Europeans and their ancestors in the New World. This is not an argument that any subsequent projects aimed at racialising identities are imposed by Europeans on passive Others. Groups use racialising strategies for defence, solidarity and to pursue political projects around obtaining recognition and material resources. The point made here is that the unmarked nature (which we have referred to here as 'invisibility') of whiteness derives from it being the centre point from which everything else can be viewed, but which can see itself only if reflected in another. So, typically, when making claims about another 'race', the white speaker is simultaneously listing characteristics whose opposite he or she feels are applicable. So when Fine and Weis's blue-collar interviewees (1996), and those of Weis *et al.* (1996), like Lamont's (2000), assert that their African-American and Latino counterparts are lazy and feckless, they are implicitly arguing that this is a boundary along which 'race' is measured, and that they themselves are industrious, careful and responsible (i.e. the exact opposite of the groups they have been talking about).

'With some exception', contend Weis and Fine (1996: 504), 'the primary function of discourses about welfare abusers, by these white men, is to draw the boundaries of acceptable receipt of government services, *at themselves* – the hardworking white man who is trying to support his family'.

So how does this help us understand the visibility and invisibility of whiteness? By demonstrating that both are true, unless you understand the process of racialisation as a static one (which is a tautology in any case). The part of the equation which consists of the dominant groups racialising Others, which we are interested in here, also entails self-racialisation. You reveal your own values when describing (or more accurately ascribing) those of other people. The role of social scientists is to listen to this, and the invisibility (or 'inaudibility', to pursue this imagery more faithfully) of whiteness dissolves. We shall see more on values in the following chapter.

Realisation of a subject's whiteness comes frequently when that person experiences an unusual setting through mobility, and may also be expressed as national belonging. Let us take two brief statements from our research project on the UK (Clarke and Garner, forthcoming).

Elsie, an elderly respondent in our survey from the South West of England, narrates the coach journey to her daughter's home on the other side of the country, a trip which she makes a few times a year. The coach passes through the main road out of East London, the A11. At the City of London end, there are areas of shops and street markets reflecting the districts' relatively high British Asian population:[27]

> When you leave London [. . .] as far as Stratford . . . when you go along there, it's all sort of market [. . .] and you don't really see a English person, it's all like Muslims and you know . . . The first time I did that on that coach, I mean, I got a bit more used to it now, I thought, oh, my, it was just as if you were in a different world, you know. Once you got past Stratford, it was okay of course.

Elsie is shocked by the absence of white people on the streets, and the look of the shops and goods on sale. She uses the term 'English' to cover white, indicating an ambiguous understanding of nationality. Elsewhere in her interviews she contradicts this. She also conflates all the religious backgrounds of the people, describing them as 'Muslims and you know . . .'. The area to negotiate in this state of anxiety was bounded, ending after the suburb of Stratford, where the coach stops before continuing its journey East.

Another interviewee, Brian, makes frequent business trips from the South West to London, and bemoans the overwhelming presence of Others that he encounters there:

> I do find it, I'll be honest, mildly irritating because you hardly see what you would call a normal white British person on the street,

because it is just full of foreigners, foreigners in inverted commas, sorry . . .

Brian's comments indicate a common culture-shock expressed about travelling from a provincial city to a big cosmopolitan one, which is seen as racialised space vis-à-vis 'normal' spaces. He is even more explicit in linking colour to nation. Moreover, his awareness of political parameters on 'race-talk', allied to the linking of phenotypical difference with unbridgeable and unsettling cultural difference, is a frequent theme in how many white people talk about multicultural Britain. On more local levels, research in Britain has elucidated the way younger people think about the spaces they travel through and to in terms of safety. This understanding can be multifaceted, involving gender, class and 'race', and complicated combinations of knowledge about individuals who use those spaces. Thus Paul Watt and Kevin Stenson (1998), and Watt (1998), found that young white people in provincial Southern England see particular spaces as dangerous for a number of reasons, such as fear of crime and violence. This anxiety is heightened when they do not know individuals resident in the areas they are crossing. Their working-class interviewees, a substantial proportion of whom had gone to schools with racially diverse populations, often based their assessment of risk on such acquaintances. However, the white suburban middle-class youth emerged from Watt and Stenson's survey as the group most concerned about safety, lacking as they did the networks and experiences of multi-cultural space and settings to enable them to make nuanced risk assessments. The other side of this coin was that young minority people avoided certain areas and even whole towns because they are seen as fearsomely white. However, we should also be wary of generalising anxiety into a norm, because other white subjects find that mixed occupation of space can become, or already has become their norm, and their ontological security is unbalanced by an *excess* of whiteness. 'Jim' in Katherine Tyler's (2004) study of Coalville in Leicestershire (a small former mining community in central England) notes a big difference between the midlands city of Stoke-on-Trent (where he went to college) and his home town, in that Stoke's multiculturalism pushed him to question prevalent ideas on 'race' when he returned to Leicestershire.

Similarly, two of our respondents in the city of Plymouth, England, commented on such disjunctures. The first, a health worker from London, who had moved to the South West, remarked that local people had 'strange ideas about colour' that struck him as such because of his own formative years in a multicultural school and neighbourhood. The second, a professional, got involved in anti-racist work in the city when he realised that he had become used to Plymouth's whiteness, a landscape that contrasted with his schooldays in another midlands town. From these examples it appears that whiteness as a *reflexive* identification, as opposed to a taken-for-granted *invisible* one, may emerge from structural relations (i.e. the generation and maintenance of their norms) clashing with the individual's frame of understanding. In answer to Helen (charles)' question, some white people do know they are white, but this revelation comes at particular moments.

Conclusion

Whiteness has been theorised as both invisible (to white people) and very visible (to others). While this appears contradictory, it can also be understood as logical, but the key to this is recognition that white is not a location like any other but the linchpin of racialised identities, granting privilege to the bearer. It is only the specificity of white as linked to power that enables it to imagine that it is of so little importance as an identity. Because of the absence of obstacles encountered, white people tend to think that what happens to them is what happens to everyone else, and importantly, they imagine that everyone is treated as an individual. This clearly is not the case: one of the ways in which racism works is to treat people as the opposite of individuals, to deny this and instead produce them as merely representations of a form of person; any Asian can stand in for Japanese car-manufacturers, any black man can be a murder suspect, any woman wearing a veil can make Muslim attitudes to women apparent and underline the threat of Islam to the West's values, etc. Even while it is acknowledged that individuals are not responsible for what others do, the mechanism still functions. In Adams and Burke's research on post-9/11 attitudes in England (2006: 992), 'Andrea' addresses exactly this:

> PB: How do you feel about the media coverage?
> Andrea: They was showing [Muslim people] being quite scared to go down the street, because they were getting attacked, Muslims over here, and spat at. I must admit, if I was walking down the street and I would see one of these, you know those dresses that they wear from head to toe, and I'd get angry 'cause I'd think, you know, 'your bloody beliefs, and all the rest of it, that did all that'. Even though I'd know they weren't personally to blame I'd still feel 'if it weren't for you bloody people'.
> PB: You felt an anger towards . . .?
> Andrea: But it is a contradiction because I did, yeah, but at the same

time I do know there are normal nice people that don't agree with it as well.

A liberal response to this conundrum is to emphasise that everyone is an individual, that to see 'race' is to be racist. Here, being white is thus equated with being human, universal, the Greenwich Mean Time of identity. So when white people gaze on their racialised Others and note difference (three hours ahead, five hours behind, etc.) they are implicitly expressing their own position. By making explicit the characteristics of the Chinese, African, etc., they are inadvertently making implicit their own understandings of who they are. The invisibility sought by the subject is therefore belied. Only a relatively small proportion of white people seem to realise what being white means about their social location. This is why McIntosh (1988) suggests that one starting point for white people interested in equality is to think about what privileges whiteness bestows upon *them*, as well as how it impacts negatively on people of colour.

3   Whiteness as values, norms and cultural capital

WHAT ARE VALUES, NORMS AND CULTURAL CAPITAL?

In this chapter I will show that whiteness has been conceptualised as consisting of cultural elements, and how this emerges as such in some examples of fieldwork drawn from Britain and the USA. However, in order to do this convincingly, we have to understand what 'values', 'norms' and 'cultural capital' actually mean in sociological terms.

A 'norm' refers to a practice or an idea viewed as constituting what is normal in a given place at a given time among a given group of people. I stress the verb 'viewed' here because it is subjective rather than objective. The term 'value', on the other hand, means an objective that is seen as one that is preferable to aspire to, something that is considered an important goal in society. The material values of late capitalism express themselves in aspirations to the accumulation of capital, the consumption of goods, the ownership of property, individual self-realisation and liberty among others. These values can be contrasted with those of collective well-being, the sharing of goods and the non-existence of personal property found in indigenous people such as First Australians and Native Americans for example. I suggested in the previous chapter that when people talk in interviews of what they admire, aspire to, and what they dislike, or feel is incorrect behaviour, they are implicitly stating their own values. Others are more explicit. Many of Michèle Lamont's blue-collar interviewees (2000) state that their values are family- and outward-oriented, and they seek to differentiate themselves from white-collar workers and managerial staff they see as selfish, money-obsessed, and poor communicators.

So there is a distinction between 'values' and norms. People can hold quite different values from one another, but it is likely that their understanding of prevailing norms in their society (i.e. their conception of whether behaviour or ideas falls within the parameters of what is normal) will be fairly similar, even if they adopt a critical stance towards some of these norms.

Cultural capital is a more complex concept. It was coined by French sociologist Pierre Bourdieu in his famous study of the upper and middle classes in France, translated as *Distinction* (1984).[28] Bourdieu was attempting to construct a more nuanced model for understanding social relationships from within the Marxist tradition. To this end, he developed the idea that there were three types of capital, including the obvious economic form. The other two are 'social' and 'cultural' capital. Cultural capital is quite a general theory and those interested in its critiques should refer to the reading suggested (Lamont and Lareau 1988, Reay 1998).[29] In its most basic terms, cultural capital is an acquired set of values, beliefs, norms, attitudes, experiences and so forth that equip people differentially for their life in society. As certain types of such capital facilitate access to the higher echelons of the education system and therefore confer privileged access to higher-paying employment, this capital can be 'cashed in' for material goods. Bourdieu argues that the dominant (upper middle-class) culture reproduces its dominance by rewarding children in the education system who speak its language, and share its assumptions and aspirations. The greater one's cultural capital, the more one is conversant with ruling-class culture's norms. In the discussion of whiteness below, we are using the term removed from the context of the education system, but its general applicability at this level remains.

I shall first give an idea of how values, norms and cultural capital have been deployed to explain whiteness at an abstract level before looking at some case studies drawn from the USA and England.

CONCEPTUALISING WHITENESS AS VALUES, NORMS AND CULTURAL CAPITAL

The idea that whiteness encapsulates a particular set of norms is raised by Matthew Jacobson's reading of the senate debates on US citizenship in 1870 (1998: 73–74). He finds a capacity for industriousness, Christianity, a high degree of freedom, exercise of independent thought necessary for democratic government, and complexion. Paynter's (2001) list reads: Christianity, hypocrisy, cultural gentility (i.e. cultural chauvinism).

Dyer (1988, 1997) sees norms of obsessive self-control, rationality, order and the repression of emotions, which manifest themselves somatically in rigidity. This creates the norms of the Others as sensuality, vivacity and childish disorder. In the film *Jezebel* (1938), for example, the heroine's failure to comply with the order of whiteness is symbolised in her choice of a red dress to wear to the ball instead of a white one, a failure to comply which is later reversed and manifested in her giving the dress away. Such sensuality is not appropriate for white bourgeois womanhood, yet it is suitable (and we assume 'natural') for the lead character's black maid, who is ultimately given the dress to wear.

Henry Giroux (1998) interprets a similar white drive towards order and repression of disorder in popular American culture. According to his reading, the film *Dangerous Minds* (1995) demonstrates a sustained attempt to devalue and homogenise minority urban experience, and inculcate white middle-class values, presenting them as rational vis-à-vis irrational inner-city youth. The film, he contends: 'functions mythically to rewrite the decline of public schooling and the attack on poor, black, and Hispanic students as part of a broader project for rearticulating whiteness as a model of authority, rationality and civilized behaviour' (Giroux 1998: 63).

Indeed, this myth of the colonial saviour (subverted in Dyer's reading of the British television serial, *The Jewel in the Crown*) is underscored in American big screen representations of 'white messiahs' (Vera and Gordon 2003a, b, Queenan 2007), who provide charismatic leadership for the oppressed Other. The fiction is to present whiteness (and virtually always maleness) as benevolent and selfless, and the people of colour encountered as in need of uplift and direction.

We noted in a previous chapter the corpus of writings by people of colour about their experience of whiteness. This resource is utilised by Marilyn Frye (2001 [1992]) to develop the concept of 'whiteliness' (a personal, socialised behaviour that tends towards racism). In setting this up, Frye draws a parallel between maleness and masculinity, with the latter constructed as a set of behaviour whose 'monotonous similarity' encapsulates whiteness as a collective experience. The works she draws on are principally the narratives of African-Americans in John Gwaltney's (1980) anthropology, *Drylongso*, and the collected edition *This Bridge Called My Back* (Anzaldúa and Moraga 1983). These accounts contain a set of stringent critiques of white ethics and abuse of power that cannot be adequately summarised in this space. The key point for Frye, however, is her assertion that these critiques demonstrate how the very ethical being of what she terms 'whitely' people is utterly undermined, since it is actually premised on the idea of the ability to assert authority, preach, teach, tell right from wrong, judge and make peace. Unsurprisingly, then, after centuries of domination, whiteness is often seen by those dominated as embodying a nefarious raft of values.

Indeed, in hooks's classrooms (1992), she observes that the process of even looking at whiteness through Others' eyes generates anger and defensiveness among the white students. The racialised power imbalance is caught here, when white students realise that their classmates have looked anthropologically at them, and have collectively returned the dominant gaze. This type of challenge is the beginning of the undermining process that Frye addresses. It holds up a mirror in which 'whitely' behaviour appears, to the beholder, distorted, ugly, pathetic even. Values are approached from very different points in Gwaltney, hooks and Anzaldúa and Moraga. The point that Frye is arguing is that 'whiteliness' does not mean natural attachment and allegiance to the values associated with domination, quite the opposite: it suggests that the project of detaching the white self from whiteliness is altogether possible.

The idea of whiteness as a 'knapsack' (McIntosh 1988) of free rides and a 'possessive investment' (Lipsitz 1998) has already been looked at in previous chapters. Paynter (2001) goes so far as to characterise whiteness as *primarily* cultural capital. Ghassan Hage (2000) argues forcefully that whiteness is a form of cultural capital that can be exchanged for Anglo culture by incoming immigrants in Australia. The earliest formulation of this thesis however is that of Du Bois, who terms the non-material deferential advantages gleaned from whiteness as 'a sort of public and psychological wage' (1998 [1935]: 700). So on one level, it might not be so surprising that whiteness has assumed such an allure that it can even be aspired to by black Others trapped in the colonisers' construction of them. Fanon (1967) explicitly deals with the psychological deficit whiteness inscribes in the non-white subject, causing a desire to mimic or inhabit whiteness, while Winddance Twine's study of Brazil (1998) indicates that people whiten up in the Census to satisfy personal (yet collectively refuted) desires for privilege.

Culturally, the concepts are relational: whiteness without blackness, freedom without slavery, civilisation without barbarity? The former devoid of the latter becomes meaningless, and this is the key to understanding how whiteness works, by continuously redefining itself as the polar opposite of non-whiteness. Similarly, 'freedom' for some depends on the 'unfreedom' of others, a relationship that Morrison (1993: 57) terms 'the parasitical nature of white freedom'. If the holding of privilege is anchored in such shaky ground, the insecurity inherent in basing one's identity on such privilege may be identified. Given that whiteness is a phenomenon unthinkable in a context where white does not equal power at some structural level, the oppositional nature of whiteness–otherness begins to assume some clarity. The economic and psychological wages of whiteness may be more meagre (and thus more precious) the lower down the social hierarchy the white subject is located. Yet this should not be seen as deterministic, but simply more likely.

These diverse trans-disciplinary studies generate sketches of the structurally uneven field upon which whiteness and blackness are constructed and relationally experienced. To divorce analyses of whiteness from the power relationships that frame it is to commit a cardinal error: it bears repeating that whiteness has historically functioned as a racial supremacist identity, fleetingly suspending the power relationships between genders and classes within the self-identifying 'white' group in order to unite them. This does not mean that acknowledging this caveat grants a licence to fall into the opposite error: that of supposing that whiteness actually suspends these relationships on a permanent basis. I shall now turn to some examples of fieldwork to illustrate some of the ways in which values become codified into racialised discourse.

CASE STUDIES: FROM LONDON TO NEW JERSEY

The Other within

Paul Hoggett's (1992) study of Tower Hamlets, in the East End of London, demonstrates the predominance of values as a battleground in racialised inter-communal tensions. The East End has traditionally been an area of first residence for new immigrants to London. The Bangladeshi community in Tower Hamlets dates back to the late 1960s. In Hoggett's study, Bangladeshi incomers in this borough are perceived as displaying values formerly characteristic of working-class East End communities. The sense of loss of such values thus coalesces around the physical presence of a group of new migrants and therefore causes a degree of jealousy.

> The resentment the whites feel toward the Bengali community is made poignant by the fact that the latter community has many characteristics – extended and intensive kinship networks, a respect for tradition and more seniority, a capacity for entrepreneurialism and social advancement – which the white working class in the area have lost.
>
> (1992: 354)[30]

The modernisation of a tower block, in which many Bangladeshis live, leads to a cockroach infestation. Their physical presence in Tower Hamlets, occupying not only geographical territory but also ethical space into which whiteness used to extend, becomes embodied in local discourse as the figure of the 'cockroach'. The recurrent notions of associating dirt and potential disease with out-groups (Douglas 1966) will be looked at in more detail in chapter 6. The Bangladeshis' status as matter-out-of-place is thus emphasised, in contradiction to the social values and shared history of class oppression, objectively binding them to local working-class white East Enders. Yet the point that emerges is that because of the values they are seen to embody, this group of Others constitutes an 'identification'. That is, the out-group is seemingly 'stealing' these values from the white working class. Thus what follows is a series of projections and identifications. 'The local white is engaged in one sense in an envious attack upon the Bengali within him', writes Hoggett, 'an attack which twists and corrupts him into its opposite' (1992: 354). Indeed, the traumatic experience of racialisation evokes recognition of loss of place, standards, and status in unpredictable locations. White even finds a local British National Party organiser in Oldham who concedes that 'we can learn something from the Asians about family values and looking after our own' (2002: 54).

American working men

The white ethnic 'backlash' of the 1980s and 1990s in the USA (Winant 1997) has provided a backdrop to the American research referred to in this book, while the 'politics of backlash' in the UK (Hewitt 2005) performs the same function in chapters 8 and 9. Indeed, Margaret Andersen (2003: 22) explains the establishment of 'whiteness studies' partly as a product of debates in America about increasing conservatism, racial politics and the idea of Whites as a declining majority. Whiteness as a particularly defensive identity vis-à-vis that of minority Others is a core theme of illuminating studies such as Weis *et al.* (1996), Weis and Fine (1996) and Hartigan (1999). However, as with affirmative action, this 'nodal point' of discourse marks one parameter of distinctiveness of the field of study in Europe. While current debates there on immigration and asylum, with their undercurrents of racialised closure, can arguably be conceptualised as 'backlash' politics, the idea of Whites as a declining majority is irrelevant. So in the following synthesis I am seeking useful overriding themes rather than supposing that the debates and experiences map directly onto one another.

Weis and Fine's (1996) de-industrialised white males in New York State and New Jersey define themselves as bearers of the traditional values of patriarchy, industriousness and patriotism, being engulfed and subsumed by amoral, family breakdown-ridden welfare-sponging minorities.

They set themselves up as hardworking and deserving users of occasional welfare, which they contrast with African and Hispanic Americans. These groups are viewed as not prepared to take up jobs (unless they are handed to them on a plate through affirmative action), but instead indulging in regular welfare abuse (1996: 499). As the authors comment, this discourse about the deserving and undeserving poor has a history (Katz 1998, 1989). Moreover, this discourse is coming to represent the transition to the period when the industrial family run on a single (masculine) wage – that covers the purchase of a house – has ceased to be the norm.

As these workers find themselves sliding towards the type of behaviour they had connected with moral failings (sporadic employment, use of welfare, incapacity to save to buy a home) they do not associate the decline with structural factors but with pathologically unethical behaviour by the men seen as their competitors: minorities. The contrast between African-American and White-American interviewees' comments to Weis and Fine reveals the formers' structural understandings of the workings of the labour market and institutionalised racism, the existence of the crack economy and police harassment (1996: 505). The latter construct individualised explanations of their failure to follow the American dream, in which personal responsibility is paramount.

The American section of Michèle Lamont's comparative study of the USA and France (2000) covers geographically similar territory (New York State and New Jersey). A rather fundamental discrepancy about self-definition emerges from it. Although there is a degree of overlap between African- and White-American workers that their shared class values are family- and solidarity-oriented, there is a revealing gap. This manifests itself in the emphasis placed on various aspects of morality, a distinction that Lamont refers to as the 'caring self' *v.* the 'disciplined self' (2000: 20–21). The difference is not absolute but relative. The black workers expressed greater attachment to group solidarity and generosity, the Whites more on self-reliance and the work ethic. This is not to say that either group spurned the values of family and responsibility, but that this was seen more as the province of the group by the Blacks, and of the individual by the Whites. Lamont (ibid.: 135) concludes that '. . . self-reliance, laziness and responsibility are important in framing whites' stigmatisation of blacks'. When asked to identify traits (ibid.: 28) that they liked and disliked in others, 70 per cent of white workers and 40 per cent of black workers stated that they did not like irresponsibility; and 59 per cent of Whites and 40 per cent of Blacks said they liked people who were hardworking. Most revealingly, when asked to provide a definition of success 20 per cent of white workers, but none of the black workers, used 'work' as a criterion.

Indeed, it is primarily through these values that the white workers defined themselves and their minority co-workers. Naturalised difference expressed in routine behaviour is cast as a moral flaw. Lamont concludes that this enables the white worker to transform a racialised judgement into an objective ethical one:

> for white workers, moral and racial boundaries are inseparable from each other. Whether they focus on differences in the area of work ethic, responsibility, family values, or traditional morality, interviewees move seamlessly from morality to race, effortlessly extending these moral distinctions to broad racial categories. They view these moral boundaries as legitimate because they are based on the same universal criteria of evaluation that are at the center of their larger worldviews. They are thus able to make racist arguments and feel that they are fundamentally good, fair people.
>
> (ibid.: 68)

CULTURAL CAPITAL AND RESPECTABILITY

Academic and journalistic practice has been to characterise working-class communities either as the sole source of racism, or as the most stubbornly racist section of an otherwise increasingly tolerant society. One counter-example is provided by John Hartigan's study of self-styled 'hillbillies' in inner-city Detroit (1999, 1997a,b), who are far more ambivalent about their class location and their relationships with Whites and minorities from better and worse-off neighbourhoods across the city. Commenting on the social mixing he observed in this area in public spaces, Hartigan concluded that the degree to which people were geographically and thus socially 'at home' greatly influenced the role that racialisation appeared to play in their interaction. He reports that when he told some interviewees that he was studying 'race relations', they directed him to a housing project across the highway, indicating that it was a zone too dangerous for Whites (1997a: 191):

> In this [their own] neighbourhood, they were one family among many, white and black, who held elaborate and lengthy knowledge of each other reaching back over the tumultuous past three decades. But across the intersection [i.e. in that particular project] they were simply 'whites', partly for their skin color and partly in terms of location and being out of place.

The invisibility feared by Hartigan's white respondents thus thematically mirrors that of the black people who are objectified by whiteness (see chapter 1). He notes that the Briggs area, where he was based for fieldwork, is one in which black and white residents are, unusually for the USA, permanently thrown together spatially, and that the general peaceful co-existence is based on local understandings of codes about how to do 'race', class and gender. Yet this is predicated on long-term familiarity. One of the black residents, Marvin, explains to Hartigan that people get along well in Briggs because so many of them went to school together and have known each other for twenty years or more (Hartigan 1999: 96). Indeed, what strikes the reader of Hartigan's account is the contingency of the extent to which 'race' was, or was not, interpreted as significant in a given situation, and the plural registers of language and action in which particular terms and behaviour are acceptable in some contexts and not in others. Additionally, the way 'race' is read through frames such as class. An example of this is a multiracial baseball game. Hartigan's main informant is Jessie, whose family like to play baseball on Sundays. They arrange to play a serious game (for a case of beer) against a team of local black people whom they had met the week before. One of Jessie's brothers, David (who lives elsewhere), refuses to play because he doesn't want to play against Blacks. His decision is viewed by the Briggs-based family as more evidence of David's weirdness and efforts to distance himself socially. More people are absorbed into the game as the afternoon advances, and it ends up with racially mixed teams. At this point, Sam, another of Jessie's brothers, tells Hartigan enthusiastically that 'this is family' (ibid.: 140). Unfortunately, Becky, who is Jessie's son's girlfriend, and lives in a white suburb of Detroit, sparks trouble by expressing her discomfort about the proximity of black people. This manifests itself in her leaving early and not wanting to lend her glove to 'niggers', the explanation that she gives Jessie. In the event, they return only once more to Briggs during Hartigan's stay. The resulting feud is interpreted by the family as being about Becky's incapacity to socialise in this surrounding, her feeling that she, like David, thinks she is better than them, and her ambition to 'spoil' Jessie's son: 'Their (David and Becky's) striving for social mobility and higher class standing was articulated through an assertion of the need for careful racial boundary maintenance by avoiding interracial situations' (ibid.: 142).

Hartigan suggests that in emphasising Becky's use of the term 'nigger', Jessie might well have been attempting to end his son's relationship with her. He sees the fact that neither David nor Becky are criticised for being racists, but only snobs, by Jessie's family, as demonstrating that white raciality is understood in this case through class (ibid.: 142–144).

While the majority of studies are spatially located in working-class neighbourhoods Katherine Tyler's ethnography of the English village of 'Greenville' in Leicestershire (2003) shows that semi-rural space is defended using the development of middle-class values of belonging through adherence to ways of being and behaving. While the class distinctions within the village are not neglected, she focuses on the ways in which racism is articulated there. The Asian families in Greenville are produced as 'abnormal' (2003: 394) because they do not fit notions of respectability and normality, such as not getting involved in charity activities (women) and not going to the pub (men). One family extended its house (against local opposition) and the anxieties of the villagers reveal the prism of abnormality through which the Asians are (mis)-understood: the potential over-use of space; as a residence, business and prayer room. One villager states that: 'They are very nice people but eyebrows are raised when the hordes of friends and relatives come from Leicester. It isn't done in Greenville' (ibid.: 405). Tyler concludes that 'wealthy Asians are thought to live in extended families, are perceived to be excessively wealthy, extravagantly religious, run disruptive businesses from their homes and cook smelly foods' (ibid.: 409). For the middle classes in semi-rural Leicester, tranquillity is a prized value. While solidarity (for the poor elsewhere) is demonstrated through the routines of charity work, the real test of belonging is to attain invisibility. Talking of a particular Asian family in the village, one resident tells Tyler (ibid.: 400): 'They are as good as gold . . . we never see them'. Hiding oneself and keeping the noise down is viewed as the correct way to behave, a value that contradicts the justification for not forging more intimate relations: Asians 'don't mix'.

The other side of this insider/outsider problem is emphasised by Garland and Chakraborti (2006), who argue that there are problems militating against involvement in village life for minorities, particularly those who are not Christian or secular, and do not drink alcohol (ibid.: 164–165). While some ethnic minority village residents' professional status may obviate a degree of the hostility, they still cannot own the cultural codes required to function 'normally'. For community 'insiders', they contend, 'rural villages can be places where kinship and shared identities can be played out and enjoyed; for those subject to the "othering" process, such places can be cold and unwelcoming' (ibid.: 169). Daniel Miller's conclusion about cultural capital is worth noting here: 'The relationship between the two kinds of capital – cultural and economic – is uneasy [. . .] Society, then, is not to be understood in terms of a simple hierarchy, but as a continual struggle over the hierarchy of hierarchies' (Miller 1987: 152). The hierarchy of economics can apparently trump that of culture: the Greenville Asians literally cannot buy the requisite cultural capital.

In Watt and Stenson's (1998) exploration of the contingency of racialised space and young people's leisure-related mobility, some places, especially more rural Buckinghamshire small towns and villages, are viewed as 'whiter' (i.e. more dangerous for minorities) than others. If cultural capital can be understood not simply as elite high culture, as Reay (1998) suggests, then there are different classed and gendered forms of such capital that are more or less valued. The cultural capital of the black and Asian respondents in Watt and Stenson includes security-oriented knowledge of dangerous, excessive whiteness. Moreover, minority spaces, however safe, are not always emancipatory for members of the minority, e.g. for young Muslim women, who prefer to go somewhere more anonymous for nights out, an experience echoed by young Sikhs in Kaur's (2003) study of Southall. Watt and Stenson's young people's leisure itineraries are shaped by intersections of class, raced identities and gender. Middle-class suburban white youth are fearful of both white working-class neighbourhoods and an Asian area in the town, whereas non-whites steer clear of particular areas in 'Townsville' unless they know white people who inhabit them through school or shared leisure activities. Indeed, most of the inter-ethnic friendships were among the working-class respondents on estates (Watt and Stenson 1998: 256). The middle-class suburban youth, more advantaged in many areas of cultural capital, are in this respect impoverished in cultural capital that they have not accrued (in contrast to their working-class peers) from 'personal contacts across the ethnic divides which were so important for moving confidently about the town' (ibid.: 257).

Yet some middle-class parents appear to be positioning themselves in order to fill their children with the same thing through investment in selected state secondary schools. Reay *et al.* (forthcoming) identify one strand of the British middle class that is not engaging in white flight, but on the contrary seeing the diversity of urban secondary schools as a resource that will enable their children to compete on the labour market and develop social skills that will be useful in later life; a form of (multi)-cultural capital. The trade off against poorer average grades than private schools is an advantageous one. The search for the 'right mix' (of people) is taken up at primary school level in Byrne's (2006) work on South London, where mothers assess local schools in terms of the various types of cultural capital available. Working knowledge of diversity figures on the list, but only if the proportion of non-white pupils is manageable (somewhere below half).

Cultural capital in ethnographic work looked at here is understood to encompass far broader settings than that of the upper echelons of the middle class. This interpretation enables us to grasp the complexity of the situations, or 'predicaments' to use Hartigan's term, in which 'race' assumes meaning at a local level.

Respectability and entitlement

One cultural battleground over which competing versions of hierarchy coalesce is the question of respectability. Beverley Skeggs argues that respectability is 'one of the key mechanisms by which people are othered and pathologized', something to 'desire, to prove and to achieve' in order to be valued and legitimated (1997: 1). Of course, what this covers varies from setting to setting, but its potency as a racialised as well as a classed boundary marker is undiminished. The Greenville Asians are seen as not respectable vis-à-vis norms of charity, religiosity and quietness. This is in contrast to those in Oldham, who are viewed by White as repositories of old-fashioned values now measurable against those of poor Whites described as an abnegation of standards 'once confined to the very lumpen fringes of white working-class culture' (White 2002: 53). In terms of whiteness, cultural capital can involve, among other things, shared expectations of behaviour on the part of minority groups, a belief that one is part of a tradition of dominance including Empire, knowledge of norms and behaviour patterns that will produce intended outcomes in particular situations; including the right to question certain people's eligibility for various resources without this being countered, and the assumption of rationality juxtaposed with the irrationality of Others.

Anoop Nayak's study of youth subcultures in Newcastle (2003) points to differing versions of whiteness and a reading of them based on entitlement and respectability. The family and/or occupational histories of the 'Real Geordies'[31] tie them into the region's manufacturing and mining employment base, and allegiance to Newcastle United FC consolidates this local-centred expression of belonging. This leads them to view hard work as the keystone of respectability, which then grants entitlement. Yet they promote 'the values of a muscular puritan work ethic (honesty, loyalty, self-sufficiency, "a fair day's work for a fair day's pay") in a situation where unskilled manual *unemployment* was increasingly the norm' (Nayak 2003: 309). The values of their parents' and grandparents' generations have thus seeped into the post-mining and manufacturing present, just as their loyalty to a football club whose players are drawn from all over the world and who earn high multiples of the local average working wage sits unproblematically for them, despite it being based on the era of local primarily working-class players performing in front of mainly working-class supporters whose worlds were not so far apart.

The other two groups looked at by Nayak are held in contempt by the Real Geordies. The 'Charver Kids' unemployed or casually employed status, involvement with petty crime, and their relationship to black music and dress, drain them of respectability in the eyes of the 'Real Geordies'. Moreover, the 'White wannabes' ' explicit search for vicarious blackness and their allegiance to international culture places them outside the fields of the local and authentic. Respect, as defined by the Real Geordies, can only be derived from these fields.

Sophie Wells and Karen Watson's London shopkeepers (2005) also implicitly posit some of these respectable values of industry and authenticity. They perceive their position as jeopardised by groups of people receiving State resources at the expense of people like them (i.e. on the basis of cultural otherness per se rather than through hard work). Even some local spaces previously seen as neutral, or as resources formerly accessible to the whole community, have been turned into mosques, for example, indicating for the respondents, the neighbourhood's demographic shift away from Britishness. This 'decline' can be charted in alternative ways. One of Wells and Watson's respondents, a butcher (2005: 269–270), narrates the area's transformation through the types of meat available. The white working-class clientele's demand for rabbit has long given way to the appearance and proliferation of halal, and before that, kosher butchers. The expectations of civilised and classed familiar meats have been overturned by 'smelly' and alien meat preparation methods: a microcosm of the invasion narrative that is told in the rest of the interviews. Bridget Byrne's interviewee, Emma, also depicts a struggle for Englishness against such a London background:

> if you go round the back there are some . . . in the marketplace you get all this halal meat and all sorts of stuff. I wouldn't touch that with a bargepole. Not because it's different, or because of anything. But just because I think it smells funny.
>
> (Byrne 2006: 149)

This is a similar response to the one found in Hoggett's (1992) study in which the meanings attached to change overlook, ignore or downplay its economic rationale. In the butcher's case, many local outlets have been forced to close down because of competition from supermarkets, so only those who specialise, for example, in organic meat or halal, can survive in a niche market.[32] Despite good reason given for the cockroach infestation in Tower Hamlets – improvements in ducting and central heating that caused a veritable breeding ground and motorway for cockroaches – psychological Othering takes precedence, and attaches to cultural manifestations of difference. Moreover, rather than global forces of capital, the local minority populations are seen as agents of change, bolstered by the state and local government.

So expressions of racism can be understood additionally as forms of self-valorisation, and a key in understanding this process is to anchor it in notions of respectability. Performing respectability means, among other things, paying dues that entitle a person to compensation in social esteem and/or other benefits. In cultures where working for payment, productive employment, is the norm, failure to do so can easily be pathologised as individual failure (all the more so when local narratives have constructed benefits as individual consumer rights as opposed to collective norms in the Thatcherite project, as Skeggs (1995) claims). In this context, respectability plus work leads to entitlement. Not paying dues in either or both of these areas is seen as queue-jumping. Just as the unemployed and single mothers in the 1980s, pathologised as feck-less underclass and irresponsible over-breeders respectively, were potent figures representing failure and excess, so now are racialised Others: asylum seekers who 'won't work' and get everything on a plate; migrants who get jobs 'we' can't get, local authority funding to build places 'we' can't use; whole migrant communities (forget they have been living in Britain for generations) who can't/won't speak English and want 'us' to give up Christmas, etc.

The neo-liberal agenda of immigration control and managed migration across Europe posits desirable migrants as only short-term labour-providers. Any other type of migrant is unwanted and defined as suspicious.[33] The emphasis on migrants being productive emerges from contemporary work in England as a mantra of banal neo-liberalism, as the example taken from our research (Clarke and Garner, forthcoming) below demonstrates:

Q   So to you what are the most important criteria for deciding who should be allowed to come into Britain as an immigrant?

A   I would say they have to be able to add some value in some respect. You're going to ask me to say what I mean by adding value, aren't you?

Q   Yes.

A   Well, to give something really, whether that be, I mean they have to be prepared to sort of work really. And that probably sounds quite harsh, but I mean you, we can't become a country

that just is inundated with just massive numbers of people constantly coming in, because there's not going to be enough
resources and jobs and whatever to go round, and I think we
have to set some kind of criteria first and foremost.

Even a respondent in this middle-class residential district who was laud-
ably indifferent to the topic of immigration as a political problem stated
that it was 'not something I feel especially strongly about . . . what's the
problem *if they have something to contribute* . . . the amount of political
hoo-hah over it seems daft'.

So norms help structure the forms of difference seen as threatening,
and these may well place the interlocutor in a position to define him/
herself as valuable and respectable vis-à-vis the group being described.
In the cases of the USA- and the UK-based research referred to in this
chapter, those enunciating this type of position are white people talking
primarily about people who are not white, and implicitly denying the
racialised Other entitlement through respectable norms.

In this chapter I have traced the conceptualisation of whiteness as
a set of values, norms and as forms of cultural capital through various
examples of fieldwork carried out in the USA and England. Despite the
differences in content between the two countries, some parallels can be
drawn: the notion of respectability is a convenient hook on which to
hang this assertion. Respectability orders the values and enables people
to identify devalued behaviour (of Others) and valued behaviour. The
latter is viewed as the norm for the white 'us', and is discursively created
in speaking of the devalued behaviour. Moreover, deleterious social
change can therefore be interpreted through the prism of individual
responsibility and blamed on people of colour who are actually also on
the receiving end of such change. As respectability is valuable only to
those who lack it (Skeggs 1997), it becomes a particularly loaded idiom in
which to discuss change, throwing up as it does a series of contingent
and cross-cutting class, gender and racial hierarchies.

4 Whiteness as contingent hierarchies

It has been argued so far that whiteness has been conceptualised in a number of ways. Primarily we have looked at the intersection of whiteness and its Others, the racialised identities created by white world's military, commercial and ideological domination of the globe since the sixteenth century. Yet at the beginning of the book I suggested that the way in which whiteness served to reproduce social hierarchies was not simply along this border, but also by creating and maintaining internal borders between the more and the less white. Immediate examples here include Southern, Central and Eastern European immigrant groups, Jews, Gypsy-Travellers/Roma, as well as the numerous divisions based on class, gender, sexuality, region, etc., identified in the literature on America and Britain (Hartigan 2005, Nayak 2003, Daniels 1997). There may well be trepidation about the extent to which we are encroaching on other areas of work. We already have concepts like anti-semitism, sexism and homophobia. Class divisions are already covered in other literatures. Considering that European migrants are white anyway, how is this to do with 'race'? Isn't it ethnicity, another area abundantly, if not excessively, analysed already? I do not want to be proscriptive. There are plenty of perspectives that can bring fruitful analyses to bear on these identities and social hierarchies, and using the whiteness problematic is one of them.

What the whiteness problematic has to bring to the table is a set of associations and a pathway that cross-cuts the other sources of identity seen as the key ones. Take the 'White Australia' immigration policy (below) as an example. The concepts of class and ethnicity could well be operationalised to look at this phenomenon. However, using whiteness suggests that a border is constructed by the state, in its definitions, that ignores both class and the specific cultural content of the ethnic groups in question. The individuals within those groups are bundled together as 'not white' according to ideas about civilisation and barbarity, the pre-eminence of a particular strand of Northern European culture and the political objectives of the Australian state aimed at improving labour capacity. The whiteness problematic may miss out on some elements of this complex situation, of course, but so do class and ethnicity alone. We should recognise throughout that hierarchies are always in the process of construction, deconstruction and reconstruction: nothing is fixed. The hierarchies I refer to are expressed in terms of patterns of power relations; that is, the power to name, the power to control and distribute resources.

What I will do in this chapter is give a brief outline of the history of white as a racial identity, then look at three broad areas of study dealt with in the literature:[34] immigration into America in the nineteenth and early twentieth century (the 'inbetween peoples' thesis); the White Australia immigration policy (1901–1972); the idea of 'white trash' in America and the working class in the UK.

WHERE DID WHITENESS COME FROM?

Although from the vantage point of the twenty-first century, the terms 'white' and 'black' seem to go without saying, these words have not always been used to identify human beings. Indeed the term 'white' used to describe people dates back only to the sixteenth century (Taylor 2005). At that time however it was one of a range of labels, and not the one most frequently used. Religion, nation, social class were all deployed more than colour. The literature on early modernity arrives at a rough consensus: the co-existence of religious labels of identity; 'Christian' and 'heathen' in the American colonies (Jordan 1968, Frederickson 1988, Paynter 2001) rendered colour distinctions redundant until slaves began to convert to Christianity. Elsewhere in the New World, Naipaul (1969) notes that after the slave revolt in Berbice (Dutch Guiana, South America) in 1764, the dead were divided up in official reports not as 'black' and 'white', or even as 'slave' and 'free', but as 'Christians' and 'heathens'. Additionally, although slavery is now irrevocably linked in popular understanding of history to Africans, the status of 'free' and 'unfree' labour in the anglophone New World did not correspond perfectly to European and African workers, respectively, until after white indentured labourers became numerically inferior due to their access to land-ownership. So it was around the last decade of the seventeenth century that colony-level legislation against voting rights for Blacks, 'race' mixing and restrictions on property ownership for Black people was enacted. We can thus start the clock of whiteness as an explicit legitimised social identity in North America and the anglophone Caribbean (Beckles 1990) from that point. This was clearly not a historical coincidence. The sixteenth and seventeenth centuries was the period when Europeans were beginning to encounter people from Africa, the Americas and Asia on an ongoing basis, and notice the obvious if cosmetic differences between groups alongside the cultural ones.

In the period between then and the mid nineteenth century, the idea that some people's identities were 'white' came to be attached to the new ways of understanding mankind that developed out of the Enlightenment (Eze 1997), and were enshrined in elite scientific discourse as empirically provable racial differences that explained cultural, political and technological inequalities. Indeed, as racial science and philosophy garnered credence, increasingly complex schemas were produced, in which there were subdivisions of whiteness. Notions of Anglo-Saxon supremacy began to gain intellectual support, bolstered by an amalgam of the press, a network of scientists engaged in somatic measurements (Horsman 1981) and internationally read work by such as that by Robert Knox and Joseph Arthur Comte de Gobineau.[35] The latter two developed the notion that within the white 'race', Anglo-Saxons were particularly capable of civilisation in comparison to Celts, Slavs and Latins. This hierarchy within a hierarchy is the basis of the thesis developed by US labour historians David Roediger and James Barrett, whose work we shall look at next.

'Inbetween peoples'?

Nineteenth-century emigrants to America did not walk into a social hierarchy and corresponding taxonomy invented specifically for them. In a set of influential publications (Roediger 1991, Barrett and Roediger 1997, 2004, 2005), Roediger and Barrett argue that in the period from the 1850s to the 1910s, incoming migrant Europeans were exposed to a situation where whiteness exerted forces that pushed Europeans to claim whiteness and gain privileged access to resources, psychological and social capital (Du Bois's 'wages of whiteness'), while playing off national groups against each other in an effort to be whiter than the other. They are not alone in positing whiteness as an overarching mainstream value of Americanness; Horsman (1981), Saxton (1990), Bernstein (1990), Almaguer (1994), Allen (1994b), Ignatiev (1996) and Jacobson (1998) all suggest this to varying degrees. Barrett and Roediger (1997, 2004) maintain two principal and connected points:

1   'Whiteness' is to do with cultural and political power and those who appear phenotypically white are not equally incorporated into the dominant groups.

2   Migrants from the various Catholic, Southern, Eastern and Central
    European countries, they argue, were not immediately accepted
    socially and culturally as white. Differential access to this resource
    was sought by successive waves of migrants learning the rules of the
    game, 'this racial thing', as one of their respondents puts it (1997: 6).
    These groups of less dominant Europeans, who are disadvantaged in
    the US context by class and culture, are labelled 'inbetween people'.
    Not white, but not black either.

Scholarship in dialogue with the writers above has debated the extent
to which various ethnic groups such as Jewish- (Brodkin 1994, 1998) and
Italian-Americans (Guglielmo and Salerno 2003) can be considered
'white'. These arguments suggest some parallels between the Irish and
the Italians in America in that over time they 'became' white. However,
there is a counter-argument developed by some historians such as Eric
Arnesen (2001) and Thomas Guglielmo (2003) that European immigrants did not actually have to 'become' white, relative to Blacks and
Mexicans, for example, and that the 'inbetween people' theory does not
withstand scrutiny. I think the keys to resolving this knot are reasonably
straightforward. They are to do with understanding the priorities and
assumptions of the protagonists (Garner 2007a). The first thing to realise
is that the 'inbetween people' thesis does not claim that Irish, Italian
and other European immigrants were really 'black', but that they were
literally 'denigrated', likened to black Americans (in terms of civilisation
and social status), and they temporarily occupied the lowest positions
on the economic and social ladder. So the point is not to suggest that
immigrants were not phenotypically white, which is why Guglielmo
(2003) correctly identifies 'race' and colour as often separate but overlapping criteria in late nineteenth- and early twentieth-century American
institutional definitions, but that ideologically and culturally they were
indeed considered different and lesser 'white races'. The corollaries of
this categorisation were not a set of life chances equivalent to those
of Blacks, Native Americans or Hispanics, rather the obligation to define
themselves as 'white' in a society where that mattered a great deal,
whereas in their countries of origin, it had mattered scarcely at all.
European immigrants thus 'became' white on arrival in the New World
because they disembarked into a new set of social identities that articulated with those they had brought with them, and one overarching
identity was whiteness.

Yet not being white, and being black, are two very different things: the
Catholic Irish were always salvageable for whiteness in a way that black,
Mexican, Asian and Native Americans were not (Garner 2003). This is

because legally they were definitely white, in as far as they could become naturalised citizens, and were not treated as imports (Haney-López 1996, Jacobson 1998). The second problem is an interesting one that illustrates divergence of interpretation of similar material. The protagonists in this debate prioritise different arenas as the source of their claims. On one side, Barrett and Roediger see the cultural domain as the one in which perceptions of 'inbetweenness' are made explicit, while Arnesen and Guglielmo pragmatically see the legal domain as predominant. Whatever people said or did, argue the latter, in law all white people were white. However, this reasoning is open to the criticism that in socio-logical terms, the law can just as easily be deconstructed as can popular culture: it is not a superior level of discourse. This is exactly what Cheryl Harris (1993), whose work we examined in chapter 1, argues. The legal domain was utilised from the nineteenth century to inject scientific rationality into decisions about who belonged to which race: and these decisions had material impacts. Yet the basis of the law was spurious, reliant as it was on unfeasibly accurate records about people's ancestry, and understandings of definitions of 'race' that were not empirically provable. The result of this was that the legal concept of ' "blood" was no more objective than that which the law dismissed as subjective and unreliable' (Harris 1993: 1740). Guglielmo (2003), for example, refers to material suggesting that Italians (especially from the South) were subject to the same kind of racialising discourses, placing them at a lower level of civilisation to Anglo-Saxons as were the Irish. Yet it is worth reiterating that 'not white' does not necessarily mean 'black'. Even if it did, how can we explain the court ruling referred to by Jacobson (1998: 4) in which an Alabama court found that the State had not proved beyond doubt that a Sicilian woman was white?

Used sociologically, the term 'white' can be interpreted as encompass-ing non-material and fluid dominant norms and boundaries. Within the white racialised hierarchy were, as Guglielmo rightly points out, a number of 'races'. Using the distinction of 'white' as an institutional starting point is a legitimate historical argument, yet this sees the terms 'white' and 'black' themselves as naturalised *givens* transposed into law, rather than products of the processes of racialisation that a sociologist ought to view as part of the puzzle itself, instead of an outline of its solution.

What emerges from this is that there are various contexts: economic, social, legal, cultural, for example, in which meaning is attributed to types of difference. In practice, it is impossible to completely separate these dimensions, but it is useful as a way of thinking through these issues to start from this basis. Moreover, the period covered, around

70 years from the mid nineteenth century to the First World War, enables us to see that understandings of who fits where in the social hierarchies can change. Why this happens when it happens can only be answered by reference to the historical record. We might put forward a few important structural items such as the Irish Famine, which altered the complexion of Irish migration to America; the Civil War, Reconstruction and after, which provided the framework both for black/white relations and for the formation of a 'white vote' in American politics; the development of the US economy to a stage which required so many manual workers that the labour supply was exhausted within the country and meant that there was plentiful work available for migrants; the consequent slump at the end of the nineteenth century experienced by Western Europe, which meant that the availability of employment that had absorbed some of the workers from Southern and Eastern Europe was diminished. Place all these together with the framework for understanding difference established by racial science in the nineteenth century, and outlines of the problem we have seen conceptualised using the shorthand 'inbetween peoples' or the process of 'becoming white' emerge more clearly. Bear in mind that being white was not just about a certain range of phenotypes, but claims on culture and values.

The next case study also looks at migration policy, but across the Pacific from America, in Australia: the set of practices and legislation that came to be known as 'White Australia'.

White Australia

Between 1901 (when the Commonwealth of Australia became a dominion, with a federal government) to 1972, Australia's immigration policy was based on the objectives of:

1   Protecting indigenous (i.e. white) labour from competition with Asian and Pacific Island labour, and
2   preserving an Anglo-Celtic majority in the country.

The term 'White Australia' was coined in 1906, as an assertion of this objective. The point of looking at this policy and the problems it ran into later in the twentieth century is to highlight both the haziness around who is considered white at a given moment and why, and give an idea of some of the contextual, structural considerations that frame such hierarchical modifications. In other words, to give an account in which neither the material nor the cultural predominates.

'White Australia' was not a single piece of legislation, but a doctrine underlying an accumulation of laws and practices that restricted immigration from outside the country (except Europe) and excluded foreign nationals in Australia from various benefits and elements of citizenship. The 1901 Commonwealth Immigration Restriction Act (IRA) was the first piece of legislation passed by the new Federal Government. Its most well-known features were its provision for a written test in any European language, at the discretion of an immigration officer, to determine a prospective immigrant's fitness for approval, and the categories of person whose entry was prohibited; the physically or mentally ill, categories of criminal other than political prisoner, prostitutes, those living on prostitutes' earnings, and those likely to be a charge on the communal purse (Tavan 2005: 7–8). In addition, various other laws provided for the repatriation of foreigners (Pacific Island Labourers Act 1901), excluded foreigners from voting (Commonwealth Franchise Act 1902; Naturalization Act 1903) and from benefits like pensions (Old-Age and Invalid Pensions Act 1908) and the Commonwealth maternity bonus (1912).

However, to properly understand the combined fear of usurping by foreign labour and 'racial contamination', as Labour leader J.C. Watson put it during parliamentary debate, it should be noted that blueprints of White Australia were already embodied in the legislation of the various Australian colonies before they joined to form the Commonwealth of Australia in 1900. Asian and Pacific Islanders had been working in Australia since the first half of the nineteenth century, primarily in the mining and sugar industries, respectively. Hostile political agitation as a response to the migration of Indian, Chinese and Pacific Islanders into various parts of the country had led to state governments passing restrictions in a number of waves during the second half of the century, particularly intensely in the late 1880s. By the end of the century, a model of indirectly discriminatory policies had been introduced. The IRA 1901 was therefore recognition on a national level of a set of practices that had been going on across Australia. What was at stake was a conception of Australia as a unique civilisation of Europeans encountering and overcoming a natural environment that other Europeans did not have to tame. The combination of whiteness, Britishness and Australianness that this embodied was most clearly defined in its dealings with Aboriginal Australians and with Chinese, not only through the physical differences shorthanded as racial, but the underlying values that Australians saw themselves as having and the other groups as lacking: vitality, industriousness, purity, cleanliness. The idea of geographical vulnerability added urgency to turn-of-the-century Australians' view of themselves as the pioneers of civilisation surrounded by potential adversaries.[36] In the prevailing social Darwinist ideological context, they were the spearhead of the white race forced into proximity with lesser races and, in the ensuing struggle, they would prevail as the stronger, fitter race. This is why although non-Europeans had their uses, mixing with them and allowing them citizenship was seen as counter-productive. Governments did not attempt the mass deportations provided for in the IRA, and particular industries such as pearl diving enjoyed, de facto, special dispensation to employ Pacific Islanders and Chinese, who were seen as 'naturally' more suited to the work. Tavan (2005: 15) sees White Australia as a populist and popular device for generating nationalism in a fledgling society that garnered support from all interest groups despite tensions of gender, class and religion. She goes on to contextualise it as central to the specific form of social liberalism that was the national ideology of the emergent State: this required state intervention to mitigate the excesses of the market, to ensure fairer distribution of wealth and to provide minimum living conditions. The cultural homogeneity putatively anchoring this set of values was seen as essential to successfully building a civilisation geographically remote from the epicentre of world civilisation (Europe). Within this, the labour movement's opposition to the conditions of Kanaka workers in the sugar industry on the grounds of their virtual slavery was not viewed as contradictory to its support for repatriation of the foreign element of the workforce.

Indeed, it was the tropical part of Australia, the Northern Territories, that most exercised Australians' minds in the first half of the twentieth century. While the baseline for Australian immigration was to build on British and, to a lesser extent, Irish stock, the idea of 'race' and its relationship to climate and space proved problematic. Simply put, the association of different 'races' both with particular types of climate and innate characteristics militated against Northern Europeans flourishing in this tropical environment (Anderson 2005). Yet with the forced departure of the Pacific Islanders in the first decades of the twentieth century, the North required a substitute labour force. The settlement of the North needed not just white supervisors, as had been the case in other tropical areas of colonial expansion, but a white labouring male tropical workforce. Was this a contradiction in terms? Alison Bashford (2000: 255) argues that tropical medicine debated the question, 'Is White Australia possible?' between 1900 and the 1930s. The problem revolved not around white men colonising other people in the tropics, but 'as colonizers of a difficult and resilient space' (2000: 258). In this debate, Aboriginals had been made invisible. The focus was on how whiteness could be adapted to overcome the tropical environment. Indeed, suggestions of how to accomplish this contributed, maintains Bashford, to producing 'an idea that whiteness was not only a characteristic of skin and colour, but was also about how one lived, how one arranged one's moment by moment existence in space and time [. . .] the capacity to live in the tropics had to be learnt in minute, detailed and constant ways' (2000: 266).

At least for those engaged in the public health discourse, the environment could be overcome (Anderson 2005). A more pressing problem for employers in the Queensland and Northern Territories sugar plantations was to remain economically viable. Here the niceties of the public health debate were ignored by workers intent on retaining a standard of living promised by the dismissal of competition in the form of Pacific Island labour. Yet in the mid 1920s, migrants from Italy were arriving in their thousands to work on the estates. This triggered a hostile campaign led by the Brisbane-based *Worker* newspaper against Italian immigration (Sheills 2006). The Italians occupied a position straddling the lines of whiteness. Officially categorised as 'white aliens', they became the object of a discourse aimed at presenting them as a threat not just to jobs, but to living standards (being willing to work for lower wages) and the cultural future of Australia (due to their clannishness, corruption, backward civilisation and unfitness for vigorous pioneer activity required to settle and develop empty land). By 1925, the Queensland government had set up a Royal Commission to look into the impact of the increased number of aliens in North Queensland (Shiells 2006). The Commissioner charged with producing a report made a sharp distinction between Northern and Southern Italians, castigating the latter for their clannishness, resistance to assimilation and propensity towards crime and violence vis-à-vis their Northern counterparts. He was not alone in this, either in Australia or elsewhere. Italians themselves debated the North–South divide in terms of culture and civilisation (Verdicchio 1997), and the characterisation of the Sicilians as 'inferior types' represented a boundary line between whiter and less white aliens.

Indeed, while the 1901 Immigration Act had been primarily aimed at keeping out the Chinese, the second- and third-largest groups of 'prohibited' immigrants (i.e. those refused the right to land) were Southern Europeans: Maltese and Italians. Distinctions within the 'white race' meant that Latins were lower down the racial pecking order than Anglo-Saxons, Alpines and Nordic peoples. Added to this complication was the reclassification of Axis member nationals (from Bulgaria, the Austro-Hungarian Empire, Germany and Turkey) during World War I as hostile aliens. There was even a temporary internment camp in New South Wales. As York (n.d) argues, bans continued for at least five years after the war. In the specific context of Australia between 1912 and 1946 (the period when separate figures on the Maltese were kept), the prevailing practice of immigration officers was to question the right of Southern Europeans to land, even if, in the case of the Maltese, they had British passports. Perceived racial difference here overrode nationality. In the most well-known case 208 Maltese were kept out of Australia in 1916 (York 1990) by Melbourne immigration officials who gave them the dictation test in Dutch: all failed.

What this reveals about the workings of whiteness is its lack of solidity and stability. Even the taken-for-granted visible signs can be misleading, or be irrelevant to those wielding power in precise situations. Cultural and political factors can override the phenotypical ones. Moreover, the capacity to centre problems around whiteness per se can make other people invisible (or visible only in particular ways, as noted in chapters 1 and 2). Despite Aboriginals living in Northern Territories and Northern Queensland, for example, public discourse obliterated them from the picture. The space was read as empty.

The basis for anxiety about shades of whiteness is expressed again through competition, or at least perceived competition, for work and conditions. It is not feasible to extricate the material from the cultural aspects of whiteness if we seek to understand it in its lived context.

Changing economic and social conditions led to different appraisals of who was allowed in and why: what are the criteria? This, as well as the example of the 'inbetween peoples' thesis, are clearly about the parallel boundaries of whiteness; the one separating white from its non-white Other, and those separating the really white from the less so.

WORKING-CLASS CULTURES: ABJECT 'WHITES' AND 'WHITE TRASH'

The ethnographic writing on white racialised identities has focused disproportionately, as has much of the academic work on class, on working-class men. This is a reflection of the academy's middle-class composition and of ethnography's colonial heritage. Since Victorian times, middle-class academics and philanthropists have conducted surveys of the poor, the work of Engels (1969[1844]), Mayhew (1967[1861]) and Booth (1902) being the best-known examples.[37] The objective may have been to reform them, evangelise them, draw parallels between them and colonised peoples, but the common strand was to reveal their failings, and create an inventory of what they did not have. Anthony Wohl, on the web resource 'Victorian Web',[38] notes that a number of characteristics were applied to the nineteenth-century working classes,

Irish immigrants and colonial subjects. They were: unreasonable, irrational, and easily excited, childlike, superstitious (not religious), criminal (with neither respect for private property, nor notions of property), excessively sexual, filthy, inhabited unknown dark lands or territories and shared physical qualities. Wohl has clearly identified an overlap between the language of 'race' and that of class: positioning both as fixed on the body and culture.

Indeed, despite the counter-narratives of working-class writers from both inside and outside the academy, from Hoggart (1957) to Collins (2004), and the new studies and problematisation of 'white trash' in the USA (Wray and Newitz 1997, Hartigan 2005, 1999, 1997a, b, Wray 2006), the same theme resonates: the displacement of contemporary anxieties and guilt about structural poverty and racism onto those at the foot of the hierarchy. This process of valuing working-class habitus negatively can be seen in the post-industrial era of structural un- and underemployment by the internalisation of such values. The identifications with, and dis-identifications from the working class by working-class subjects themselves, are highlighted by Skeggs (1997), whose respondents define working class by reference to values they personally do not or no longer have, or to economic predicaments they do not face. The age of readily-sanctioned reference to a working-class 'us' appears, outside particular work milieux, to have disappeared. The anxiety around white working-class subject positions is explored in this section, as a reflection of white middle- and ruling-class attempts to pathologise and racialise them as an underclass.

Chris Haylett (2001) argues that sections of a white 'underclass' are constructed in turn-of-the-century Britain as the effects of relations that 'produce people who are outside/beyond/beneath the nation' (ibid.: 358). This process involves devaluing social actions carried out by them, so that the protagonists in the Autumn 1993 'white' riots (in Oxford, Cardiff and Newcastle) 'were not hailed as class revolutionaries or even righteously angered disenfranchised minorities, rather they were an embarrassing sign of what the white working-class poor had become – a disorganized, racist and sexist detritus' (ibid.: 358). Indeed, blame for this 'decline' in the working class, in the de-unionised post-Fordist landscape, is placed on the working class themselves, or at least the poorest sections of it. Explanations, argues Haylett, have become increasingly less structural, and more individual, and fixed around pathological working-class masculinities, and backwardness: in short the exact opposite of the expanding multicultural, cosmopolitan middle classes. Working-class Whites are in these narratives culturally disposed to degeneracy, crime, over-fecundity, fecklessness, etc. Indeed, the identity work here is relational: the multicultural moderns depend on the 'abject unmodern' white working class (ibid.: 365). The latter represent an anomaly in the symbolic order.

> Poor whites thereby come to reveal the symbolically 'worked at', socially produced nature of the order of things. For governing elites, the contradiction that a mass of poor whites embodies has to be dealt with if social systems are to maintain credibility.
>
> (ibid.: 361)

Whiteness in this account is significantly mediated by class. A topic elaborated on by the work on 'white trash' that has been undertaken in the USA (Bettie 2000, Gibbons 2004, Morris 2005). The theme of productiveness–unproductiveness is also central to it. Hartigan's tracing of the development of the phenomenon of 'white trash' in the USA (2005) demonstrates some interesting points of comparison. Using the conclusion of travel writer James Gilmore,[39] he distinguishes between elements of the working class: 'The *poor* white man labors, the *mean* white man does not labor: and labor makes the distinction between them'.

So the 'fundamental basis for objectifications of this group', concludes Hartigan (2005: 67), 'arose from this moral categorization of those who will and will not work'. Writing from the 1860s evidenced the struggle between those for whom such 'meanness' was in the blood and those who recognised a degree of environmental input. These competing logics developed into the twentieth century. Racial theorist Madison Grant, for example, understood 'white trash' as a combination of natural habitat and bloodlines: to do with sexuality, urbanisation, crime, rather than just immigration (Grant 1916). Eugenics discourse stressed the perils of mixing with bad genes, and responsibility for policing the border. It argued that a host of antisocial and expensive behaviour derived from poor family etiquette and practices. The result of this discourse in popular outlets, contends Hartigan, was heightened middle-class awareness of threat from below, and of their racial selves. In the scenarios popularised in the press, the idea of 'racial poisons' dominated discourse, with the weaker blood multiplying faster than the stronger. Gertrude Davenport (the wife of leading eugenicist Charles Davenport) wrote in April 1914 that 'the greatest menace of imbecility is not that the imbecile may break into our house and steal our silver, or that he might set fire to our barn, but that he may be born of our flesh' (Hartigan 2005: 95).

Similarly, Winthrop Stoddard's (1922) Freudian fight for civilisation taking place within the Self sees class status coincide with racial value:

Let us understand once and for all [he warns] that we have among us a rebel army – the vast host of the unadaptable, the incapable, the envious, the discontented, filled with instinctive hatred of civilization and progress, and ready on the instant to rise in revolt. Here are foes that need watching. Let us watch them.

(1922: 87)

The figure of 'white trash', like that of 'Chav' in the UK (Hayward and Yar 2005), is therefore a way of making 'explicit and emphatic the perception of pollution that plays such a critical role in racial consciousness' (Hartigan 2005: 104). The bodies thus categorised are excessive, and display the innate behaviour that both confirms the depths to which the working class has collapsed (so far from work, so far from respectability), and the industriousness and respectability of the middle-class subjects that fill the signifier 'white trash' with meaning. However, there is more to it than this, as Haylett seems to suggest, and Hartigan concurs:

The meanings, effects, tendencies and images that the name assembles do not simply reside in individual bodies or groups of bodies, but rather are generated in complex coded struggles between classes and races and over what will count as sexuality and gender.

(Hartigan 2005: 116)

Moreover, Hartigan's (1999) study of inner-city Detroit clearly highlights the class-specific inflexions in the deployment of 'race' there. Class influences the way 'race' is spoken about, the meanings attached to it, and the ease with which racelessness can be invoked. Clearly, while enjoying the 'wages of whiteness', Americanised nouveau-white workers were, and many of their descendants are still, on a considerably lower 'wage' than other whites. Among the economic relationships between gender, class and 'race' since World War II, Henwood (1997: 178) finds statistical evidence that 'most officially poor people are white', and that white males 'have watched their inherited skin and sex privileges wasting away for two decades' (ibid.: 182). This, as Henwood stresses, is occurring in the context of greater racialised polarisation and enduring racial discrimination.

Plural trajectories of whiteness

Behind the gross figures then there are trends that alert us to the need to think more contextually about some forms of racialised power relationships. Du Bois's 'psychological and social' wage may well still be on offer, but for some, the differential is a lot less impressive than it was a generation ago. This perception of diminishing funds, resources and access to them, held particularly by people on lower incomes across the EU, may go some way towards explaining why the 'asylum seeker' emerges from opinion polls as an envied competitor (see chapter 8). Their insecurities have compelling material bases. Ethnographic fieldwork carried out in Britain has illuminated what we could call the plural trajectories of whiteness. In other words the internal and external boundaries of the white 'we' are shown to be contingent. People make sense of the social material we use to understand 'race' in differing ways. We are going to look briefly at two pieces of British ethnographic fieldwork to illustrate some aspects of these 'plural trajectories': Katherine Tyler's discussions with Coalville residents (2004),[40] and Les Back's study of young people on the 'Riverview' estate in South London (1996).

Tyler's (2004) inter-generational dialogue among small-town Leicestershire inhabitants shows how personal biographies profoundly shape how people perceive 'Others'. Among the interviewees, no homogenous representative voice is expressed: white superiority is contested by some, just as it is accepted unthinkingly by more. Identification can take the form of empathy, for example, as in 'Sarah's recognition of her own narrative – the experience of her Czech immigrant father's struggle to run a business – in critiques of Asian businesses' (Tyler 2004: 304). Moreover, a person may develop a critical angle through mobility and return. Another of Tyler's respondents, Jim, returns to the town after three years doing a degree in another small and more multicultural Midlands city. He reports that his recognition and awareness of racism increased dramatically when he was reabsorbed into family circles and heard the types of discourse that he previously listened to uncritically. He can now reflect on the older generation's assumptions and dissect them. When his grandmother died, the house she had lived in was bought by an Asian family, something that his uncles were unhappy about. 'The presence of Asians in the home where they were brought up signifies an intolerable and unacceptable transformation', paraphrases Tyler (2004: 299). Here we see a crucial element of the mechanism of enacting and critiquing whiteness: the attachment of a perceived negative change (in this case the retrospective tainting of the family) to an effect (the Asian buyer) rather than a cause (the grandmother's death, the psychological toll of memories of childhood in that home, the broader global changes that brought the family in question from Asia to Britain).

Inter-generational and gendered differences are also revealed by this study: the older people are generally less reflexive about whiteness and quicker to deploy racialised discourse, as are men as compared to women, many of whom see more positives where the men see only negatives. In this survey, the plural trajectories of white people come even closer to the surface. There are clearly a number of places to be located ideologically in the racialisation process, a process that becomes even more interesting in the London estates where Les Back worked in the early 1990s.

Back's (1996) ethnography of youth culture on South London estates suggests that values determine the salient borders of identity, and that culture becomes the modality through which they are racialised. Black and white youths there put aside sporadic but real differences in order to ally against Vietnamese and Bangladeshi newcomers on their estates (1996: 240–241) in what Back terms 'neighbourhood nationalism'. This alliance assumes the form of verbal and occasionally physical attacks. While the black youths are well aware that in other circumstances they could, and indeed have been, the victims of such aggression from their white counterparts, in the context of defining membership of the estate, their secular, linguistic and music-based coalition with white youth in 'Riverview' estate appears to predominate. They thus become what Back terms 'contingent insiders' (1996: 240), while their counterparts in 'Southgate' estate seemed to enjoy a qualitatively different relationship with their white peers, who had 'vacated concepts of whiteness and Englishness . . . in favour of a mixed ethnicity that was shared' (ibid.: 241). So while there is frequently tension, there is also often alliance, through personal relationships drawing on shared knowledge and experiences. This can also be seen in Watt and Stenson's work (1998), discussed in the previous chapter.

Indeed, a recurrent topic in British ethnographic studies is the heterogeneity and elasticity of the category 'white' in its members' affiliations with black and Asian cultures, to the point where terms such as 'black' or 'white' culture become almost ideal-types. In their study of the East End of London, Paul Hoggett *et al.* (1996: 113) remark on a similar set of provisional allegiances, noting the large Afro-Caribbean presence in a demonstration following the fatal stabbing of a white schoolboy by a Bangladeshi boy:

> The paradox is that whilst Afro-Caribbean soccer players can still be the object of crude racial abuse at nearby Millwall Football Club, Afro-Caribbeans can nevertheless also be included in an imaginary community of English-speaking Christian Eastenders which stands opposed to the alien Muslim threat.

These groups of young people illustrate a paradox that resurfaces else-where in British fieldwork. In their survey of shopkeepers in a London borough, Wells and Watson (2005) find that not all those championing 'white values' are white, while some champions of white rights include their black neighbours in their embattled and beleaguered 'we'. In these cases the Other is Muslim/Asian. Clearly, the power relationships at a personal and local level allow for whiteness to be expanded to incorporate those not phenotypically white beneath its cultural canopy for the enactment of both rhetorical and physical violence. People who are not white can be absorbed into honorary whiteness in particular circumstances, yet this invariably involves othering different groups. In fact this othering appears constitutive of the process of redrawing of the boundary of whiteness in terms of values, so that it embraces British black or Asian people, depending on the context. In confirming shared values, both the groups that share and do not share them are defined.

CONCLUSIONS: HIERARCHIES OF CLASS AND WHITENESS

The focus on the borders at each end of whiteness, between white and non-white, and between the constituent groups of the white whole, serves to keep in mind the contingency of the political and social hierarchies thrown up.

> Part of what the epithet white trash expresses is the general view held by whites that there are only a few extreme, dangerous whites who are really racist or violently misguided, as opposed to recognizing that racism is an institutional problem pervading the nation and implicating all whites in its operation.
>
> (Hartigan 2005: 118–119)

While racist ideas do abound in the working-class communities studied – although this label is contested in Midtown (Kefalas 2003), Corktown and Warrendale (Hartigan 1999) – academics play a significant role in creating a selective picture in which only the working class express such ideas and live in segregated neighbourhoods. Studies of whiteness in middle-class circles, residential areas or workplaces, or at all, are few and far between (Hall 1992, Ware 1992, Pierce 2003, Johnson and Shapiro 2003; Hartigan's (1999) section on Corktown; Reay *et al.* (forthcoming); Clarke and Garner (forthcoming)). Whiteness is neither just for the wealthy, nor the poor. Yet the people who have engaged in defining the desirability of including particular segments of their compatriots in the civilised, right-thinking mainstream have been middle- and upper-class British and Americans (Hartigan 2005, Hall 1992).

Moreover, under certain conditions, whiteness (as a dominant set of values and assumptions that make various groups problematic) is not even only for white people. It is clear from survey research (Lewis 2005) that minorities generally have more sympathy for immigrants and asylum seekers, and tend to understand racism as structural rather than individually generated (Lamont 2000, Weis and Fine 1996), yet from the examples of Back, Wells and Watson and Hoggett *et al.*, there is enough to suggest that there might occasionally be a strategic overlap of values between white and black people that coalesce around defending neighbourhoods, and possibly jobs.

We have looked in turn at attempts to understand whiteness as terror and supremacy; invisibility and visibility; norms, values and cultural capital and finally, as a set of contingent hierarchies. In chapters 5–7 the focus will change to specific historical and geographical contexts, and 'borderline Whites'.

5 Whiteness in the Caribbean and Latin America

The geographical focus placed on Latin America and the Caribbean in this chapter serves three purposes. First, it extends comprehension of whiteness as a global and historic property of social relations into contexts that differ from the American and British ones. Second, it shows the distinctiveness of national and regional 'racial regimes'. The countries referred to here differ in history and social composition, but the equation of whiteness with power, which is the constant in this sea of variables, speaks with local accents. Third, it enables us to examine the processes used to construct racialised identities and their relationship to bodies.

In the first two sections, we shall look at two societies to obtain an idea of what purchase slaveholding had on the development of whiteness by using two examples: the Irish in the early anglophone Caribbean, and the Portuguese in British Guiana in the post-abolition period. Then in the next section, the focus will fall on how the process of nation-building in Latin America (with special attention paid to Ecuador) has historically been organised around whiteness, and excludes non-white Others in different ways in different places.

THE IRISH IN THE CARIBBEAN[41]

Irish people arrived in the Caribbean from the 1630s as political prisoners, indentured labourers, administrators and priests. Their status in the Caribbean was ambiguous, plural and dynamic. At the outset, the Protestant English and Scots occupied higher positions in colonial society, and they generally held more land and slaves than the Catholic Irish by the eighteenth century. Using sources such as the 1678 Census, we can assume that maybe 30 per cent of the white inhabitants of the anglophone Caribbean colonies *in toto* were Irish in the mid seventeenth century (around 20 per cent of the whole population).[42] Governor Modyford's 1678 survey revealed that the Irish owned 10–20 per cent of the property in Jamaica (Silke 1976) and substantially more on Montserrat (Akenson 1997). Within 25 years of the arrival of the first political prisoners in Barbados they had risen to become free labourers, land-owners and slave-owners. The rights and power inherent in these locations should indicate the error of consigning the Irish to an undifferentiated subaltern slot in the New World hierarchy. Yet by the 1690s they had evaporated into the category 'white', or 'European', which meant dominant.[43] The last two decades of that century saw the African element of the population overtake and then dominate the European, a point that both relegates the precise proportion of Irish inhabitants to a lower level, and means that this question became increasingly immaterial. In the eighteenth century, the rising proportion of enslaved Africans to Europeans meant that the latter group could no longer afford to be split nationally in the face of the constant potential for rebellion. The terms English, Scots and Irish thus diminished rapidly *in importance* to be replaced by 'white' or 'European'. This is not to say that individuals no longer identified themselves in national terms, but that in the Caribbean context the national divisions lost salience in contrast to whiteness as an overarching identity. The fact that compared to their English and Scots counterparts, the Irish owned relatively small holdings and few slaves proves merely that there was a status gap between those groups.

Irish indentured labourers and enslaved Africans worked side by side in the fields for years in the New World. It is not surprising that planters were watchful for signs of collusion between them. Yet ultimately, reports of alliances between Irish indentured labourers and slaves appear to have been mainly expressions of English planters' paranoia.[44] The picture emerging from the texts studied by Hilary Beckles (1990) is that planters were extremely fearful, both of Irish–African alliances and Irish allegiance to Catholic European powers, and that this anxiety led them so far as to request the reduction or elimination of the supply of labour from Ireland at a time when such labour was still relatively important (i.e. until the 1680s) and a shortfall still existed. Governor Willoughby of Barbados wrote to the Privy Council in 1667:

> There yet remains that I acquainte your Lordships with the great want of servants in this island, which the late war hath occasioned. If labour fayles here, His Majesty's customes will at home; if the supply be not of good and sure men the saifety of this place will always be in question; for though there be noe enemy abroad, the

keeping of slaves in subjection must still be provided for. If your Lordship shall offer a trade with Scotland for transporting people of that nation hither and prevent any excess of Irish in the future, it will accommodate all the ends propounded.

(Beckles 1990: 509–510).[45]

Moreover, Michael Craton (1997) maintains that although white servants in Barbados were certainly treated worse than contemporary agricultural labourers in Britain, this was a transitional phase: ultimately the lower rungs of white society in the Caribbean provided 'managers, voters and militiamen for external and internal defence' (ibid.: 166), and enabled the planters to dominate in societies in which they represented a tiny minority.

Planters' anxiety sometimes led to the implementation of distinct social control systems for the Irish, such as passes (Barbados, 1657) and the withdrawal of the right to bear arms (Antigua, 1689). Indeed the Irish on English-held islands were actually more likely to side with the French than the slaves. There is evidence of this in St Kitts and Montserrat in the 1660s for example (Beckles 1990: 519–520).

The same Governor had, a few months earlier, pleaded with the King for servants other than Irish, expressing his preference for the 'downright Scot who, I am certain, will fight without a crucifix round his neck' (ibid.: 508).[46]

Many of the Irish originally sent to Barbados later migrated to the USA and other Caribbean territories. In Jamaica, Montserrat, Trinidad and British Guiana, for example, white Barbadians accessed land more cheaply and were able to rise to intermediate positions in a hierarchy predicated upon black disenfranchisement. Again, after the initial two decades or so of testing living conditions, the Irish evaporated into the dominant white elites in the anglophone (and some parts of the Spanish-speaking) Caribbean.[47] The point then is that in the New World setting, the social category 'white' itself is indigenous, if we can use that term provocatively, to the slave mode of production. Its outer boundaries may have been set phenotypically, but in terms of privilege and correspondence with labour force positions, it took generations for the joint interests of the Irish, Scots and English to coincide, in other words for 'free labour' to refer unequivocally to Whites, and 'unfree' labour to refer to Blacks, the freedom of the former deriving explicitly from the unfreedom of the latter.[48]

THE PORTUGUESE IN BRITISH GUIANA

In the post-abolition period, sugar planters in British Guiana sought to replace their labour force by using indentured labour drawn from a variety of sources: India, China, Africa, other West Indian territories. Around 35,000 people also arrived from the Portuguese islands of Madeira and the Azores in the 1840–1880 period (Tinker 1974). At the first Census, in 1891, they were classified as 'Portuguese', a category distinct from 'European'. The Portuguese cannot be considered to fall geographically outside the category 'European', so we can take the latter to include British and other Europeans who arrived in Guyana neither as indentured labour nor descendants of such workers. They became 'Portuguese' in Guyana just as Hindus and Muslims of various castes became 'Indians' there, and Hausa, Yoruba and Wolof, etc., became 'Africans' on reaching the other side of the Atlantic. The cultural construction of the Madeirans and Azoreans as 'Portuguese' highlights the distinctiveness of each receiving country's racial regime. Immigrants constructed historically as Portuguese in North America have also been black, as in the case of the Cape Verdeans (Halter 1993), and as poor Catholics in Catholic France.

Like many of the Irish two centuries before them, Portuguese indentured labourers rose to become important elements of the colonial business elite. Their social ascendance resulted from their seizing opportunities provided by a colonial policy aimed directly at creating an indigenous buffer group between the British administration and planters, and the African- and Indian-descended workers who comprised the majority of the population.

The colonial state opened options for Portuguese economic advancement through the accumulation of capital. This avenue had been closed to other groups: former slaves attempting to establish themselves as independent farmers in the 1840s onwards suffered as a result of land prices, taxes and the state's refusal to be responsible for irrigation (Adamson 1972).[49] Although Indians at the end of the century were able to benefit from cheaper land and free irrigation, they were not granted licences for business outside the rice-growing sector (Nath 1950).

However, the Court of Policy (colonial assembly) created a virtual Portuguese monopoly in the granting of licences to open 'rum shops' (small bars). By 1852, the Portuguese held 70 per cent of the licences issued in the colony, and the value of their property destroyed during the riots in 1856 was an estimated £60,000. By 1865, they owned more than 90 per cent of rum shops in Demerara (the most highly-populated county) (Wagner 1977). In addition to the rum shops, over 50 per cent of all shops in Georgetown and the second city, New Amsterdam, belonged to the Portuguese by 1851 (Premdas 1995). Not only did the Government grant commercial licences to the Portuguese, but they were also the only group outside the 'Europeans' to be authorised for bank loans.

British Guiana was a multiethnic society in which different statuses cross-cut ethnicity at different times. By the mid 1850s, the planters were forced to reassess the system of indentureship in relation to the behaviour of the various groups. In January 1855, the Court of Policy (British Guiana's legislative body) met to discuss the problem of runaway Portuguese indenturers. The following debate (which resurfaced in 1856) illustrates the sets of logic inherent in the construction of the colonial ethnic hierarchy, in which 'whiteness' draws specific and implicit meanings, and the different ways in which this logic was applied. From the establishment of indentured labour in 1834, a recruitment fee had been paid to the planters for each labourer. During the 1855 meeting, the idea of no longer paying out if a worker breached the contract by running away was floated for the first time. The idea was amended to establish the criterion of working for three years rather than the 12 months provided for in the original contract.

Despite their frequent desertions, the Portuguese escaped being cast as pathologically 'idle' as were other runaways in official discourse. On the contrary, during the same meeting in 1855, they were referred to as a 'very valuable class of people'. Local press articles on the 1856 riots, in which Portuguese-owned premises were ransacked by Indian and African crowds, demonstrate official attitudes towards the Portuguese, as conveyed by the press. 'The rioters', states the editor of the *Colonist*, 'actuated by blind and savage feelings of jealousy and fanaticism, destroyed the property of their more industrious fellow citizens.'[50] Yet an estate manager for planter Henry Barkly alerts us to a more abiding concern. He had stated in a parliamentary commission on rioting in the colony in 1847:

> I think the safety of the whites depends very much on the want of union in the different races of labourers, and I should be glad to see some more Madeirans and, if possible, Chinese coming in: the Coolies too would always hold by the whites.[51]

In the 1850s, there was an ongoing financial re-assessment of the ethnic groups in relation to their capacity for work. From the evidence available, the Portuguese held a privileged position within the sometimes contradictory hierarchies established in the post-emancipation period, shielding the ruling minority from the rebellion of the Africans and Indians, as was to be the case, for example, in the widespread rioting of 1856 and 1898.

The efforts made by the authorities to seek and punish Indian runaways (and slaves prior to abolition) lead us to another conclusion as regards the Portuguese community. Portuguese runaways hid with their compatriots in urban areas and disappeared. Yet pursuing them was economically unviable because they comprised only a small minority and were more useful to the colony in business. This conclusion is borne out by the new recruitment fees set after the 1855 meeting referred to above. In this new set of tariffs, Chinese workers were worth $G60, Indians $G30, and Portuguese only $G15, that is, a quarter of a Chinese indenturer and half an Indian one: a 'very valuable class of people' maybe, but not in the literal sense of the term.

These figures were based on planters' assessments of each group's productivity. Eighteen months later, in June 1856, the Court of Policy met to re-set the fees, in a kind of 'ethnic labour audit'. According to the consensus expressed at the meeting, the Chinese accomplished 20 per cent more work than the Indians in a given period, which led to the setting of a new fee at $G100 per worker, compared to $G35 for each Portuguese worker, that is, a higher amount and proportion than in 1855, but still much less than a Chinese worker.[52] The Portuguese, by the criterion used to judge the various ethnic groups in British Guiana during the nineteenth century, were the least productive, *sensu stricto*, yet they ascended to an intermediate position above the Africans and Indians who had preceded them there.

By this stage, the Portuguese were nearly white. Indeed, due to their privileged position, they attracted the hostility of subordinate groups. The Portuguese were viewed as greedy and selfish in popular attitudes. In 1856 and 1905, because of their refusal to grant credit to striking Indian and African sugar workers, Portuguese premises were attacked and looted.

Yet success in business enabled the Portuguese to accrue political power. They qualified for the restricted franchise and the right to stand for election through property-ownership, and later earned membership of decision-making bodies through elections. The juxtaposition of the electoral roll with the 1915 Census (see Table 2) highlights both the disproportion between the number of 'Europeans' and their actual political power, and the privileged position of the Portuguese vis-à-vis other subaltern groups. Comprising just 2.9 per cent of the adult male population, 17.7 per cent of the Portuguese figured on the electoral register. They thus accounted for 11.4 per cent of all eligible voters. Their

Table 2 Relative proportions of the Guyanese ethnic groups and their potential voting power 1915

Ethnic group	Percentage of adult male population	Percentage of eligible voters	Percentage of adult males in each group on electoral register
Europeans	1.7	17.0	46.1
Portuguese	2.9	11.4	17.7
Indians	51.8	6.4	0.6
Africans & Coloured	42.3	62.7	6.8
Chinese	1.3	2.4	12.3

Source: Clementi (1937).

standing should be compared to the Indians and Chinese, with whom they arrived contemporaneously in the colony.

Indeed, throughout the twentieth century, many Portuguese accessed the liberal professions, the civil service and the ownership of pawnbrokers' licences in greater numbers (Moore 1975). By the 1950s, most Portuguese were part of a business elite represented in the Guyanese establishment, e.g. Peter D'Aguiar, owner of Banks' Beer and head of The United Force, a political party that shared government from 1964 to 1968. Vis-à-vis the other subaltern groups, they were clearly white by local criteria.

This type of social climbing was much more unlikely for Black Guyanese even if their children became 'Mixed' after a few generations. There was no argument that the Portuguese were ever black, but they did occupy types of work associated with Blacks and Indians for a generation before being offered a ladder out. The privileges they attained were obviously not always gained through fair competition. Like the Irish of the seventeenth-century Caribbean, the Portuguese had accessed white status and the advantage in life chances this conferred in a social hierarchy founded on systemic racialised inequalities of labour: in a mode of production that was both post-slave and pre-slave, based on parallel cohorts of free and 'unfree' labour.

NATION-BUILDING IN LATIN AMERICA

Even a cursory reading of available texts on racial and ethnic diversity in Latin America suggests a thoroughly absorbing and complex phenomenon, with national, regional and sub-regional factors combining to produce a series of relationships that cannot and should not be analysed using only tools developed from US and European sources. Bourdieu and Wacquant (1998) claim that US imperialism has extended into models for understanding group relations, by presenting its American models as universal. Indeed, each society has its own norms, values and specific history of 'race', in short, its own racial regime. Yet a convincing international history of the development of ideas and practices of racial discrimination could also be written. Bourdieu and Wacquant are also correct to draw attention to the US focus on Brazil, particularly in comparative perspective. That nation has the largest black population of any country after Nigeria, and has of course interested scholars and activists interested in civil rights and the African diaspora (Skidmore 1993, Winant 1994, Hanchard 1998, 1999, Marx 1998, Winddance Twine 1998, Sheriff 2001). Brazil has also figured in the sights of scholars focusing on the prevalent policy orientation of eugenics (Stepan 1991, Dávila 2003). This literature is fascinating and the epistemological issues raised by Bourdieu and Wacquant are indeed crucial ones. In the light of this familiarity with Brazil, and the fact that Brazil is in some ways atypical (the combination of a relatively large population of African descent, Portuguese language, plus modern immigration from Asia), I have opted for a different approach. What we shall try to do in this short section is make a case for an interpretation of nation-building in Latin America based on what I will label a 'moral economy of whiteness'. This is not to argue that this is the only dimension of nation-building, yet the latter is a particularly apposite site for understanding what Omi and Winant (1994) term 'racial formation', in which the state plays an important role. Indeed, what we are interested in is exactly what Appelbaum *et al.* (2003b: 9) identify as 'a processual and contextual understanding of nation-building and race-making'.[53] Ecuador will be the main, but not exclusive, basis for this exploration. Its proportions of people are arguably more representative of the continent as a whole (white, mestizo, indigena, black), and it is also much less familiar to anglophone readers. Focusing solely on national territories is not the only or even the best way to conceptualise whiteness, but it does offer a way into ideologies and practices centred on the nation-state. The themes under which we will examine the issue of whiteness are cleanliness, redemption and the moral economy.

Cleanliness

All the processes looked at in this book can be loosely gathered under the term 'othering' (i.e. the construction of boundaries between groups in which particular characteristics and values are imputed to the 'other' group). These characteristics and values are usually the opposite of those believed to be those defining the group that does the othering. At the root of othering process, argued anthropologist Mary Douglas (1966), are the binaries of order/disorder, purity/impurity, cleanliness/dirt. Indeed, in social science work on othering (Sibley 1995) dirt becomes the general metaphor for matter-out-of-place that dis-orders the place-based social order.

In Latin America's racialisation processes this is very clear. First, the construction of identities in which elites came to designate peoples and whole areas as backward, uncivilised and dirty. This doesn't mean that only the elites constructed identities, but that they held the power to enforce definition and operationalise such definitions. Second, state policies were aimed at remedying these problems through public health and education. So from the anxiety about dirt it is implicit that the question of purity is a central one. As Anderson-Levy (2005: 3) argues in her reflection on social relations in Jamaica, whiteness represents itself as pure and 'can be contaminated in a way that, for instance, blackness cannot be'. In the Latin American context, the signifier 'white' and the bodies thus signified may well not correspond in the way that North American and European racial regimes allow. This is a point that alerts us again to the contingency of whiteness, and is also a point clear to the actors such as Grace Schubert's black respondents (1981: 576) who retaliate against racist comments by rejecting the commentator's basis for calling him or herself white in the first place.

At the heart of the demographic 'problem' as viewed by nineteenth-century Latin American elites was the diversity of what were seen as 'races'. The continent's already diverse indigenous populations sat alongside Europeans and the descendants of enslaved Africans, plus the mixed European/indigenous/African people broadly labelled *mestizo*. The Spanish rule of blood purity, *limpieza de sangre*, which maintained a social class and racial hierarchy in Spain, was transposed as the corner-stone of early colonial rule. It granted higher social position to those with 'pure' noble lineage. This concept underwent changes, particularly in its relevance to class, but remained an important obstacle to social mobility and access to democracy. As elsewhere, the sliding scale of 'fitness for democracy' (cf. nineteenth-century USA) was believed to encompass Whites at one end and Blacks at the other, with Mestizos and Indigenas below the Whites. Not having *limpieza* meant you were barred from office-holding, some forms of property-holding, voting, citizenship, and were obliged to pay extra taxes.

So the idea of purity generated its obverse: impurity. Mixing, and the possession of blood from other 'races', equalled impurity. Degenerate behaviour could be read from this corporeal evidence. Ann Twinam (2005) quotes Peruvian officials in 1586:

> in these provinces there are many Blacks, mulattos and mestizos and people of other mixtures and that each day the number of them increases and . . . many of them do not know their parents and they grow up in great vice and liberty without working, they have no occupation and eat and drink without order and mingle with the Indian men and women and join in their drunkenness and witchcraft and do not hear mass.
>
> (Konetzke, Vol. 1, Doc. 427, 1586)

These kinds of official ideas were developed in a specific colonial economic context. The perceived vices of the people described above are notably geared to unproductiveness – a feature central to the construction of 'white trash' in the USA and asylum seekers in Europe. In a context where the colony's *raison d'être* was basically to produce wealth through its mineral resources, people with no occupation were morally reprehensible. In the specific Andean context here, enslaved Africans had been put to work in mines.

In Ecuador, black people were also brought in from neighbouring Colombia and the West Indies in the nineteenth century in order to work on building the coastal railways, and the line linking the capital Quito, to the major port, Guayaquil. They have historically been concentrated in the Northern province of Esmeraldas, and the Chota-Mira Valley. These two areas, asserts Jean Rahier (1998: 422), 'are looked down upon by the white and white-mestizo urban citizenry as places of violence, laziness, backwardness and unconquered nature'. The ideological labour involved in associating dirt and disorder with these characteristics is a vital prong of racism. In imputing violence, laziness and backwardness to their black compatriots, white Ecuadoreans assert their civilisation, industriousness and modernity. Moreover, certain geographical spaces are constructed as naturally home to black people. When the latter migrate to the urban spaces of Ecuador, they are seen as matter-out-of-place, as dirt in clean places. The senior policemen quoted by Rahier (1998: 423–424) view them as incorrigibly delinquent and criminal, bringing their dirtiness and disorder to a space of cleanliness and order.

A similar process can be observed even more explicitly in relation to Indigenas. Some groups have traditionally lived in the Highlands of the country and some in the Amazon rainforest. De la Torre's interviews with middle-class highland Indians tell a story of confrontations with racism when moving into urban space. For these people, as for bell hooks, travel may well equal terror. Indian students, professionals and businessmen are transformed into 'dirty Indians' in white-mestizo spaces. Two female students for example recount their experience of being approached and offered domestic work (De la Torre 1999: 101–102). The man who did so assumed that any young Indian women in an urban space could only possibly have been looking for menial work. Indeed the association of Indians with dirtiness reached such intensity that there was a successful bus boycott in Otavaleno (in the Highlands) in 1986. Drivers had made a practice of insulting locals, and de facto segregation had developed, where Indians felt obliged to sit at the back of the bus, leaving the white-mestizo clientele to monopolise the front (Colloredo-Mansfeld 1998: 191–192). Colloredo-Mansfeld argues that the theme of dirt/cleanliness is the principal racial marker between white-mestizo and indigena cultures and people. This is expressed in physical repulsion over smells of hard physical labour and the places where this labour occurs, which trigger white-mestizo association of dirt/work/backwardness: 'images of filthy Indians and clean whites carried a discursive force, inducing white-mestizo reactions of condemnation, confrontation and separation' (ibid.: 192).

What is more striking in this fieldwork is the degree to which Indians have internalised this racialising trope. In order to be socially mobile, cleaning up one's act means overcoming this obstacle. Otavalenos' industriousness and recent successful involvement in international trade has led to a complex reconfiguration of this relation between dirt and Indians. Recognised by whites as the 'cleanest' of the Indios, many Otavalenos have bought their own land (from the haciendas that dominated the Highlands) and seek a separate existence from coastal (white and urban) society. Their very autonomy has led to a burgeoning indigena middle class that engages with white-mestizo society and recognises the importance of cleanliness. This has two important side effects identified by Colleredo-Mansfeld. The first is the transformation of the taunt of 'dirty Indian' into a way that successful Otavalenos differentiate themselves from those Indigenas they see as backward, lazy, and ultimately dirty. If they do so with a Quechua rather than Spanish term (ibid.: 196), the central mechanism of differentiation is maintained. A cholera scare reignited the intensity of the clean/dirt border in the 1990s (ibid.: 198–199). Second, since the idea that Indians are incapable of anything other than manual and menial labour, or of making a success out of business, is clearly unfounded, the ideological boundary has to shift. This is accomplished by tainting Indians' material success with suspected corruption. Colloredo-Mansfeld reports being involved in a conversation in a doctor's waiting room with white and mestizo Ecuadoreans in which the idea that Indians were actually doing narco-trafficking (with handi-craft trade as a cover operation) was expressed. Indian success is thus seen as a 'threat to the purity of the proper (white-mestizo) national economy' (ibid.: 188).

The notion of dirt (experienced in the sense of smell and touch) is inextricably embedded in conceptions of superiority and inferiority. Whiteness is identified with odours of cleanliness and otherness with odours of dirt. While whole regions are identified with backwardness and dirt in this type of discourse (as we shall see below), 'race' in *purely* biological terms is absent from the arena. The racialised constructions of Latin America then are expressed at least as much in cultural as in biological language.

Redemption

It has been argued from the outset that all racialised identities are con-structed, that is, flexible and contingent, and open to criteria that fix people's identities culturally rather than inflexibly and biologically. In the previous section we have seen that particular themes are used to fix racial boundaries in Latin America, and have focused on cleanliness. So, if the argument that identities are constructed stands up to scrutiny, there must be ways in which people can move between the categories, or in the language of the previous examples, become clean (more civilised). Such discourses have historically been infused with ideas about the dif-ferences between social classes and gender, as well as about 'race'. I have identified three responses to the problem of how to clean up the national population: individual effort, collectively imposed uplift, and the social erasure of people. They allow for both individuals and groups to become white, or even whiter, and therefore access the resources available from that social location.

Individual effort

The example of the elements of the Ecuadorean Otavaleno population which have developed into a entrepreneurial middle class demonstrates that concerted action involving the adoption of some white values, allied with financial backing, can propel individuals into whitened social loca-tions. The clean and successful Indigena can develop a different, white, identity in particular contexts. These identities are always problematic and subject to others' ascriptions. Indeed, the movement of darker com-plexioned people towards a social location to do with paler complexions, and other forms of cultural, economic and social capital, is a constant theme in the history of the New World. From 'whitening up' through marriage in the Caribbean, to self-classification as white in the Brazilian census (Winddance Twine 1998) and the famous Brazilian saying: 'money whitens', individuals engage reflexively in strategies aimed at producing social positions for themselves and their children that enable greater access to all kinds of resources. What is aimed for is the *status* of 'whites'. The physical properties of whiteness do not necessarily have to correspond to the status, nor are the criteria agreed (Stutzman 1981). In Anderson-Levy's studies of Kingston, Jamaica, white middle-class respondents try to construct barriers between themselves and other black and white middle-class Jamaicans using appeals to representing good (as opposed to bad) models of citizenship and their authenticity as long-standing upright moral agents.[54]

The breadth of criteria bearing on the ascription of whiteness is all the more apparent when we observe a little known practice established in Spanish America 1795. Ann Twinam's exploration of *Gracias al sacar* whitenings by decree (2004, 2005, 2006) and their surrounding negotiations reveals some of the options that people who were classified as *pardos* and *mulattos* might secure. The petitioning of local colonial government in order to be granted white status was usually the final step of a process by which individuals had negotiated niches, then toeholds, then footholds, then given service to the Crown through government or business. Although only a few were successful in their bid to become white after the establishment of the grant, the very existence of this mechanism reveals the disjuncture between the biological and the cultural in racialisation. In the New World, rules could be bent, and in the bending, they reveal the constructed nature of racial categories. Yet recognising that there are factors that can mitigate racial identities does not change the paradigm of 'race'. Cultural reasoning only goes so far. At the end there is still a 'white race' for applicants to join.

A major policy response to this assumption in Latin America has been to build new nations on the edifice of *blanquiamiento* (whitening). This takes the form of improving the white and *mestizo* lower classes, black and Indian people in order to inculcate the values seen by the ruling classes as white.

Collectively imposed uplift

The aim of state policy can be effectively attained through a combination of whitening through demographics and/or education. The intellectual elites of Mexico, Brazil and Argentina for example (Stepan 1991, Stern 2003, Rodriguez 2006) found social Darwinism and eugenics compelling frameworks. These ideologies argued that the stronger genes overcame the weaker, and that this is reflected in social and cultural hierarchies. In order to strengthen the gene pool, maintained the eugenicists, stronger genes must be brought into it. White European culture and genetics were the ideal, and the strategies for whitening the nation involved European immigration and education to clean the others and morally uplift them. There are a number of variations on this theme. Stern (2003) shows that in Mexico the twentieth century saw a challenge to the idea that the elusive European immigration should be the target. Race-mixing could indeed achieve the same goal, given the inherent strength of the white gene. He cites Dr Rafael Carillo's talk to the Mexican Eugenics Society in 1932: 'It is also certain that if *mestizaje* continues indefinitely, it will disappear over time, given that the white race, being superior, will prevail over the inferior black and Indian' (2003: 193).

While *mestizaje* was thus seen as long-term whitening, other elites were interested in more concrete and short-term measures. In fact, Weinstein argues that the São Paolo region provided a 'new discursive context' in which: 'Even as discourses of civilisation, modernity and progress replaced earlier preoccupations with race mixture and degeneration, notions of difference based on race (broadly construed), far from fading, flourished' (2003: 240).

The theme used in São Paolo was the fight of civilisation against underdevelopment as a proxy for 'race'. The coffee boom had enabled state government to subsidise massive European immigration and industrialisation (ibid.). The elite fashioned a narrative of São Paolo's development and modernisation in which blackness was simultaneously eliminated and used to illustrate whiteness. Folklorist Dalmo Belfort de Mattos, writing in 1939 on the region's black majority during the coffee boom, stated: 'This soon passed. Mortality and mixture gradually eliminated the African *excess*' (ibid.: 244). While in the campaign of the revolutionary constitutionalists (in 1932) São Paolo is constantly portrayed as white and modern, the North East (containing Bahia province) is depicted as degenerate, backward, the 'perfect foil for claims about São Paolo's vast superiority' (ibid.: 249).

Claims were made sometimes on clearly racial terms (slavery, degeneracy) but usually through models of development in which São Paolo is the only modern area. Appeals to the whiteness of modernity (or the modernity of whiteness?) are thus fashioned by moving between registers. Similar striving for conquest of backward space and peoples through European immigration was successfully satisfied in Argentina and Uruguay, but less so elsewhere.

Nicola Foote (2006: 263–264) describes how European immigration as a civilising process was encouraged in Ecuador. Early access to citizenship was offered for European settlers (in return for their perceived character-istics of industriousness, attachment to the soil and responsibility) in order to fill empty land, and to enable administrative costs to be min-imised (as full citizens could staff their own state bodies). This can be contrasted with the treatment of West Indian immigrant rubber and railway workers and Chinese immigrants (ibid.: 264). In Ecuador's case, immigration did not whiten the population, because Chinese and black migrant workers outnumbered the white. These two populations were each constructed as morally threatening to the nation, Foote argues. The Chinese were viewed as entrepreneurial competitors and sources of opium, prostitution and gambling. Indeed, Chinese immigration was banned in 1899. The West Indians building the Quito–Guayaquil railway line were similarly constructed as violent, gambling alcoholics. However, after the 1895 liberal revolution, indigenous Afro-Ecuadoreans were not granted the same rights as Indigenas by new President Eloy Alfaro, even though the Blacks played their part in the armed revolt for a longer period. Additionally, no official recognition was accorded to the military efforts of black and mulatto troops in retrospective narratives of nation-building. Afro-Ecuadoreans, contends Foote (2006: 266), were thus written out of 'the founding covenant of the Liberal state'.

Social erasure of people

This theme of strategic neglect leads to the third way of whitening the nation: by non-inclusion or writing over of people or space, like a social palimpsest. We established earlier that a set of associations have been built up in Latin America between geographical space and 'race' through linking particular people and the places they inhabit to dirt and cultural backwardness. Yet while the cultural deficit may be redeemable (Highland Indigenas in Ecuador) or not (Afro-Ecuadoreans, see below), it is also pos-sible to redeem a region by violent usurpation, settlement and/or post-facto selective narration. This strategy is by no means new or limited to Latin America: see, for example, the English and Scots colonisation of Ireland in the sixteenth century (Garner 2003), as well as forced removal of indigenous people from land in nineteenth-century North America and Australia. However, one such case is that of Cauca province, in the western coffee-growing region of Colombia in the 1846–1948 period (Appelbaum 2003). Appelbaum's study of the town of Riosucio demon-strates highly contested versions of the region's history, coalescing around the privatisation of communal lands in the establishment of the coffee industry. Competing local mestizo and indigena versions of the area's history detail their oppression by and resistance to the immigrants from the neighbouring Antioquia province from the late nineteenth century onwards. White stories, on the other hand, assert the hard work and well-deserved economic success of pioneers who tamed nature.

Another result of such over-writing can be complete erasure. In the case of Afro-Ecuadoreans, Foote maintains, the black element of Ecuador's population was subject to a policy of malevolent neglect. In addition to the exclusion of their participation in the revolutionary war, their inclusion in the state project of uplift and cleansing through education was minimal. They were racialised as black, not deracialised as poor, as Wade (1997) argues is the case of Afro-Colombians. Separate strategies were implemented regarding highland and Amazonian Indigenas and Afro-Ecuadoreans in the early nineteenth century. The two latter groups were considered irredeemable because of backwardness and savagery, while the former became the object of extensive educational efforts. While civil war raged in black majority Esmeraldas province in the 1912–1916 period, the supply of teaching staff dried up, leaving unqualified locals needing to work two jobs as the only possible workforce. On the basis of Ministry of Education documents, Foote contends that it was not the dangerous politics but the inherently dangerous people that were cited as reasons why teachers did not want to go there. The effort of incorporating a group felt to be incapable of change into the whitening project was not worth the time or the money in the pre-World War II period.

Schubert's anthropology (1981) of San Lorenzo, a coastal railroad town in the midst of changing from a black- to a white-dominated place in the 1970s, shows that local economic changes towards a cash economy, under a different regime, and the arrival of white highlanders (Serraños) with capital to develop businesses, alters the racial dynamic of the city. Where previously there had been no need to pursue whitening strategies because economic independence was feasible, with modernisation (i.e. control of business and, increasingly, of local politics, by Whites) comes a reconfiguration in racial politics. The new economic conditions require new racial strategies: those that want to get ahead must be prepared to 'whiten up' in terms of values, speech patterns and behaviour, at least publicly. The central state then is not the only agent of change or of whiteness.

A moral economy of whiteness

Civilisation – in the form of rationality, development, and Europeanness – has been contrasted with barbarity – in the form of irrationality, backwardness and nature – by successive generations of white Latin American intellectuals and governing elites. There are a number of ways in which this has been worked out, and the positing of white identities is as much part of this process as the construction of Others. The position of Ecuador's elites is illustrative. With one eye outwards, they deployed the equatorial location and the associated scientific research carried out by the nineteenth-century Condemine mission to establish Ecuador's modernity. Yet they wanted also to distance themselves from association with the equator as a region per se, since most of the territories around it were African. Domestically, they worked to create a nation comprised of distinct geographical/demographic/economic spheres. 'Just as independent elites were "de-colonizing" their identity, they were doing so on the basis of several pernicious racializations, as they attempted to maintain "whiteness" and racial exclusions' (Radcliffe and Westwood 1996: 60). In the case of Argentina, for example, Joseph (2000: 341) cites work by nineteenth-century political ideologist and later President, Domingo Sarmiento, who imputed civilisation to ideas, policies, regional and global geography and physical bodies.

São Paolo's intellectuals forged a founding origin myth that depicted the place as qualitatively different from the rest of Brazil: more modern and held back by the rest (Weinstein 2003: 244). The emblematic figure in this story was the *bandeirante*, a risk-taking adventurer and proto-capitalist. In this discursive manoeuvre, the São Paolo elites glossed over the region's slave plantations (that had generated so much capital), which were portrayed as parasitical relics of outmoded economics in other areas of Brazil.

Arguments about whether Latin America has structural racism, either because of the lack of slavery (e.g. Argentina), and the ease with which it was abolished (e.g. Peru (De la Cadena 1998)), or the difference from North American racial systems are, as Appelbaum *et al.* indicate (2003b), red herrings. The absence of discursive markers identical to those of the US model should not be confused with their absence *tout court*. Even the literature on Brazil, which was North American academia's favourite test case, now looks at how racism is configured rather than questioning its existence. What is clear is the normative role that whiteness plays at national and local levels, and how it is grounded not merely in the exploitative labour and political relationships that have existed since the Portuguese conquest. Racialisation has always included a component of attributing cleanliness, decent behaviour and progress to whiteness as a moral characteristic: we might label this the 'moral economy' of whiteness. So the journey to nationhood involved attempts to valorise European heritage at the expense of indigenous and black ones, and/or construct *mestizaje* as a whitening process (evolving towards normality). Yet this linking of goodness and whiteness is disrupted by the meanings attached to it by subaltern populations. Indigenas in Ecuador believe Whites to be violent, corrupt, rapacious, and obsessed with material goods. Indeed, Colloredo-Mansfeld reports that the Otavalenos of Ecuador believe Whites to be 'naturally – even supernaturally – untrustworthy' (1998: 198).

There is a further, psychosocial, issue raised by De la Torre: 'Given that only a few Ecuadoreans can be certain of their European descent, each act of aggression against the Indian and black "Other" is a form of denial and hatred of the *mestizo* self' (1999: 93). This uncertainty and ambivalence about purity permeates the emotional drive towards the European ideal, which means moving away from rural, agricultural, family and community orientation, dirt and squalor. The purity of whiteness makes it unattainable, and the distance between European whiteness and the form of whiteness engineered by Latin American elites is papered over by attention to staying clean. In Argentina, for example, Joseph (2000) argues that a degree of ambivalence was exhibited about the rural 'indio' President Carlos Menem representing the country abroad.[55] The dissimulation exercise necessitates abnormal intellectual and physical labour. Colloredo-Mansfeld (1998: 187) comments on the role of odour in constructions of 'race' in Ecuador, as Whites expend effort expunging all smells to do with physical labour and rural settings, which define Indigenas: 'the odours, textures, and materials of rural life become racial emblems as the white-mestizo elite constitute themselves and their national authority by pursuing an elusive physical and moral ideal: cleanliness'.

This pursuit of cleanliness as moral economy recalls David Sibley's summary of nineteenth-century London:

> The middle classes have been able to distance themselves from their own residues, but in the poor they see bodily residues, animals closely associated with residual matter, and residual places coming together and threatening their own categorical scheme under which the poor and the defiled are distinguished.
>
> (1995: 56)

Clearly, we have moved away from 'race' as comprised of exclusively somatic properties. It is not just blood but habits that make people 'dirty'. For White and mestizo urban Ecuadoreans, menial and manual labour in rural (backward) settings is both the cause and effect of Indigena poverty, and the smells associated with it must be avoided by Whites at all costs.

Racialised identity overlays class: residues betray poverty and the distance from whiteness. Here, extra ideological and purifying labour must be performed because the whitened object does not begin pure.

At a national level, the community imagined as a nation represents a series of sometimes contradictory strategies in which pluralism is both avowed, by the Ecuadorean army, for example (Radcliffe and Westwood 1996: 70–71), and disavowed. The division of the country's territory and peoples into distinct blocs is a powerful abstraction: 'Different cultures are mapped as "grounded" in particular and un-overlapping locations. Population and place are represented as equivalences, places become defined by populations, discursively linked with bounded, sub-national places' (ibid.: 74). So despite the reality of internal migration and the mixing of populations, the racialisation of Ecuador continues in the form of official representations, where 'populations are represented as belonging to *one* geographical location – identities are assumed to be constituted in direct, unmediated and singular relationship with one place' (ibid.:78). Moreover, this is not a neutral division, but one in which 'whiteness and moves toward whiteness are most valued' (ibid.: 68). The black Costeños in Schubert's study, for example, are keenly aware of the advantages to be gleaned from strategically acting white (1981: 574), yet this is not purely a cultural matter, but an identity ploy that responds to a material shift in the local economy. Only when white Serraños begin to dominate the business and political worlds of the black Costeño, does *blanquiamento* appear a worthwhile objective: and then only in selected arenas.

6 Whiteness at the margins

In chapter 4 I argued that one of the borders of whiteness is placed between the dominant and subordinate groups within the nominally 'white' collectivity. This historically contingent practice has been studied in the greatest depth by the American labour historians whose work we discussed in the previous chapter, and will look at again in the next, in relation to the Catholic Irish in America. The argument I drew from this was that not being white (i.e. being 'inbetween' to use Barrett and Roediger's terminology) is not supposed to be an equivalent of being Black, Asian, First Australian, Indigena, etc. So this intermediate zone of 'inbetween-ness', if you like, highlights the qualifications required to be considered approximate to the dominant culture at a given moment. It is a space of peripherality, of being marginal to the dominant culture. However, there are margins and there are *margins*. Being a member of an 'inbetween' group (two examples of which we shall look at below) is not the same type of peripherality as that experienced by groups categorised as neither white nor 'inbetween'. The members of 'inbetween' groups have the option of identifying as white, either as a medium to long-term goal or as a common practice in the present, when the context is such that the border between white and non-white is the most important. This is a thorny and nuanced argument to make. I have already attempted to start the ball rolling by identifying class as a significant arena for quasi-racialised distinctions. Here, I will try to establish the argument about marginal Whites in relation to Jews and Travellers/ Gypsies. This is not going to be an exhaustive and sweeping historical analysis of anti-semitism and anti-nomadism. The object is to indicate how each group has been positioned as marginal to dominant cultures, as not-quite-white.

Jewishness and whiteness in the USA

Within the literature explicitly referring to whiteness, Jewish experience has received attention in the American setting (Lerner 1993, Brodkin 1994, 1998, Jacobson 1998). Karen Brodkin (1998) inserts Jews into the American inbetween-ness position through her innovative interlocking of historical research and family histories. Parallels are drawn between the passage of Jews from outsider to insider with the journey undergone by the Catholic Irish in America, as they assimilate to the American value system. What is striking is the centripetal force working in the communities she describes, caught between recognising other minorities as versions of themselves in earlier, relatively powerless situations on one hand, and on the other, taking advantage of the opportunities earned through adherence to the values of industriousness, both in business and education. This exemplifies Charles Mills's assessment of the relationship between African-Americans and Jews (Mills 1998: 88) in which what distinguishes the social position is that the latter have attained a position whereby they *have the option* to identify with whiteness. The difference between Blacks and Jews, he argues, could be described as that separating 'outside outsiders' from 'inside outsiders'. The former are 'unambiguously nonwhite', and the latter 'ambiguously white' (ibid.).

Jacobson's chapter on Jewish identity in *Whiteness of a Different Color* (1998: 171–201) focuses on the passing and non-passing of Jewish-Americans in and through whites-only domains from the late 1870s to the 1940s, using examples drawn from film, literature and current affairs. Jacobson's chronology for Jewish identity in the USA sees the period up to 1920 as a search for Jewish specificity. This period is marked by Jewish intellectuals' use of racial science to define Jews as a racial group as valid as others: a source of solidarity in the wake of the Eastern European pogroms of the 1880s and the discrimination faced by Jews in America. Physical appearance becomes a fetish, both for anti-Semites and Jewish racemakers who appeal to essentialist categories of difference. From the 1920s, the stake is no longer Jewish distinctiveness, but the drift into becoming Caucasian. Here, the primary motor of change is economic, with World War II as the key experience. 'Postwar prosperity and postindustrial shifts in the economy, too, tended to disperse Jews geographically', argues Jacobson, 'either to outlying suburbs or sunbelt cities like Los Angeles and Miami – in either case, to places where whiteness eclipsed Jewishness in racial salience' (1998: 188). This process, wherein whiteness overrides ethnic distinctiveness, was exacerbated by the GI Bill of Rights, and the practices of the Federal Housing Authority, which meant that where no covenanting system existed, Jews were grouped with others under the heading 'white', and thus given access to residential areas forbidden to Black, Asian and Hispanic Americans. Within this location, the tensions remain between insider and outsider. Arthur Miller's novel *Focus* (1945) shows how, when an anti-semitic human resources professional is misrecognised as Jewish, '. . . the social category "Jew" becomes aligned with the visual category "Jew" ' (Jacobson 1998: 191).

Jacobson also examines the lynching of Leo Frank in Georgia in 1915 as a way of exposing the normativity of lynching as a white-on-black form of collective violence. Frank's Northern-ness, his middle-class location and his physical conformity to the 'visual category "Jew" ', combine to place him in a position so vulnerable that he is temporarily decoupled from the protection of whiteness, in that a black employee is allowed to give key and ultimately fatal evidence against him in the Mary Phagan murder trial. Jacobson summarises that:

> even in the strict white-over-black social bifurcation, complete with its own imperatives, rituals, etiquette, and patterns of deference and domination, Jews could be racially defined in a way that irrevocably set them apart from other 'white persons' on the local scene.
>
> (1998: 62)

Frank was found 'inconclusively white' (Jacobson 1998: 65), and inscribed into the role of sexual pervert lusting for Gentile women.

Jacobson's most recent work (2006) situates Jewish-Americans as one of a number of hyphenated ethnic groups seeking to revalorise their difference in post-civil rights America. He highlights this tension of white ethnics, being trapped in the bind of being both identified with whiteness by non-whites and having to defend oneself using two strategies. The first is the 'shared oppression' argument, and the second the 'my people arrived too late for slavery or the Indian Wars' response. He quotes Melanie Kaye/Kantrowitz on the meaning of the Holocaust for American Jews: 'As Jews, afraid of the myth of Jewish power . . . guilty about our skin privilege, we are so hungry for innocence that images of oppression come almost as a relief' (2006: 22). On the second argument, he notes that Michael Novak's reassurances to his Native American interlocutor that his ancestors never 'saw an Indian' (ibid.) rely on a narrative ploy identified by McKinney (2005) among her white students, which consists of fossilising oppression in the past and arguing that, implicitly, there is no longer any benefit accruing from being white.

What can we learn from this? Extrapolating from relatively short periods of historical oppression into the contemporary field provides a carapace of virtue that ought to crack under the scrutiny of the whiteness problematic. Whatever social formation *generated* discrimination against Jews and Native, Asian and African-Americans, has altered to the point where the discrimination against Jews in America is no longer structural.

The racialisation of Jewishness in Britain at the turn of the twentieth century

Tony Kushner (2005: 208) summarises what is at stake in Jewish whiteness in the British case. Looking at the various migrations into Britain in the last two centuries and analysing the responses to them highlights the distinction between two key problematics: 'race relations' and 'racialisation'. The former was the dominant paradigm in UK academia until the 1980s,[56] when it came under challenge (CCCS 1982, Miles 1982, 1989, 1993, Miles and Phizacklea 1984), and, under the guise of ethnic relations, remains the dominant paradigm in public policy. Racialisation in the British context has thus been deployed by Miles (1989), Solomos and Murji (2005), as well as US academics David Goldberg (1990), Howard Winant (1994), and Stephen Small (1994). What is at issue is the epistemological basis for understanding racism, whether 'races' can be assumed as given entities, and whether they relate to each other, as such. The formulation of this problem can be traced back to Robert Park and was developed from his analysis of the way different groups behaved in the early twentieth-century Chicago housing market. The racialisation paradigm (as distinguished from the process), which can be traced back to Fanon (1967) and Banton (1967) or earlier, according to Barot and Bird (2001), sees 'race' as inherently unstable, fluid and subject to pressures exerted by actors such as the state and civil society. The emphasis thus shifts from the pathology of 'races' and onto the broader structural terrain of explaining how the ideas of 'race' are used as bases for oppression, solidarity and political manoeuvring. What we are trying to accomplish with the whiteness problematic is an examination of the transformations in the meanings attached to racialised identities. It is not necessary for any of the actors to specifically use the vocabulary of 'white people' for us to consider how Jews are the object of a particular racialisation process at a particular time, in which the indigenous English differentiated them from themselves, differentiated between types of Jew, and how British Jews differentiated themselves from the new immigrants at the end of the nineteenth century in a range of ways.

We might pick up the British story at the moment referred to in Jacobson's account as that of 'becoming Hebrew' in America. As the pogroms in Eastern Europe got underway and people fled to the West,

Britain was one of the destinations for sanctuary. In Britain, as elsewhere in Western Europe, Jews had been for centuries viewed as deicides, heretics, and perpetrators of ritualised murder (Wistrich 1992). They were represented as cliquey, and tight-fisted. The structural explanation for this may well be their exclusion from guild membership and the availability of the money-lending niche in the market in early medieval times. British Jews had integrated successfully into British society and the professions, yet by the turn of the twentieth century, the figure of 'the Jew' had come to represent an amalgam of threats thrown up in modernity. They were hyper-mobile and transnational in a context of nation-states and undivided loyalties. The Wandering Jew – whose mobility is an eternal punishment – was simultaneously inside and outside the nation, constructed as a fifth columnist because of his loyalty beyond the state. Contemporary Catholic nationalists in France, such as Maurice Barrès (in *Les Déracinés*, 1897), at the time of the Dreyfus Affair (1894–1906), could use the theme of rootedness to demonstrate the distinction between good Frenchmen, uprooted Frenchmen (open to alien influence) and aliens, of whom the epitome is the Jew (in a permanent state of uprootedness). Robert Zaretsky (1996), commenting on David Carroll's (1995) book on French Literary Fascism, contends that the true nation (*le pays réel*) is always defined by what the Jew is not. Indeed Barrès's definitions of 'race' are formulated through culture, as nothing is offered in terms of physical appearance. This use of a straw man to define the nation might lead us to acknowledge Zizek's (1989) argument that it is not the specific content of the Other that is important, rather it is the structural practice of what this represents. The 'Jew', he argues, is

> just the embodiment of a certain blockage – of the impossibility which prevents society from achieving its full identity as a closed, homogenous totality … Society is not prevented from achieving its full identity because of the Jews: it is prevented by its own antagonistic nature, by its own immanent blockage, and it projects this internal negativity into the figure of 'the Jew'.
>
> (Zizek 1989: 127)

I wonder to what degree this insight can be taken at face value for somebody interested in the ways in which power is racialised and the idea of 'race' injected with salience. Alongside the clarity that Zizek provides, and his argument's epistemological rupture with contemporary positivist social science, go a wilful downplaying of the specifics of time and place. It is one thing to argue that societies construct scapegoats for their failure to cohere, and another to say that it is not important whether this *pharmakon* figure takes the form of Jews, Catholics, asylum seekers, or 'coloured immigrants'. In order to examine what Zizek's thesis leaves out, we shall look at the opposition to Jewish settlement in London's East End which led to the passage of Britain's first immigration legislation, the Aliens Act (1905).

The process of racialisation was triggered by the arrival of many poor Yiddish-speaking East European Jews fleeing pogroms from the 1880s. This high level of immigration over a short period altered the composition of the long-established 'Anglo-Jewry', much of whose membership occupied high-class positions (Phillips 2001). Indeed, in the 1880–1906 period, the British Jewish population increased by a factor of five (to 300,000), the majority of whom were living in London (Feldman 1994: 24). There was a very high concentration of Jews in a small part of the East End of London (Spitalfields), covering less than one square mile – called 'Jew-town' by contemporaries (ibid.: 167). In addition, there were several hundred thousand transient migrants stopping in England en route to the Americas (Phillips 2001: 5). So what was at stake was control of the direction of the racialisation process. British Jews saw that uncontrolled immigration of foreign Jews would negatively alter the way they were viewed by their Gentile British compatriots. Hence the community efforts engaged in over the last two decades of the nineteenth century. Phillips (2001) argues that Anglo-Jewry ran de facto immigration control in the period until 1905, providing funding for some, discouraging others from coming, and repatriating and shipping on many people. They realised that it was important not to provoke hostility against them *as Jews*, and that these newcomers risked doing just that. These efforts, however, were not enough to completely neutralise the situation's potential for racist activism. The racialisation of Jews in Britain, but primarily in the East End of London, revolved around four interlocking areas: threats to native male employment levels; physical concentration in housing; threats to health; and alien values. The theme of dirt as an indicator of moral depravity operated as a binding nucleus.

By the end of the nineteenth century, London's Jewish employees were concentrated disproportionately in the clothing trade, which employed 60 per cent of them. The employment pattern in 1897, according to Feldman (1994: 164), saw about 9 per cent of them as employers, 20 per cent self-employed and about 71 per cent employees. As is commonly the case, particular niches of employment were closed to some groups. Saturday working in factories militated against Jewish employment, while areas of casual employment such as the docks and the building trade were dominated by informal networks (Phillips 2001).

The new wave of Jewish workers accepted lower rates and much poorer conditions than the local workforce. As the British economy experienced contraction in the last quarter of the nineteenth century, unemployment struck the less skilled element of the workforce harder than the skilled. This had the result of pushing unskilled male labourers out of the job market, and drawing the lower-paid (immigrants and women) into it. As the principal area of new Jewish settlement was in the already poor and working-class East End, hostility was expressed by the vulnerable section of the workforce who perceived themselves as being ousted by alien labour that did not comply with local rules. This meant Sunday working, but also the construction of 'sweating' as an 'alien' rather than indigenous practice. 'Sweating', which involved substandard and often insanitary working environments, together with the lowest pay and longest hours, was a practice confined neither to Jewish employers, nor to the clothing trade. It predated Jewish immigration, but by the end of the nineteenth century, came to be associated in anti-alien campaigning solely with Jewishness, so that it was presented as a kind of paradigm of Otherness, as removed as possible from the English aspirational norm of unionised and regulated labour (Kershen 2005).

Gainer (1972) notes that the housing conditions into which large numbers of Jewish immigrants settled were already marked by overcrowding. Yet the population density of Spitalfields rose through the 1880s and 1890s. Not only were there physically more people in the same space, the proportion of the population who were Eastern European Jews rose also. While the area in which most of them settled remained small and restricted, this did not limit the degree of antipathy expressed, either over the changing public face of the area, or the practices with which the newcomers were most closely identified: rack-renting and insanitary behaviour. Gainer documents a number of complaints over the practices of Jews buying up houses and renting them out to immigrants, who would over-occupy them, and whose experiences of housing were not up to the relatively poor but more sanitary ones of East London tenements. Claims that toilets were not used properly and that refuse was thrown into the backyard fuelled concerns about health as well as cementing the image of the 'dirty Jew' invading the hitherto respectable and clean working-class quarters in which they lived. Again, the presence of the new immigrants served to exacerbate already difficult conditions rather than cause them per se.

These different standards of hygiene were a major source of anger. In a culture of public health awareness, routine exposure to refuse of all kinds was guaranteed to spur health scares. When official reports found similarly insanitary conditions in the infamous sweatshops, the threat of epidemics was expressed. Although the 1903 Royal Commission in fact found that such claims of 'sweating' and associated conditions were exaggerated and not more prevalent than they were in non-Jewish industry, the link between Jews, dirt and illness had already been established to the point where it was a key claim in anti-alien agitation (Kershen 2005).

Moreover, certain poverty-related illnesses were over-represented among Jewish immigrants: *plica polonica*, syphilis, and trachoma (Maglen 2005) were linked to poor living conditions and poverty, so it was unsurprising that groups of very poor people should exhibit them. Additionally, the malnutrition also located in the lower orders of society was highlighted by leading eugenicist Karl Pearson, who claimed, on the basis of his findings of physical development among the first generation of children born to Jewish immigrants, that the parents were 'inferior stock' not to be used to regenerate the British nation. The new Jewish Eastenders were seen by many as congenitally dirty, risks to public health, and displacers of labour: in short, an unassimilable invading force.

Yet at the root of this interpretation were cultural differences, or alien values. Considering the amount of ideological labour that has gone into depicting Jews as physically different from Gentiles, primarily by the latter but also by Jewish theorists seeking racial solidarity, relatively little of the early twentieth-century discourse in Britain revolved around the phenotypical. We should be wary of generalising this statement however. Gilman (1991: 172–176) argues that in popular mid to late nineteenth-century European representations, the Jew was 'blackened', and that particular parts of the body: noses and feet, were also projected as pathologically Jewish throughout the early twentieth century. This led to the popularity of rhinoplasty practised by the pioneering Jacques Joseph in Berlin in the 1920s. Importantly, the darkness of the Jew's skin (which was open to debate) was associated with illnesses, both *plica polonica* (Polish plait) and syphilis. In this combination, proof that Jews were not white was thus indelibly linked with immorality, the lack of whiteness exaggerated into moral failing legible on and in the body.

Yet while the British debate was less about appearance,[57] it was more about difference expressed through values. This was a more complicated arena. On the one hand, a number of cultural practices had, by the early 1900s, become fuel for anti-alien campaigns in England involving trade unions, parliamentarians and candidates, as well as individuals such as Joseph Banister and Arnold White, and lobby groups like the British Brotherhood League. The first, 'sweating', confirmed the view of Jews as simultaneously money-grabbing exploiters of labour, and blackleg workers lowering the industry bar. Moreover, Sunday working encapsulated this excess, as forcing people to work on the Sabbath and agreeing to work on the Sabbath were seen as cultural slaps in the face by the British workers. At both ends of the scale, Jewish behaviour was perceived as exceeding the local norms. Another point of moral discrepancy was the lesser-known topic of white slavery (Holmes 1979: 44–46). Jewish involvement in this appears to have been primarily at the organisational level, distributing poor Eastern European women across the New World, yet accusations that Jewish prostitution in the East End was flourishing, and that indirectly, the overstocking of labour supply forced British women into prostitution surfaced and resurfaced from the 1880s (ibid.: 45). Clearly, as with the other accusations, Jewish immigrants did not instigate the institution they are later blamed for, but their involvement in it is given a higher profile and lent one-dimensional and explanatory form. This projection of sexual depravity and moral failings onto an identifiable Other is a frequent element of anti-immigrant discourse. What is important about this particular version is its relationship to an ambiguously white population, and the fact that the pro-alien arguments were couched within cultural terms.

Support for the Jewish immigrants among the Gentile population (Gainer 1972, Holmes 1979) can be traced to the middle classes, and the dominant liberal ideology of the day. Religious toleration, individual industriousness leading to the accumulation of capital, innovation, entrepreneurial spirit, and intelligence were traits admired by both the established Anglo-Jewry, and the newcomers. The example of the former showed there was promise in the latter. Indeed, Deborah Cohen (2002: 461) goes so far as to argue that racial difference was used as a discourse in relation to British Jews precisely because they had become so hard to distinguish from the Gentile population the higher up the class structure they climbed – a version of the 'money whitens' approach noted in Latin America. 'White middle-class Jews', she states, 'were the most able chameleons' (ibid.: 469). Cohen uses the 'mistaken identity' case of Albert Beck, a Norwegian falsely imprisoned for crimes perpetrated by the Jewish Englishman John Smith, to assert that physical differences as a means to distinguish Gentile from Jew were fallible, despite popular notions to the contrary. Indeed, the overriding characteristic detected by Cohen in British discourse about Jewish identification is uncertainty. This corresponds to the most insidious difference: the somatically undetectable kind. Adaptability thus becomes essence. 'The only characteristic that definitively signalled a Jew was mutability. John Smith's many disguises attested more reliably to his Jewishness than his outward appearance could ever have' (ibid.: 477). Yet even this adaptability is both a liability and an asset, as Jews could be depicted as both unpatriotic and self-serving, or extremely integrated patriots.

We have argued throughout this book that whiteness is to an important extent to do with cultural norms. In late nineteenth- and early twentieth-century Britain, Jewish norms corresponded to the dominant ideas of the (white) ruling classes (a scenario also exploited by Brazil's Jewish community (Grün 1998)). Yet clearly not all Jews are of equivalent standing: some Jews are 'whiter' than others, and this was a distinction made by both Gentiles and British Jews at the time. The diluted contents of the 1905 Act are testimony to the prevailing liberal hegemonic ideas: the Act's restrictions bear only on the poorest immigrants. Yet, the Aliens Act of 1905 is merely the beginning of an increasingly restrictive pattern of immigration laws from 1914 to the early twenty-first century. More indiscriminate blocking of Jewish refugees occurred in the 1930s and during World War II than after the class-oriented 1905 Act.

Sander Gilman's (1991) compelling argument that wealthy European Jews strove to efface their physical difference is developed primarily from the German and Austrian context – their Jewishness still could not be hidden in the 1930s, even with Joseph's rhinoplasty. Britain's Jewish communities thankfully did not have to withstand such violence, but it is also clear that the racial assumptions of the Nazis were not completely absent from the situation. The 'most Jewish' characteristics (i.e. those furthest from Western European norms) were those of the East: the *Ostjuden*. Michael Burleigh (2000: 575) remarks that the Germans moving eastwards through Poland and the Baltic States encountered different Jews from those they had grown up with as fellow Germans. The extent of cultural difference must have facilitated their process of dehumanisation. Burleigh quotes Goebbels in Poland in 1939: 'These aren't human beings any more. These are animals. This is therefore not a humanitarian but a surgical task. One must make cuts here, moreover really radical ones' (ibid.). Soldiers trained to think of Jews as being physically and sartorially different could tell immediately who, among the people they encountered, were Jews, as their clothes and language set them apart from the indistinguishable German Jews. The readiness of locals to join militias and participate in pogroms and round-ups indicates that long-standing hostilities and racialised understandings of difference required a context in which to be transformed into collective action. The paradox is that in anti-semitic propaganda, all the things that tied European Jews into Western European culture: physical appearance, capital accumulation, involvement in the arts and intellectual life, the capacity to utilise networks and resources to flourish in business, also later served to distinguish them from Gentiles. European Jews inhabit both a marginal and a mainstream space in terms of their place in Western societies;

while successfully negotiating particular spheres of business and achieving above average education levels, they are also vulnerable to identification as beyond Christian and secular societies. They have thus been in the firing line of far-right propaganda seeking to scapegoat them for the excesses of capitalism, just as during the communist period they were linked with Bolshevism. At particular moments, as we have seen here, a convergence of factors means that the way a nation sees its Jewish members can come under intense scrutiny. Yet this can only happen because there is a pre-existing idea of Jews *as a group* being different. This is clearly recognised by the British Jews in the 1890s who organised onward migration and the distribution of funds to their Eastern European co-religionists at the end of the nineteenth century in order to manage potential fallout.

So, what the whiteness problematic enables us to do is focus on the process of racialisation and how it creates and maintains types of borders based on ideas of innate capacities and behavioural traits *within* the larger groups understood as constituting 'races'. By focusing on the racialisation processes we can see how such marginal groups move across the borders at particular moments, thus producing a more nuanced and flexible picture of the way 'race' functions than can be procured by deploying 'race relations', or using binary maps of identity.

ANTI-NOMADISM

Another group in a marginal position in relation to dominant white culture are nomads, whether Travellers, Gypsies, Roma or Sinti. Nomads have been the targets of state policy at local and national levels, aimed at eliminating them from particular areas of space and relocating them in others because of the threats to order and purity they represent (Hawes 1996, Sibley 1995, Helleiner 2000, Barany 2001, Bancroft 2005, Sigona 2005). Between half a million and a million nomadic people died as a result of the Nazi operations in Eastern and Central Europe and in the concentration camps, in '*O Porrajmos*', the Gypsy Holocaust.[58] Gypsies were listed in Nazi race laws as a group that were forbidden from marriage with Aryans, but they had been identified as a degenerate 'race' centuries before the Nazis took over. A number of laws had been passed against Roma over the period since the sixteenth century: a law in England having proclaimed the death penalty for Travellers (and their companions) in 1554. Yet the first documented law goes back to Lucerne in 1471 (Kenrick and Puxon 1972: 42), initiating a trend that spread throughout Europe by the end of the seventeenth century.[59] Nomadic peoples have consistently been characterised as un-Christian, immoral, dirty, and subhuman.

The central characteristic of nomadic society – its rejection of fixity – appears to have given rise to the constructions of nomads as both anti-modern and anti-capitalist. We are going to look at two national cases here – Ireland and Britain – to illustrate some of the borders that have been developed to set Nomads apart as racially distinct. Not all the treatment of Nomads has been as extremely violent as that referred to in the work cited above, yet the underlying ideas about difference are similar, and still salient in the contemporary period.

Ireland

There is now a growing corpus on racism in Ireland (Lentin and McVeigh 2006, Garner 2003, Fanning 2002, McVeigh 1998b, 1992, Mac Laughlin 1995) in which Travellers have been identified as central to the problematic of racism as it is played out on the island of Ireland. To go by opinion polls alone (which is usually inadvisable), Travellers are the subject of the most hostile attitudes of any Irish racialised or ethnic minority in the attitudinal survey work done between 1972 and 2001 (Garner 2003). Despite the presence of refugees and Black people in growing numbers, antipathy towards whom is identified in the Eurobarometer 1997 and 2000 (European Commission 1998, 2001), and the sporadic newspaper polls, Travellers were still the most 'socially distant' ethnic group in McGréil's work (1996); 52nd of 59 groups. They also constituted those whose presence is found to be 'most disturbing' in the named surveys above. They record the highest frequency of physical and verbal attacks among the minorities in the 2001 Amnesty International survey (Amnesty International/FAQs 2001), and experience discrimination principally in the areas of accommodation, leisure, health services and education. Travellers' mortality levels are well in excess of those of the settled population, and life expectancy far lower (Barry *et al.* 1989, CSO 1998). A series of state attempts to reassess the nature of the problem and propose action between 1963 and 1995 (Garner 2003: 144) have still not brought about either the infrastructure required to provide adequate living conditions, or the cultural change required to see Travellers as equal members of the nation. The Department of Justice's Monitoring Committee on the 1995 Task Force's recommendations even acknowledged in its report (Department of Justice 2000: 13) that the numbers of families on the roadside had increased rather than diminished since the 1995 report, and that one in four Travellers still had no access to toilet facilities or running water, etc. So clearly, the results of whatever relationship exists between Travellers and settled populations at the beginning of the twenty-first century are detrimental to the former in a number of areas.

Yet Travellers have gained the status of officially-recognised ethnic minority in the Republic.[60] As one of the arguments goes, Travellers are a white ethnic minority, so they cannot be the victims of racism (which is assumed to be a property only of white/non-white relations). What I want to do in this section is emphasise the significant elements of the border between Irish Travellers and sedentary society, to argue that the former are, at best, marginal Whites.

The exact status of Irish Travellers[61] only comes under scrutiny at particular moments in history: when stages of modernity are at stake. This first comes in the push to attain statehood from the British. Sinéad Ní Shuínéar (1994) notes that although references to Irish tinkers are traceable as far back as the thirteenth century, the appearance of the 'Irish Traveller' as a distinct grouping in academic circles occurred in the 1890s (during the Gaelic Revival, when Irish indigenous culture was being revalorised in order to provide fuel for claims for independence). An Irish variant of the discourse equating nomadism with barbarity had existed since Giraldus Cambrensis's twelfth-century treatise, *History and Topography of Ireland*. It was modified over the following centuries and intensified from the 1570s onwards. Moreover, Jim Mac Laughlin (1995) asserts that anti-nomadism assumed new dimensions in the conservative and aggressive forms of 'blood and soil' nationalism of the nation-building nineteenth century. Attachment to land in the form of individual (not communal) property relations was posited as the keystone of modernity. So part of the process of Irish nationalists ideologically transforming the Irish nation-in-waiting to a modern one, the equal of other European nations, is to designate those without claims on land ownership (Travellers and the peasantry, the Irish versions of 'abject whites') as outside, or at least marginal to, the nation. What the Travellers represent in addition to the landless peasantry, however, is hyper-mobility in a Western culture where sedentarism is valued.

Since its inception in 1922, the Irish State has responded to the Travellers by wavering between assimilation (the elimination of cultural differences through housing policy), expulsion (the elimination of bodies from territory)[62] and a recognition of cultural difference. Robbie McVeigh (1998b) asserts that the overall orientation of the policy is underpinned by a genocidal logic: Travellers' very culture is the target of criminalising legislation. As we shall see in the case of Britain (below), the state can act to shrink the space available for the enactment of Traveller culture, and turn normal cultural practice into crime. The most important of the state's instruments are the 1998 Accommodation Act, Section 32; and the Amendment to the Criminal Justice Act 2002, making trespass a criminal (rather than a civil) offence. Powers conferred on the police in the cases of what is interpreted as 'illegal encampment' allow on-the-spot fines and confiscation of vehicles. So it is possible for Travellers to lose their home and means of transport for parking temporarily in an unofficial roadside site. Yet at the same time, local authorities have consistently failed to provide the targeted number of halting places, thus leaving a proportion of Travellers with no option but to use unofficial sites, therefore putting themselves in jeopardy.

One of the principal functions of racism, the ordering and government of movement into and within physical and imaginary spaces, is thus starkly apparent. The Irish State has transformed spaces central to the maintenance of Traveller culture into no entry zones, as a quid pro quo for the provision of some (but not the agreed number of) accommodation sites.

The relationship between the authorities and Travellers is played out at both national and local levels. Bryan Fanning (2002: 112–151) explores the institutionalisation of anti-Traveller racism in one local authority: Clare County Council in the West of Ireland between 1963 and 1999. He argues that Councillors prevaricated around the statutory obligation to provide accommodation for Travellers. When accommodation was provided, it was only in spaces where Travellers did not want to stay (e.g. close to a cemetery). Councillors used putative distinctions between 'local' and 'outsider' to argue about Travellers' eligibility for housing. Even if individual Travellers felt they were from Clare, they were likely to be categorised as being from another county because the proof of residence within the Council's jurisdiction was difficult for Travellers to provide. This bureaucratic procedure ran parallel with a de facto policy of only rarely offering council housing to Travellers.

Indeed, Councillors helped create a climate of antipathy to Travellers by giving popular leadership to residents' fears of Traveller settlement in their areas. They would criticise voluntary sector initiatives aimed at ameliorating Travellers' living conditions, and they contributed to focusing attention away from the Council's failure to initiate policy and onto Travellers' behavioural norms. This was despite senior local authority officials' warnings that the Council risked being overridden by central government in the case of non-compliance with directives. The occasional minuted suggestion by councillors that Travellers should not be dealt with by the same criteria as others indicates the degree to which they could be successfully excluded. Popular discourse on Travellers is saturated with assumptions that they are inherently violent, thieving cheats. This has the dual result of enabling them to be thought of as an especially undeserving case, and a priori invalidates any claim that they have been discriminated against. These claims draw responses that they are actually being given special treatment, and/or are even engaging in a massive extortion racket enabled by the equality legislation that was adopted in the Republic at the end of the twentieth century. Proof of their special case status is that the Minister for Justice, Equality and Law Reform ruled in 2003 that Travellers' claims against discrimination by pubs, restaurants and hotels could no longer be dealt with under the Equal Status Act, 2000 (the only group for which this exception has been made). Yet the Equality Authority's 2005 Annual Report (Equality Authority 2006: 60–62) shows that Travellers are still the group making the largest number of claims under the Equal Status Acts 2000 to 2004 (which deal with discrimination in the provision of services) (29.1 per cent).

There has been a dual movement in settled Irish society on its relationship with Travellers. While since the mid 1990s, the official language used has assumed the more moderate and equality-based model (couching references in terms of 'ethnic' difference; using capital 'T' for Travellers; including a question on 'membership of the Traveller community' in the 2002 Census), the policy to support this linguistic gear-shift has remained wedded to a framework of criminalisation. There has been a failure to translate established and agreed housing, health or education targets into reality, in tandem with legislation that simultaneously recognises Travellers' citizens' rights to non-discrimination and other laws that criminalise and delegitimise the basis of their culture. Moreover, the sporadic anti-social (and highly publicised) behaviour of small groups of Travellers is used as a justification for legislation impinging on the rights of all Travellers unrelated to these incidents, treating them collectively as potential litterers and vandals per se.

Ní Shuínéar (2002, 1994) comments that Irish settled society has internalised anti-nomadic ideas that were first put into circulation centuries ago in the British colonisation of Ireland. Just as indigenous people in the Americas and Australia, for example, were displaced and excluded from the project of nation-building because their relationship to land did not involve individual property ownership, so too have European Travellers, Gypsies, Roma and Sinti suffered progressive exclusion from the land and the cultures of the countries they move within. The treatment of Travellers, Native Americans and First Australians derives from the common assumption that the irrational, nomadic, non-landowning, non-capitalist organisation of collective life is backward and inferior to rational, modern, capitalist society, and that the individual members of the groups share a pathology of degeneracy. This is therefore a justification for controlling and decimating it through passive or active state intervention. The aim of policy has therefore been to control movement, exclude and eliminate the Other from national space as they have been excluded from the imagined space of the nation.

Britain

Mary Douglas's insight that people, like dirt, can be seen as 'matter-out-of-place' (1966) is frequently referred to in cultural geographies. In the logic of 'out-of-place' there is always an implicit 'in-place', which enables the 'out-of-place' categorisation to make sense. However, the case of British Gypsy-Travellers lends itself to a less clear-cut interpretation. Competing narratives at the national level sought to locate Gypsies in their appropriate environment in the nineteenth (Holloway 2003) and early twentieth centuries (Sibley 1995). By the contemporary period, it is questionable whether there is an 'appropriate' location at all (Halfacree 1996, Holloway 2005). This is due to a combination of state-driven legislation and enduring representations of Travellers as thieves and con-artists.

Sarah Holloway identifies two explanations of the geographical location of British Gypsies posited by nineteenth-century elites. The first imagined them as exotic and romantic Others in the countryside. They were bearers of traditional pre-industrial values and could be compared to the noble savage of colonial lands. The second viewed Travellers as a rural version of the urban criminal underclass, and as such a group who should be controlled and assimilated (Holloway 2003). Both can be seen also in the House of Lords debates on the Moveable Dwellings Bill, 1908 described by Sibley (1995: 106–108).

The insight Holloway (2003) brings from fieldwork on an annual fair in the North of England (Appleby Horse Fair) traditionally attended by Travellers is that at local level, the vocabulary and ideas used to distinguish Gypsy from non-Gypsy do not necessarily correspond to the national debates. Neither the cultural references nor the concept of Traveller in nineteenth-century Appleby fit with the elite discourse described above. The concept of the identity of particular groups at the Fair being Traveller (or Romany), rather than merely horse-traders and sharp practitioners, does not emerge until the inter-war years of the twentieth century. Moreover, this transformation accompanies the discursive ploys of distinguishing the authentic from the inauthentic Romany. The authentic are identified by activities and appearance (horse-trading, caravans, dress and dark complexion): their appropriate location is rural. The inauthentic are poor horsemen, only con-men, and do not dress or look noticeably different from the urban poor. In the hierarchy of representations, the rural and traditional trumps the modern and urban. Indeed, although Gypsies have actually always used urban space (Okely 1983) they are seen as 'belonging' only in the countryside. Yet even this belonging is contingent upon the interests of the dominant groups who seek to portray them in threatening or less threatening ways, as part of, or as a stain on, the English countryside (Sibley 1995: 106). In the contemporary period, legislation to restrict Travellers' mobility and capacity to settle were introduced in Britain, as it was later in the Republic of Ireland. Part five of The Criminal Justice and Public Order Act (CJPOA), 1994[63] successfully made the countryside a location in which not just Gypsy-Travellers but New Age Travellers, hunt saboteurs and ravers were officially matter-out-of-place. As well as granting police powers to arrest people felt to be intending to stay illegally on property, it gave them the authority to stop suspects and confiscate their vehicles and other property. The 1993 debates surrounding the Bill's introduction focused primarily on the perceived anti-social behaviour of 'New Age Travellers' (characterised as sponging welfare recipients), contrasted often unfavourably with other types of Traveller (shades of the authentic/inauthentic distinction frequently made about Travellers). The CJPOA was aimed at restoring order to types of mobility seen as dis-ordering, that is, threatening to the interests of some of those living in the countryside. However, alongside the extra police provisions enabling them to turn groups of people away, the statutory responsibility of local authorities to provide halting sites, under the Caravan Sites Act 1968 and the Local Government Planning and Land Act 1980, was abolished, thus shrinking the legal space for Travellers to stop in. What is left available are often sites under flyovers, next to dumps, lay-bys and wasteland (already viewed as polluted and dirty by settled society). British Gypsy Daniel Baker (2006) has the following to say about authenticity:

> Although our presence is felt in the contemporary cultural landscape, it is only as a form of cipher or archetype. Any sense of the real – as a community or as individuals – is left behind when popular cultural representations are set in motion, prone as they are to the seductions of romance, villainy, fantasy and myth.

Yet as Sibley points out, the marginal space in society and the marginal places of Travellers in the West are not only a fantasy, 'they translate into exclusionary practice' (1995: 69). While Gypsy-Travellers have internal social order, and very strong ideas about cleanliness, hygiene and purity

(Okely 1983), this is ignored in the dominant discourse on them, which transforms them into the source of all dirt and disorder.[64] Indeed, the British government found that around 90 per cent of legal halting sites had been closed down between 1994 and 2004 (ODPM 2004: 21). So if they are out of place in the countryside and in urban settings, where can they be in place?

In the first decade of the twenty-first century, the relationship between Travellers and settled population has risen to prominence again. Gypsy-Travellers in the twenty-first century have access to cars and caravans, and some have made money from their entrepreneurial activities. They are clearly no longer the romantic kerchief-sporting characters with painted horse-drawn caravans, smoking pipes, playing violins and performing seasonal labour (if indeed they ever were). This increase in material resources (for some), combined with a willingness to take on local authority planning committees, sparked an intense anti-Gypsy media campaign in March 2005 led by tabloid newspapers, the *Sun* and the *Daily Mail*[65] focusing on the government's dealings with illegal encampments. Use of planning regulations by local authorities to block Travellers from developing land they have bought[66] has spurred a series of conflicts between local residents and authorities trying to prevent Travellers building on land they have purchased. Two nationally prominent ongoing planning conflicts have received the most coverage: one in Cottenham, Cambridgeshire, and the other at Dale Farm, near Basildon in Essex (both counties in the South East of England). In both cases, groups of Travellers have challenged planning law and a series of rulings and appeals has ensued.

In a MORI opinion poll conducted in 2001, Travellers were the group that respondents felt 'the least positive about', placing them just ahead of refugees.[67] While such figures are only indicative, it is striking that both these groups constitute 'folk devils' in contemporary Britain. Travellers who transgress into some places make themselves symbolically inauthentic, as Vanderbeck (2003) highlights in his analysis of responses to the Tony Martin Case.[68] Both settled rural and settled urban Travellers emerge as out of place; the former because they bring the outside (crime and disorder) into isolated and quiet communities, and the latter because they are viewed as constituting an element of the abject urban underclass. When Travellers are mobile and unfixed they are suspect because they owe no allegiance to and have no investment in place. Yet when they adopt sedentary lifestyles or even purchase property, the cultural traits imputed to them remain those with which they were endowed on the road: bringers of dirt, crime and disorder. What does this tell us about whiteness? The racialisation of the Travellers tells us what has been valued in white Western modernity. Dominant whiteness is about order imposed on disorder (Dyer 1997), with groups perceived as close to nature racialised as pathologically wild and uncivilised. The order of sedentary society is expressed not only through unambiguous fixity to place (local community and nation), but through the consumption of goods, the payment of taxes, respect for the law, and avoidance of dirt. Travellers' failure to be fixed makes them dis-ordering, and their marginal location in space reinforces the symbolic ideas of them being dirty. Moreover, they are also seen as obstinately unproductive and non-compliant: their very trade of scrap-metal dealing feeds off sedentary society's residue. So even though Travellers now perform profitable (and now mainstream) recycling functions, the scrap around their encampments is interpreted as mess inside settled space.

Just as in the case of immigrants and asylum seekers, power is expressed through notions of purity and boundary maintenance, and implemented through the forces of order, legal tools and sometimes violence. As usual, not all those racialised as white enjoy the same level of access to planning regulation discourse and means of protecting the countryside, but even the white working-class subjects and ethnic minority individuals settled in rural areas are part of the sedentary 'community' that can be mobilised against encroachment.

JEWS AND TRAVELLERS: WANDERING STRANGERS IN MODERNITY?

In previous chapters we have explored some of the discourse about whiteness as it is used to demarcate the powerful from the powerless along the basis of colour, class and nationality. The examples of anti-semitism and anti-nomadism remind us that fixation with difference is an enduring element of the cultural repertoire of Western civilisation that predates colonialism. A superficial 'racial' reading, perhaps of far-right websites and manifestos, and New Right material (McDonald 2004),[69] could leave us with the idea that Jews are fully in control of the dominant elites of the West. Why else obsess about them owning everything and manipulating state policy in Europe and North America for their own ends? There is no equivalent to the *Protocols of the Elders of Zion*, nor Traveller conspiracy theory, in far-right mythology, perhaps recognition of the absence of power held by nomadic communities vis-à-vis the economic success of European and North American Jews. However, if we are interested in what it is specifically that makes Jews and Travellers marginal Whites, then there are some common elements to identify. The idea is not to suggest that experiences are parallel, but to indicate that there are parallels in the way whiteness is constructed to exclude them. It is not an accident that these two groups suffered most from the Nazis' extermination policies, justified as an act of cauterisation of a series of degenerate strands of Western civilisation.

The first is the trope of mobility in sedentary civilisation. Allegiance to place through physical location is a key idea in the construction of community. Gypsy-Travellers therefore cannot earn this type of allegiance. They move all the time, not just within the borders of the nation, but frequently across them. Like the Jewish people they are a diasporic group. Whilst not proper local citizens they cannot be bona fide national citizens either. Similarly, however much Jews might see themselves as British or French or Irish first, they are always open to the accusation of having supranational loyalties, to other Jews and/or Israel. In the world of nation-states there is little room for the really ambiguous play of loyalties identified as constitutive of the field of transnationalism. Bauman's (1998) theory that modernity cannot cope with ambivalence between categories is nowhere better borne out than in the continual misclassification of bodies viewed as out-of-place in the nation. Such bodies are a threat to the nation-state that demands unequivocal loyalty.[70] Not only is this encapsulated in ideas of Jews being unpatriotic, but in the twin twentieth-century imaginings of international labour and international capital. At various times in the last century the figure of the Jew was the representation of both of these: as the international banker and financier, and as the Bolshevik.

The theme of impurity attaches to both Traveller and Jew, who are constructed as poor, dirty and harbingers of disease. Travellers and poor Jews generate filth and live in it: this is what can be gleaned from representations of them above. Yet the most unbearable and infuriating aspect of the non-whiteness of Travellers and Jews is that they can 'pass'. Social ascendance and the dropping of names and religious practices can render a Jew unidentifiable as such. Individual Travellers outside their settings are not identifiable as such, particularly at the wheel of an expensive car, for example. The idea of mobility is not merely applicable to geographical movement through space, but of transgression into social space. Jews and Travellers are also shapeshifters, not playing by the rules. One of the rules is that the dirt of one's culture should be apparent: when it is absent a challenge to the dominant culture is advanced. If the difference between white and not-quite-white is down to dirt and disorder, and the representative of the latter is clean and ordered, then what else is left as an indelible distinguishing mark?

So finally, the combination of exclusionary practices and the drive for autonomy makes the separateness of both groups a social reality. The word 'ghetto' was coined to describe segregated organisation of urban land in which Jewish settlement was confined. Travellers' residence in marginal spaces similarly reflects power relations that dictate where particular bodies are in and out of place. Choosing to remain at arm's length from the source of power that racialises and criminalises your community is one act of resistance, but when this strategy is followed largely on the terms of the dominant culture, the spatial marginalisation of bodies becomes a self-fulfilling prophecy.

7 How the Irish became White (again)[71]

One of the key texts in the American literature on whiteness is Noel Ignatiev's (1996) study of Philadelphia, *How the Irish Became White*. It was noted in chapter 4 that one of the main criticisms of historians' construction of whiteness as a research problematic is that the process of becoming white is not proven. The European immigrant groups covered by these studies were already white. The argument in this chapter is that not only did Catholic Irish immigrants *become* white in nineteenth-century America, but that the Irish in twentieth-century Ireland also became white. To recap, it was argued in chapter 5 that the Irish in the sixteenth- and seventeenth-century Caribbean experienced a shift in their racialised status. As the major dividing lines became those separating enslaved workers from free labourers and landholders, the people in the former group were all African, and those in the two latter were virtually all European. In this context the relationship between black and unfree, and white and free, emerged as defining the social hierarchy of plantation societies. After negotiating an intermediate status as colonised, Catholic indenturers, the Irish were absorbed more readily into the dominant group. The distinction between on one hand, not being white, and on the other, being black, is central to this argument, and in the US context, particularly, we will focus on the Irish transition from the position of disadvantaged ethnic minority, to a place in mainstream American society. The last section looks at the ways in which the shift from country of emigration to a country of immigration has positioned the Irish as a dominant white group vis-à-vis minorities within Ireland, with particular reference to recent state intervention in the area of citizenship and entitlement.

IRISH INTO WHITE AMERICANS

Why and how the experience of nineteenth-century America turned Catholic Irish emigrants, from before the Famine, into White Americans, and what ramifications the process has for contemporary society, have been the subjects of increasing attention since the early 1990s, particularly among American labour historians. When few Irish immigrants in America signed up to a petition against slavery in the 1840s, Irish nationalist leader Daniel O'Connell lamented that his countrymen in the USA had eschewed the international solidarity with victims of oppression and joined what he labelled 'the filthy aristocracy of skin'.[72] O'Connell had not grasped the central social reality of American life. For Catholic Irish immigrants, becoming American meant becoming white: and proximity to African-Americans, whether spatial, cultural or political, was inimical to such a process.

The Catholic Irish in the nineteenth-century American racial hierarchy

Catholic Irish immigrants disembarked into a social structure that differed vastly from the one they had left behind. In 1790, the American constitution had opened citizenship to 'white men', while black people were defined as 'imports'. By the time of the 1870 legislative debates on citizenship, it had become defined as the right of 'civilised whites'. Jacobson's study of those debates (1998: 73–85) led him to conclude that 'whiteness' referred to four overlapping factors: colour, degree of freedom, level of civilisation, and devotion to Christianity. Ideas of culture and 'race' were thus inextricably linked: US society was constructed on a racial hierarchy, with different rungs allocated to the various groups. At the top of this hierarchy were upper-class Protestants of Northern European extraction. While from the vantage point of the twenty-first century, the differences between this elite and Irish emigrants, who were generally from agricultural backgrounds, were primarily to do with social class, educated nineteenth-century Americans would have viewed the immigrants through a specific prism.

The nineteenth century witnessed an extraordinary set of developments in the ways in which 'race' was understood and used as a determining point of social difference. Scientific racism, developing through pseudo-sciences like phrenology and craniology (Gould 1997), had, in the first few decades, attempted to reinforce the more general claims of the Enlightenment thinkers (Eze 1997) about the links between climate, appearance and collective intellectual capacity. A transatlantic network of writers and scientists sharing the belief that people's measurable physical characteristics determined their ability to reason, and achieve civilisation, grew up around the 1820s (Horsman 1981, Fryer 1984). Europeans and Americans engaged in the enterprise of racialising humanity referred to each other's work, and gradually gained dominance over the monogensists (who explained the human race as being descended from Adam and Eve) so that by the 1850s, asserts Horsman (1981: 135): 'the inherent inequality of races was simply accepted as a scientific fact in America'.

In this context, the Catholic Irish were perceived as uncivilised and degenerate because within the proliferating racial hierarchies, Celts had been posited as a less-developed white 'race', particularly relative to the Anglo-Saxon. This did not necessarily mean that they were black. Indeed they enjoyed the opportunity to become citizens, move without restrictions, and exercise rights unhindered. Yet they were not considered white, if that meant able for the responsibilities encumbent upon members of the American democracy. The point of difference between Irish and Americans on which pro-Protestant American nativist discourse concentrated was religion. The putative backwardness of Catholics, manifested in tribalism and dogma, was diagnosed as symptoms of popery. This meant questions raised about their loyalty to a Protestant state, industriousness and readiness for democracy. Irish Catholics, as we have seen, had been viewed as bearers of a non-modern culture and were thus a threat to the republic, with their alleged propensity for idleness, political corruptibility and external allegiances. Moreover, in terms of fitness for democracy, the Catholics' fealty to Rome was constructed as inculcating a slavish, childish and, above all, pre-modern mentality unsuited to the rigours of one-man-one-vote democracy. American racial scientist Samuel Morton claimed that the Celts' 'physical traits', 'moral character' and 'peculiar customs' had 'undergone little change since the time of Caesar', before going on to cite the natives of the South West of Ireland, whose 'wild look and manner, mud cabins and funereal howlings recall the memory of a barbarous age' (Morton 1839: 16). Indeed, the incompatibility of the Irish with modernity became a cliché in American commentary. After the Fenian raid in Canada, in 1866, for example, *Atlantic Monthly* stated: 'All the qualities which go to make a republican, in the true sense of the word, are wanting in the Irish nature'.

New York, anti-abolitionism and the Irish

Why did the Irish side overwhelmingly with the anti-abolitionists and vote Democrat (the pro-slavery party)? The exceptional conditions of

New York City help to explain the Irish immigrants' adherence to a cause that put clear blue water between them and the slaves. Irish emigration to the USA peaked in 1851.[73] The principally Catholic Famine Irish remained overwhelmingly in the urban setting. In the period 1 May 1847 to 31 December 1860, the Irish comprised 41.4 per cent of immigrants disembarking in New York (i.e. over 1 million), while the Irish-born made up 53.1 per cent of the city's population at the 1860 Census (Miller 1969). Indeed, the increased level of immigration, and its focus especially on New York City, is of significance in the story.

The exceptional role of New York City is derived from its close commercial integration into the Southern states' economies, and therefore, indirectly, into the slave mode of production. This meant that its business community had the most to lose should slavery be abolished. So then did those employed in its factories. Most of the Irish in work were unskilled workers, the category most vulnerable to even minor economic deterioration. Yet why did a class-based vulnerability express itself as a racialised struggle? Within the logic of anti-abolitionism and Democratic populism from the 1830s onwards, the plight of the white worker in the North and of the slave in the South had been bound by a particular message: the end of slavery for Blacks would lead to wage slavery for Whites, who would then be forced to compete for low-paid work with an influx of freed slaves. Elements of the Democratic Party and local New York newspapers such as the *New York Weekly Caucasian*, the *New York Day Book*, the *Freeman's Journal*, the *Herald* and the *Metropolitan Record* habitually linked these two ideas (Miller 1969). This reasoning was the basis of the idea that the abolitionists had fomented the war, which took root prior to the 1863 Draft Riots. As a consequence, Irish workers were, in this version of events, being recruited to fight for 'negro emancipation', which appeared to them to be counter-productive.

The majority of work done on the interface between Irish and African-Americans in the nineteenth century has been accomplished by labour historians. Some of the forms of hostility between these two groups are described by Roediger (1991), Allen (1994a, b), Ignatiev (1996), Barrett and Roediger (1997, 2004) and Jacobson (1995, 1998) and included labour organisation aimed at removing rival black workforces from specific locations and thus competition, political organisation such as Tammany Hall, cultural organisation such as the 1910–1916 Irish Race Conventions, violent protests like the 1863 Draft Riots (Bernstein 1990: 27–31); smaller-scale attacks on black homes, places of worship, and public places in which Blacks and Whites spent time together (Ignatiev 1996: 125–127, 134–139, 151–153); participation in white supremacist projects such as lynching, anti-Chinese immigration activity (in the Order of Caucasians) (Saxton 1990, Almaguer 1994); and involvement in the army's campaigns of removing and persecuting Native Americans.

Socialisation through the workforce was a crucible of Americanisation in the nineteenth century, and for 'immigrant workers, the processes of becoming white and "becoming American" were intertwined at every turn' (Barrett and Roediger 1997: 6). The economic relations between immigrant and indigenous groups became a key focus of Democratic Party propaganda under the leadership of Buchanan and Douglas. Moreover, the Democrats' willingness to enlist immigrants into 'white' America through local patronage networks saw appeals couched in terms of the 'workingman' slide into those for the 'white workingman' as the century progressed. From the conclusions of Fox (1917), Schlesinger (1988[1945]) and Bridges (1984) we might go as far as to say that the Democrats 'created' a white vote over the middle decades of the nineteenth century.

Certainly attempts to scare workers away from sympathising with slaves involved explicit calls for racial solidarity. Allen identifies the proactive role of the Democrats as one of two strategies (the other being the Catholic Church's official 'neutrality' on slavery, and anti-war position) that pushed Irish immigrants to oppose abolition. It was argued that freeing the slave population would create a massive pool of cheap labour, which would then lower wages in the Northern cities where immigrants were already pitted against each other. Indeed, the success of this strategy is that it managed to frame the debate on competition in such a way as to cast the free Blacks as the threatening rivals, whereas it was the Irish who actually usurped them. Moreover, Allen (1994a: 192–198) shows that other white immigrant groups provided by far the stiffer opposition in terms of jobs held in those occupations where the Irish were dominant by 1855, while Ignatiev (1996) sums this situation up: it was not competition but its absence (i.e. the protection of jobs from Blacks) that generated conflict.

Indeed, the free Blacks they encountered in New York and other urban areas had been improving their social standing in the 1810–1830s, accessing unskilled and semi-skilled occupations in addition to the domestic service into which, as an extension of the practices of slavery, they were accepted. Albon Man summarises the position:

> Before the spurt in immigration in the decades of the forties and fifties, such occupations in New York as those of longshoremen, hod-carriers, brickmakers, whitewashers, coachmen, stablemen, porters, bootblacks, barbers, and waiters in hotels and restaurants

had been almost wholly in the hands of colored men. Domestic maids, cooks, scullions, laundresses and seamstresses were generally colored women. They were secure in these types of employment and earned relatively good wages. But with the huge influx of white foreigners, particularly after the Irish famine of 1846, their position changed radically.

(Man 1951: 376)

Lessons learned from the Democrats' ideological labours manifested themselves in the internalisation of the American value of ethnic classification. Irish-dominated unions (such as the longshoremen) both legitimised the expulsion of black workers, and then sought to protect Irish jobs by attempting to ban Germans from the dock under the pretext of safeguarding 'white men's work' (Ignatiev 1996). Similar tactics were deployed on the west coast later in the century in the campaign against Chinese labour and employers of Chinese immigrants, led by the Order of Caucasians. It is hard to imagine a more forceful expression of assimilation of values. Indeed, Barrett and Roediger (1997: 31) detect a strategic movement from the terrain on which the Irish were most exposed to one in which power relations could be invoked in their favour: 'Changing the political subject from Americanness and religion to race whenever possible, they challenged anti-Celtic Anglo-Saxonism by becoming leaders in the cause of white supremacy'.

The fight for whiteness and the meaning of slavery

The geographical concentration of Catholic emigrants, particularly, but not exclusively, in urban areas of the Eastern seaboard, had brought them into close contact with another racialised group: free African-Americans. The ideological positioning of the two groups who shared a similar social place (concentration in the lower echelons of the workforce) was dialectical. Black Americans were abolitionists, mainly Protestant, voted for the Federal and Republican parties, and maybe even the nativist (and rabidly anti-Catholic) Know-Nothings. Moreover, they were fans of Britain, which had abolished the slave trade in 1807 and slavery in 1838. The urban Irish were Catholic, anti-abolition, supported the Democratic Party and regarded Britain as the overriding source of Irish suffering (Miller 1969). Even without the addition of difficult access to resources there was enough to indicate that some level of antipathy would develop between the groups.

In the eyes of WASP America, however, Blacks and Irish immigrants were perceived in racist discourse as being comparable, if not inter-changeable, as late as the 1870s. The simianisation of Irish and Black characters in later nineteenth-century pictorial representations created equivalence in their position at the foot of the racial chain, while their juxtaposition in publications such as *Harper's Weekly* (the self-styled 'journal of civilisation') indicated the limits of fitness for citizenship. Frequently their attitudes would be compared in terms of civilised behaviour and aptitude for citizenship. The following is an extract from a book review published in *Atlantic Monthly* in 1864:

> The emancipated Negro is at least as industrious and thrifty as the Celt, takes more pride in self-support, is far more eager for educa-tion, and has fewer vices. It is impossible to name any standard of requisites for the full rights of citizenship which will give the vote to the Celt and exclude the Negro.

Indeed, in John Appel's study of images of the Irish in *Puck* magazine (1971: 368–369) he points out that out of a number of stereotypes held by White Americans about their Black compatriots in the 1930s, eighteen are also evidenced in *Puck's* treatment of the Catholic Irish in the late nineteenth century.[74] It is in this context then that the Irish drive for whiteness must be interpreted: the attainment of whiteness meant above all the banishment of blackness. Whiteness safeguarded access to the labour market, the vote and a degree of social prestige con-stituted from its antithesis: a constant unflattering comparison with occupationally and residentially-segregated Blacks.

The theme of slavery provides an interesting focus for the complexities of the Irish–Black relationship. Irish nationalists, particularly in the era of O'Connell, developed the use of the term to refer to Britain's con-trol of Ireland. In America, where slavery had acquired a specific insti-tutional form, the two interpretations co-existed, creating a barrier to solidarity. On one hand, the Irish claimed to be enslaved, both nation-ally, and as a class of wage slaves in the American economy, a line pushed hard by anti-abolitionists. There was even an argument that white workers were worse off than the slaves, who were fed and kept by their masters, while the former were left to their own devices. Frederick Douglass (an admirer of the Irish in Ireland (Sweeney 2001, Rolston 2003)) took issue with this understanding of slavery:

> there is no analogy between the two cases. The Irishman may be poor, but he is not a slave. He may be in rags but he is not a slave [. . .] The Irishman has not only the liberty to emigrate from his

country, but he has liberty at home. He can write, and speak, and co-operate for the attainment of his rights and the redress of his wrongs.

(Foner 1999: 169–170)

Moreover, he often raised the matter in public speaking engagements, stating that he had recently vacated a position of slave that was now available, but to his knowledge there had been no applications from Irishmen to fill it.

Too much overlap between Irish and Black, both in the occupational and residential spheres, therefore militated against social advance for the former, certainly in America. This is put forward as an explanation of attacks on Blacks living in mixed areas or even neighbourhoods next to Irish ones in urban America (Ignatiev 1996: 136–137) while the theme of informal policing of racialised borders is further explored by Barrett and Roediger (2004). They observe that broader gate-keeping duties performed by the Irish were a formative experience for other white and 'off-white' European groups, whose earliest experience of urban America later in the nineteenth century and the first decades of the twentieth (Barrett and Roediger 2005) was of Irish-dominated neighbourhoods and institutions, that is, those in which control of police, political appointments, and some other areas of employment lay in Irish and usually Democratic Party hands. In other words, the new arrivals learnt the codes of racial conduct from their Irish-descended peers. The removal of Blacks from areas of proximity to the Irish thus parallels the usurpation of the former from specific economic niches within the urban setting. It also established ground rules for incoming apprentice Caucasians. Indeed, transforming 'nigger work' (that performed exclusively or usually by black Americans) into 'whiteman's work' (i.e. that from which black Americans were excluded) was a project successfully accomplished by urban-based Irish immigrants over the 1830–1865 period (Roediger 1991, Ignatiev 1996). The 20 per cent drop in the black population of New York City in the 1860–1865 period testifies to the unfavourable climate both residentially and occupationally, generated by events of the time (Man 1951: 375–405).

From Irish-American to White American

Coming from a position in which they and their culture were vilified under colonial rule, the Catholic Irish emigrants found a similar reception on arrival in the USA. Yet there were three important differences. First, the combination of the Democratic Party machinery in urban America and the strength of the Catholic Church gave them membership of two powerful networks, on the basis of which they could consolidate and then advance their social position. Second, by the nineteenth century, the distinction between 'free' and 'unfree' labour had endorsed the natural order of 'white' and 'black' worker. This both provided a glimpse of the abyss from which Irish labourers had escaped, and permitted the threat of its dissolution to assume an apocalyptic nature. The relationship of ideas about working-class freedoms vis-à-vis those of slaves was a key factor in framing and motivating the frequent outbursts of violence against free Blacks in urban America in the mid nineteenth century. Third, there were already uncivilised 'Others' in the American ideological landscape against whom they could aim to whiten themselves. The ongoing construction of Black and Native Americans as constituting savagery (Morrison 1993) was part of the process by which European Americans made themselves 'white'. Whiteness was about civilisation, taming nature, governance, religion and the exercise of power. So the overlap of these three factors from the middle of the nineteenth century created an impetus for Irish immigrants to distance themselves from black Americans in the urban areas where the groups encountered each other.

However, it would be an oversimplification to assert that the Irish merely became white through social pressures to conform. Groups within Irish America defined themselves as an 'Irish race', as Celts and as white Americans, simultaneously. The role of Irish America in developing the notion of the Irish race lay in the provision of solidarity with Irish nationalism and the creation of an interest group to further Irish causes in the States. The emphasis on an 'Irish race' tied the diaspora community to the homeland in a relationship that to a degree eliminated time and space, and made the Irish equivalent on the world stage to any other group that had not been colonised. The cultural content of the 'race' had, in America, been evacuated of its Protestant component, with the latter's collective identification as Scotch-Irish (Miller 1985). The Catholic Irish identification process is reflected in the cultural organisations, nationalist activities and newspapers produced. In the post-Civil War period, organisations such as the Fenian Brotherhood, the Ladies Land League, the Ancient Order of Hibernians, Clann na Gael, the Irish National League, and Gaelic Societies were set up, while the community's press was dominated by the *Irish World*, and the *Catholic Citizen*. There was also the Irish-language *An Gaodhal*, which was published in the 1881–1898 period (Jacobson 1995).

It was with this sense of destiny, then, that Catholic Irish America invented itself as a diasporic community bound by bloodlines to its homeland and united against its enemies, be they absentee English land-lords in Ireland or Know Nothings in the USA. The 'Irish race' in this form developed in a society undergoing industrialisation, and whose racialisation processes were derived from a different social base to those of Ireland: a neo-colonial country of mass immigration, with indigenous people and an enslaved population of African origin.

The project of racialising the Irish therefore involved virtually dialectic confrontation between those seeking to place either a generally positive or a generally negative interpretation on Irishness. In other words, the fight was for inclusion in, or exclusion from, the entitlement to be American and enjoy the fruit of that social location. The integration of Irish Americans into the mainstream of white America that would become the Caucasian 'race' in the twentieth century was thus far from complete at this time. Yet they had crossed a social rubicon. The eugenicist-inspired 1924 Immigration Act imposed no quotas on immigration from Ireland, a sign that it was no longer considered a contaminating source of manpower. This incomplete incorporation into hyphenless America entailed ambivalence over its imperial projects, particularly since they constantly recalled Britain's own role in Ireland, yet integration into the ideology of racialised difference had been accomplished long before. Not only had Irish-Americans learned what was at stake in being white, but now saw international conflicts through this same hall of mirrors.[75] The ideological struggle in which they were engaged did not involve throwing the rule book out of the window, but honing skills and playing better than those from whom they had learned the rules in the first place: this meant accepting that there was 'civilisation' and 'barbary', staking out their claim to a position within the former category, and then seeking to reach the upper echelons of it.

Conclusion

The Irish in nineteenth-century America could therefore be seen simultaneously as carriers of an inferior, less-civilised culture, and compared unfavourably to Black Americans in terms of their readiness for full membership of the republic, whilst forming the core of an army whose principal mission was to dispossess those deemed to have cultures inferior to that of White America, and be in the vanguard of a movement to drive Chinese workers out of California to preserve the labour market for the 'white man'.

In the context of the New World, new classificatory dichotomies (free–unfree, white–black) cross-cut and reinforced older categories (civilised and barbaric), thus forming unique configurations of power relationships founded on 'race'. The Irish grasped that they were capable of attaining whiteness but would have to argue their case, and that revolved around distancing themselves from Others, especially Black Americans. Passage through this transitional zone, between blackness and whiteness, was successfully negotiated over the 1830–1890 period.

Yet Irish immigrants started off as 'not white' (in terms of culture and religion) and ended the century as white (i.e. part of the dominant majority). The argument that they were basically a 'white' race as good as any other, and therefore better than non-white ones, was key to their success. Indeed, the American setting and the transatlantic network of migration could be argued to comprise part of a collective imaginary, an Irish 'American dream'. However, the glossed-over element of this history is that black and Native Americans, not to mention Asians, lost out to the Irish in this battle for privilege, whose consequences profoundly shaped the life chances and work opportunities available in America to the present day (Luibhéid 1997, Corcoran 1997, Lloyd 1999: 105–106).

WHITENESS IN THE REPUBLIC OF IRELAND

Just as Anglo-Saxon Protestantism, a specific set of racial ideologies and a moment in the development of capitalism, framed the process of group identification described above, then we can identify similar factors contouring the changes occurring in the Republic of Ireland since the mid 1990s. I suggested at the outset that whiteness spoke of power in local accents. The local accent, or habitus, to use Bourdieu's term, here is that of a Catholic-secular state,[76] which has existed only since 1921, and was itself previously a colony. At the same time, Ireland benefited from empire by proxy through trade and prestige, while a large number of Irish people held power of differing forms in empire: as soldiers, administrators and priests. Ideas and practices derived from colonial rule thus circulated in this community, as they did between the USA and Ireland (Jacobson 1995). The Irish case underscores the need to look beyond national boundaries, at flows of people and ideas, in order to understand the way whiteness functions.

In the period leading up to Independence, the Irish nation-in-waiting had developed particular Others: Jews, Travellers, the British coloniser, and was a country of large-scale emigration. Whatever the similarities between the exercise of power through whiteness there and in the USA or the UK, there are also clearly differences. One of these is the response to increasing diversity.

The idea that Ireland was somehow devoid of racism until black people arrived in significant numbers in the mid 1990s was popular,[77] but has now been successfully challenged by scholarship from the last few years. However, what is not disputed is that the transition from a country of net emigration to one of net immigration (since 1996) has had a serious impact on Irish identity (Lentin 2001, Garner 2003). Apart from challenging the Irish to rethink themselves as citizens of one of the richest countries in the world, the diversity of the country's population is now a source of reflection. In 2002, for example, work permits were issued to nationals of 130 countries (Garner 2003: 58). The response to these changes has meant the identification of new ethnicities, a rise in racism, and debate on the relationship of this new phase of Irish history to the past.

In 1996, Ireland became a net importer of labour, thus catching up with European former labour-providers like Italy, Portugal and Spain, as countries of immigration. Ever since then, the numbers of migrants to Ireland have been rising. However, the gross figures conceal three important trends. First, until 2001, the majority of migrants were 'returning emigrants' (i.e. Irish people who had been living abroad). Second, the numbers of labour migrants exceeded the number of asylum seekers in every year except 1999, and third, that the majority of labour migrants were white Europeans, either from EU member-states including the UK, or from Accession States and non-EU Eastern Europe. Overall, then, the type of migrant most represented in this wave was white. Here is the first clue to what whiteness might mean in a country with few minorities: the disproportionate emphasis on visible markers of difference. In the polling work carried out between 1996 and 2003, it became clear that one pattern observed was for Irish people to express increasing concern about the problem of immigration and asylum.[78] There is nothing country-specific about this. However, the concerns voiced indicated that particular groups were more worrying than others: black people, Roma and Muslims. The discourse on immigration has focused primarily on the minority of those migrants. Moreover, the conflation of labour migrants and asylum seekers, together with the emphasis placed on illegality in the discourse, meant that black Irish people were also singled out for abuse. The context for this enactment of whiteness is an economic boom that attracted people to the country, ever-deepening integration of the Republic of Ireland into the European Union and its own border-defending agenda.

By the beginning of the twenty-first century, racist abuse had become endemic in Ireland and its victims could be anyone who is not white, regardless of their nationality or immigration status. At the beginning of the second phase of policy making, after a new Minister for Justice, Equality and Law Reform took office, a referendum on citizenship was held in June 2004. The details of this are covered elsewhere (Lentin 2006, 2004, Luibhéid 2004, Garner 2007b, c) and analysed in the following chapter. The most important point was that a constitutional amendment was made as a result. The phases of racialisation leading up to such significant state-directed border-closing are described in the following section.

'Irish-born children'

After the 2002 election, a new Minster, Michael Mc Dowell, was appointed at the Department of Justice, Equality and Law Reform. The former Minister, John O'Donoghue (1997–2002), had not explicitly connected Irish citizenship and immigration, although he had been less than positive about immigration, stating in 1999 that Ireland was becoming a 'target' for immigrants (Loyal 2003: 75). His handling of immigration and asylum had been roundly criticised, and not just by NGOs (*Public Affairs News* 2000). Cabinet colleague Liz O'Donnell, Minister for Overseas Development, also labelled the policy 'administrative shambles' in a speech in November 1999 (McKenna 1999). The importance of the incoming Minister's agenda turned out to be crucial. The situation he inherited can be briefly summarised. The citizenship laws accorded Irish nationality to all children born in Ireland, including those born in Northern Ireland, immigrants and asylum seekers. The only *parents* to whom this was valuable were nationals of non-EU member-states, since it extended residence to parents of 'Irish-born children'.

The Department of Justice acronym 'IBC' became significant from the late 1990s, as people awaiting asylum decisions (in the late 1990s this wait lasted up to two and a half years) had children, and were advised, either by immigration lawyers or Department officials, to apply for residence through an 'IBC'. The administrative normalisation of this term indicates the way in which clearly racialised distinctions enter into Irish mainstream politics. Separating Irish children into two groups for administrative purposes, the 'IBC' classification made the most salient point about one group of Irish children the fact that their *parents* were not Irish nationals, hence implicitly emphasising the prioritisation of bloodlines over residency, a distinction not made in the Irish Constitution, but one that was the objective of Minister Mc Dowell. Because of the 1989 'Fajujonu' case law ruling (see below), it was a Ministerial privilege to grant residence to foreign parents of this category of Irish children. By the end of 2002, residence had been extended to between

7,000 and 10,000 people, with a further 10,000 pending (Haughey 2003).

It is at this point that the new Minister for Justice's agenda becomes apparent: his statement of intent having been given on assuming office, when he argued:

> Eighty per cent of foreigners in Ireland have nothing to do with asylum. We have to approach it on a rational basis. We have an immigration policy which is fair and free from wrongful discrimination against any particular group ... The asylum-seeking process costs about €200 million ($265m) annually and between 80 and 90 per cent are found not to be eligible, by a system the UN upholds.
>
> (Coulter 2002)

In this statement, Mc Dowell's linking of the various immigration statuses and construction of the problem as one of fairness, administration and good housekeeping, is key to the presentation of the subsequent referendum on citizenship as a neutral, rational non-racist process. This depiction of rationality seeks to conceal the more populist appeal of the Minister's objective, which was to make it more difficult for particular, racialised groups of people to stay in Ireland and access resources.

The change from the reactive, ad hoc approach favoured by Minister O'Donoghue to a stridently proactive clampdown was heralded by 'Operation Hyphen' in July 2002, which involved *gardai* (police) and immigration officers raiding a number of addresses in order to remove visa and asylum-process over-stayers. This cost over €100,000 ($132,000) and was criticised within and outside the Dáil (parliament) as a waste of money (Fekete 2002). The operation constituted a message to the electorate that the new Minister was determined to expel those with no right to be in Ireland. His subsequent policy manoeuvre: a challenge to the 'Fajujonu' ruling in the Supreme Court in 2003, was an attempt to close off one important avenue of settlement in the Republic of Ireland by non-EU nationals.

The challenge to Fajujonu

Under Citizenship Acts in 1956, 1986, and 2001 children born in Ireland acquired Irish nationality through *ius soli*. The status of non-national parents of Irish children was dealt with on the basis of a case law precedent set in December 1989. The Supreme Court judges' 'Fajujonu' Ruling had established a precedent for non-nationals to obtain the right of residence through having Irish children (i.e. children born in Ireland)

(*Annual Review of Population Law* 1989). The judges had agreed that Irish children were entitled to the 'company and protection' of their family (as stated in Articles 41 and 42 of the 1937 Constitution). Thus, the justification for Mr Fajujonu (who had overstayed his visa) and his wife to remain in Ireland derived from the specificity of the Constitution, steeped in the non-secular values of the Catholic Church. The absence of large-scale immigration into Ireland at that time appears, with hindsight, to have allowed the luxury of compassion.

By 2003, things had changed: Ireland was a country of immigration, and Mc Dowell was Minister for Justice and no longer a barrister defending people such as Fajujonu. In January, three asylum seekers (a Czech man and a Nigerian couple), who had Irish children, challenged their deportation on the grounds of 'Fajujonu'. By a 5–2 decision, the Supreme Court ruled in favour of the Minister: the Fajujonu precedent had thus been nullified. Among the reasons provided to support the ruling were political context: the 1989 decision had been made against a background of net emigration and tiny numbers of asylum seekers. The two dissenting judges, however, argued that the 2003 ruling addressed the rights of the *parents*, whereas Fajujonu, correctly, had been focused on those of the *child*. The rights of the parents should only be secondary (Lobe *v.* Minister for Justice, Equality and Law Reform 2003). The outcome was that from January 2003, asylum seekers' and other Third Country Nationals' access to residence rights through the so-called 'IBC route' was no longer automatic. De facto, not all 'Irish children' had the same rights: access to citizenship was henceforth contingent on the parents' nationality. Applications for residence through 'IBC's would now have to be dealt with on a case-by-case basis. The referendum that ultimately resolved this state of affairs, redrawing Ireland's citizenship laws in order to exclude these parents even from a case-by-case discussion, is covered in the following chapter.

Conclusion

The Irish had become white in the Caribbean (chapter 5), the USA (this chapter) and Australasia by the twentieth century,[79] but the question of whiteness had been posed differently in Ireland itself. The thrust of its nationalist narrative involved siding ideologically with the colonised, although this was a minority sport, with the main ideological labour being expended on carving out a niche for the Irish within the 'white race' (Garner 2003, Mac Einri 2006). Moreover, Irish nationalism has struggled to find a place for Travellers and Jews in particular, and, to some extent, Protestants. When the Republic became a country attracting migrant workers and asylum seekers from outside the EU, the racialisation process began to work differently. Among the responses ranging from solidarity to hostility by individuals and NGOs were institutional interventions from the state and the media. The latter played the role of agenda-setting, disinformation on, and distortion of, the actual benefits, entitlements and living conditions of migrants to Ireland, as well as reflecting the government's construction of the issue as an administrative and financial burden rather than an international reciprocal obligation. In the 1997–2002 period the state's interventions included racialising entry checks and the establishment of an asylum regime which imposed particular restrictions. After Minister Mc Dowell's accession to the Department of Justice, this agenda became more stringent in its orientation towards defending the nation. One of the strategies involved redrawing the rules of access to entitlements such as residence and citizenship. The first part of this was accomplished in January 2003 by overturning the practice of granting automatic residence rights to foreign national parents of Irish children. This meant that the possibility of Ireland becoming more multicultural through further settlement by people from outside the EU, most of whom are not white Europeans, was greatly reduced. The state's input into the process of racing Irish nationality, in which non-white bodies were being demarcated for verbal and physical violence, was to affirm the otherness and the threat of such bodies to Irish national cohesiveness. After being Catholics, Celts and Gaels, the Irish (in Ireland) had become white . . . again.

8 'Asylumgration': the Others blur

Since the fall of the Berlin Wall, 'asylum' has become an intensely controversial issue on the agendas of European governments and the European Union (EU). It is indisputable that more people have sought asylum in the last twenty years, and numbers have only tailed off since 2002. However, while it is important to establish trends in asylum up to a certain point, what is interesting from the point of view of analysing whiteness are the responses to asylum. I will begin by sketching the broad patterns of asylum in Europe before we go on to two case studies: the Republic of Ireland and the UK, which will analyse state action and demonstrate both the way that asylum seekers have been represented as threats, and how the various types of Other have been conflated into the figure of the asylum seeker.

CURRENT TRENDS IN ASYLUM

A number of factors might account for the increasing numbers of asylum seekers in Europe up until 2003, when overall numbers began to decline. These include the breakdown of communist regimes in the former Eastern bloc and resulting removal of restrictions preventing people moving between Eastern and Western Europe (from 1989 onwards); increasing instability due to wars; and the collapse of civil society institutions (e.g. Iraq, Somalia, Afghanistan, former Yugoslavia, the Russian Federation, Turkish and Iraqi Kurds, the Central African states involved in the Rwandan genocide and its aftermath, Sudan, Colombia, etc.). The UNHCR maintains that particular situations generating refugees are 'protracted', and that there were thirty-eight of these at the end of 2005, accounting for over six million refugees. Many of these began after 1989.[80] While absolute numbers of people 'of concern' to the UNHCR, which includes internally displaced persons (IDP), peaked at around the 20 million mark (by the UNHCR definition), the proportion of refugees (i.e. people who have left their country of origin to seek asylum) now stands at around 8.4 million.[81] The majority are located in the developing world excluding sub-Saharan Africa (47 per cent) and in sub-Saharan Africa (41 per cent). The peak for asylum seekers in Europe came in the 1999–2000 period, when more than 500,000 applied for refugee status. The year 2005 was the fifth consecutive year in which total asylum-seeking numbers had fallen globally, and the almost two million asylum seekers located in Europe (down *c.* 15 per cent on 2004) accounted for 23 per cent of the total (UNHCR 2006: 3).[82] The top two asylum-seeker receiving countries were Pakistan and Iran, which together held more than one-fifth of the total. The highest-ranked European country was Germany (third), followed by Great Britain (seventh). The top ten countries of origin of people seeking asylum in the UK in 2005 (see Table 3) (which accounted for 60 per cent of the overall numbers) provide an indication of the 'push' factors; war or political persecution is ongoing in all of these countries.

All these figures are in the public domain, including those that confirm the decrease in asylum seeking over recent years. However, in the UK (and, to a lesser extent, Ireland) the decade 1995–2005 witnessed an intensifying combined process of demonisation of asylum seekers, the racialisation of asylum, and the simultaneous conflation/collapse of statuses so that labour, migrants, students, asylum seekers and nationals perceived by other nationals as Other could be routinely grouped together and viewed as potentially threatening in a number of ways such

Table 3 Asylum applications to the UK. Top ten sending nations 2005

Country	Applications (per cent)
Iran	3,150 (12)
Somalia	1,760 (7)
Eritrea	1,760 (7)
China	1,730 (7)
Afghanistan	1,580 (6)
Iraq	1,415 (5)
Pakistan	1,145 (4)
DR Congo	1,080 (4)
Zimbabwe	1,075 (4)
Nigeria	1,025 (4)

Source: T. Heath, R. Jeffries and S. Pearce, 2006: *Asylum Statistics United Kingdom 2005: Home Office Statistical Bulletin*, London: Home Office, 10.

as through crime, competition for resources, sex, and disease. The state, the media and citizens have responded to asylum in particular ways at particular times. We shall look at two national examples – England and the Republic of Ireland – to observe how white nationals have developed discursive strategies aimed at categorising and racialising these Others.

THE 'RACIALISATION' OF ASYLUM IN IRELAND

The late 1990s represented an economic and cultural shock for Ireland. Its economy grew at the highest annual rate in the EU, and it became a country of net immigration after centuries of providing labour for other countries' economies. One of the consequences of Ireland's transition to a wealthy country status was an intensification of the racialisation of Irishness (McVeigh 1992, Lentin 2001, Garner 2003). This in itself is an interesting counter-case: the usual explanation of resource-competition-based arguments states that hostility intensifies in economic downturns. One modifier would be that it is rapid social change per se, rather than boom or bust, that exacerbates feelings of insecurity that are expressed as racist. Another point is that writers such as Allen (2000) and Kirby (2002) posit a polarisation of income parallel to a net increase. This might suggest that those feeling themselves left behind in Irish society's material advances would be most likely to experience relative loss of status, one of whose outcomes might be racist tendencies. This is an important starting point to grasp: too often whiteness is discussed in American literature as if it were tending to the universal position. The configuration of white norms in Ireland is around a Catholic-secular base, with a particular historical relationship with Britain and as a colonised country of emigration. The relationship between Travellers and the settled population is increasingly tense. There are also elements of imperial superiority that filtered down through Ireland's ambivalent position within Empire: the benefits accruing directly to some sections of the population, and the privileged power relationships enjoyed by the many Irish administrators, soldiers, priests, etc. What happened in the late 1990s then was that twin relational processes drew tight lines around Irishness, and thus around its Others, during a period of rapid economic growth. The focus for this process of racialisation was asylum, but it was not inevitable that this should be so.

The 'colour line' in contemporary Ireland

It should be understood that racialisation of the Irish resident population along colour lines long predated the mid 1990s (Nic Suibhne 1998,

Paulin 2000, Mullen 2001, Murphy 2001, Lentin and McVeigh 2002) and intensified from that point. One of the outcomes of the transition to a country of immigration was the underscoring of the line in the imaginary between national and non-national based on somatic rather than cultural difference. While anti-semitism, anti-Traveller racism and hostility towards minorities in general in the Republic have far longer histories (Mac Laughlin 1995: 85–86, Fanning 2002), the new forms of discrimination amalgamated black nationals, migrants, asylum seekers, refugees, students and tourists. Indeed, the first person killed in a racist attack, in January 2002, was a Chinese student learning English, Zhao Liutao.

Some Irish people had started to make distinctions between those who 'looked Irish' and those who did not: a distinction that could literally mean life or death. It was not a coincidence that this happened on a personal level, since state officials had begun to do the same thing as early as summer 1997. Fears of illegal immigration had spurred an official policy of assertive border-policing (Cullen 1997). The practice of immigration officials and police at points of entry involved selecting non-white passengers (and staff) for questioning (Cusack 1997, *Irish Times* 17 January 1998). Small-scale research reports from the same period (Pilgrim House 1998, 1999, African Refugee Network 1999) had also identified Blacks (with Roma and Travellers) as the groups most likely to experience verbal and physical abuse.

In October 1998, a Dublin pub was refused its licence after a case taken against it by Teresa Lynch, a black Dubliner who claimed she had been refused service when the pub changed hands earlier that year (*Irish Independent* 1998). This was the first prosecution of a defendant accused of discrimination on the basis of colour to take place in the state. The telling element of the story is Lynch's comment that despite experiencing racism all her life, 'things had got much worse since asylum seekers started arriving in larger numbers over the past few years'. Indeed, by summer 2000, Amnesty International was using a radio advert for its anti-racism campaign in which a black Irishman complains of a significantly negative change in attitude towards him over recent years. Moreover, in that organisation's study of the experiences of minorities (Amnesty International/FAQs 2001) the sub-group of minorities expressing the highest rate of discrimination suffered (88.6 per cent) was 'Black Irish'. There were erroneous arrests of asylum seekers in Dublin under the 1935 Aliens Act, for failure to provide proof of identity to police, and passengers reported black people being taken off the Belfast–Dublin train and obliged to show ID, while their foreign white counterparts were left alone (Smyth 2002). Hysterical responses to non-whites include the temporary jailing of seven Pakistani business-men in 2000 (Parkin 2000), and of a British-based Nigerian woman mak-ing an inquiry in a social welfare office in Cork in January 2003 (Kelleher 2003). These practices indicate that the 1997–1998 policy of victimising 'non-white' individuals has been continued into the twenty-first century in unchanged form.

Indeed, in a small 1998 survey of Irish people (Pilgrim House 1998), 70 per cent of those polled stated that they had formed opinions about asylum seekers 'based on what they saw', implying that without speak-ing to a member of that group (only 2 per cent said that they had spoken to an asylum seeker), they had categorised individuals as 'asylum seekers'. Those individuals might have belonged to any one of a number of categories, including that of Irish nationals. The act of equating colour with legal status is a racist act. It demonstrates that the process of assimi-lating all non-white people in Ireland to the status of asylum seeker, with all the negative connotations the term has accrued, was already well advanced by summer 1998. With such a lead being shown by officialdom, and the intensely hostile coverage of asylum (rather than labour migration) by the media (Guerin 2002, NCCRI/Equality Authority 2003), it cannot surprise us that so many people followed suit. In view of this, outbursts by public officials in more recent times are elements of continuity, representing the point of contact between underlying racist thinking and official discourse rather than isolated blips. Such attitudes were publicly articulated by various elected representatives such as Liam Lawlor (Fianna Fáil), Ivor Callely (Fianna Fáil), and Helen Keogh (Progressive Democrat) in the run-up to the 1997 General Elections and after, with Callely especially referring to 'a culture that is not akin to Irish culture', and 'the bleeding of lambs in back gardens' (Donohue 1997) in the context of an attack on refugees receiving social benefits. During her election campaign in Dublin Keogh labelled asylum seekers 'professional beggars'.[83] In January 2002, Cork North Central TD (parliamentary rep-resentative) Noel O'Flynn (Fianna Fáil) claimed that Cork's Northside area was home to many 'illegal immigrants', a supposition questioning the legal legitimacy of the presence of black people per se. How could their illegal status be determined on sight, if the implicit point was not the blanket supposition that all asylum seekers are bogus and therefore illegal? Local media[84] was supportive of O'Flynn's stance, which went unsanctioned by his party leader, the *Taoiseach* (Prime Minister).

The suddenly increasing presence of both migrant labour and asylum seekers in Ireland has produced technical discourses on visa regimes, yet the conflation of statuses with phenotype referred to above ignores the relative weight of numbers. Since 1996, when Ireland became a country of immigration, the number of people receiving work permits has out-numbered those applying for asylum only in one year, 1999. In the twenty-first century the labour migrants have outnumbered asylum seekers by a factor of at least five to one.[85] Part of this trend can be explained by the composition of each group. The majority of migrants were either returning Irish emigrants or Eastern Europeans. Yet the media have focused on asylum seekers, many of whom are from the various parts of Africa and Asia (although a substantial minority are from the former Soviet Union or Romanian Roma).

However, as we have argued throughout, 'race', and whiteness as an exemplar, are to do with ideas both of culture and physical appearance. There is an accompanying discourse that stresses culture and values as dividing lines between Irish and Others. A letter from an American-based emigrant, published in the *Irish Times* in 1998, encapsulates a viewpoint that posits an opposition between industrious, productive Irish and indolent, unproductive Others:

> we come prepared to work hard and make a go of it. We would not be allowed to claim unemployment benefits or otherwise scrounge off the state [. . .] taxes in Ireland are appallingly high – they will remain so if we keep subsidising the economically challenged from abroad [. . .] I suggest that many of the recent influx of foreigners have come to Ireland, not for the love of the country either, but because the word is out that we are suckers for a sob story.
>
> ('Letters to the Editor', *Irish Times*, 27 May 1998)

The industrious (white) Irish emigrants made a positive contribution to the economy of the host country, while the (non-white) foreigners in Ireland subtract from it and absorb without contributing. In addition to the anachronism embodied in this strand of anti-immigrant response (there was no social security in nineteenth-century America or Britain, nor were there international treaties on refugees), it demonstrates a mis-understanding of legal realities. As in most European countries, asylum seekers are prohibited from taking paid work. Indeed, there is a high degree of ambivalence as well as misunderstanding around the question of asylum seekers' productivity. In the poll carried out by the lay Catholic organisation, Pilgrim House, in July 1998, 81 per cent of those polled stated that they felt that asylum seekers should be allowed to work while they awaited their decision (Pilgrim House 1998). By the time of an *Irish Times*/MRBI poll eighteen months later (*Irish Times*/MRBI 2000), the level of support was almost identical (77 per cent). The striking thing about the latter, much larger, survey is the levels of uniformity, with virtually all the variables being more or less within the statistical margin of error. Higher levels of agreement were expressed by ABC1s (81 per cent) and those with degrees (83 per cent), and slightly lower levels by C2DEs (73 per cent). These results might be interpreted as a desire to see people earn their keep rather than any expression of support for the freedom of movement of labour. Again, we should note that the cultural production of difference (the white Irish are more hardworking than the non-white immigrants) has roots in both the economic (the defence of resources), and the affective (construction of collective self as valuable and productive).

As usual, there are competing versions of whiteness and, in Ireland, this derives from specific Irish historical experience. Asylum seekers here are recognised as the economically- and politically-persecuted Irish of other times. This idea is expressed across the NGOs, political opposition parties, trade unions, interested church bodies and more radical anti-racist organisations. A succinct example of this comes from a speech by Labour Deputy, Liz McManus, in a 1998 parliamentary debate:

> For this global celebration of Irishness [St Patrick's Day], this focus of investment, this tourism opportunity, we have to thank the generations of Irish asylum-seekers who were driven out to seek refuge among strangers. They were often poor, hungry, sick and homeless people. Sometimes they died in flight, sometimes they were political outcasts and convicted criminals [. . .] I refuse to accept that our past has no bearing on this debate. *Our history requires us to be generous and just.* [My emphasis]
>
> (*Dáil Debates*, 10 March 1998)

This however is a minority view. The majority, when offered the opportunity to redefine Irishness more narrowly, by reference to bloodlines in 2004, did so. The government held a referendum on changing the citizenship laws to introduce a qualification period on the access to citizenship enjoyed by the children of foreign nationals. The debate has been well covered in detail and critiqued elsewhere (Luibhéid 2004, Lentin 2006, Garner 2007b, c), and the vital background to the referendum forms part of the previous chapter. To summarise briefly, a 1989 Supreme Court ruling ('Fajujonu') had established a precedent whereby non-national parents of children qualifying for Irish citizenship through birth in the state were granted leave to remain in order to ensure that the child was able to enjoy her/his constitutional right to the company of family. In January 2003, the Minister for Justice, Equality and Law Reform successfully challenged this ruling. Instead of being guaranteed residence rights, such parents would now be obliged to have their applications examined on a case-by-case basis. Between 7,000 and 10,000 people had been granted residence rights like this by January 2003, and a further 10,000 had applications pending at the time of the ruling.

The 2004 Citizenship Referendum: racing Irishness

The Minister was not satisfied with the outstanding ambiguity, and sought to close what he considered a 'loophole' that allowed people to access Irish residence too easily. Such people were de facto, as the only people affected by such options for obtaining residence, asylum seekers and labour migrants from outside the EU. In March 2004, he announced that a referendum would be held on the issue of amending the 2001 Citizenship Act. Mc Dowell proposed the introduction of a 3-year residence qualification for non-Irish national parents, before their *child born in Ireland* could be entitled to citizenship. It is at this point that the racialisation of Irishness becomes starkly apparent. As the right to Irish citizenship was, by 2004, the right of any child born on the island of Ireland, the government's proposed amendment would separate these children into two groups. On one side were those with at least one Irish national parent. On the other were to be those who had no Irish parents, the so-called 'Irish-born children'. This category, accorded the Department of Justice acronym, 'IBC', were no longer to constitute an advantageous foot in the door, but were to have their right to enjoy the benefits of Irish constitutional protection stripped. Yet the right to Irish citizenship for those with at least one grandparent born in Ireland would remain, the whole package thus privileging membership of the nation through bloodlines over membership through birthplace. If the amendment were approved, Ireland's citizenship laws would be adjusted to institutionally discriminate against a portion of its citizens on the basis of ancestry.

The referendum took place on 11 June 2004, when the Minister's amendment received an almost 80 per cent backing of the voters on a 62 per cent turnout. It was later enshrined in the Citizenship Bill 2004 (which came into force on 1 January 2005). The right to Irish nationality is no longer automatic for *some* children born in the Republic. Moreover, the 3-year period does not include time spent as an asylum seeker or student, as the residence period visa must be 'without restriction'.

There were three principal interlocking arguments for amending the constitution to 'protect the integrity' of the Irish immigration system:

1   The concept of *ius soli* was posited as anomalous within the EU. Ireland should therefore comply with existing norms, an administrative reasoning not necessarily consistent with Ireland's relationship with EU directives in other areas (some of which have long been ignored or resisted). This initiative did not even stem from a directive or policy guideline issued by the EU.

2   A strong theme in the discourse of the 'Yes' campaign (in favour of the restrictive amendment) was that in the new conditions of immigration, Ireland's *ius soli* law enabled people without 'social' or 'cultural' links to the country to access membership of the nation. The content of the social and cultural links was not made explicit: the implication being that birth within national territory alone was too tenuous a bond to allow citizenship.

3   The phenomenon of 'citizenship tourism' was identified as a threat to the immigration system. The campaign began with the Minister's statement that 60,000 children had been born to foreign women in Ireland during the previous year. He also claimed to have been approached by the Masters (CEOs) of the Dublin Hospitals to prevent foreign women arriving in the latter stages of pregnancy, absorbing resources and endangering lives.

First, he had collapsed all non-Irish women into one group, and second, the Masters later challenged Mc Dowell's interpretation of their correspondence with him. However, the focus of this element of the argument extended to cover an example of a case which had been with the ECJ Advocate General since February 2004.[86] A UK-resident Chinese woman, Man Levette Chen, had gone to Belfast to have her second child in order to strengthen her case to remain in the UK (as the child would have an EU nationality). Although Chen was not an asylum seeker, never set foot in the Republic or cost Irish taxpayers a penny, her case was brandished as a cautionary tale of 'citizenship tourism'. While no official figures were produced to enumerate the size of the problem, its impact was clearly felt by pregnant non-Irish women in Ireland who suffered physical and verbal abuse in public spaces (Lentin 2003). Thus the predominance of the administrative argument: the need to assume responsibilities in regard to EU neighbours; and the chance to weed out the bogus from the genuine applicants for Irish nationality emerge as the key criteria for constitutional reform of the border separating Irish from non-Irish.

It might be argued that the Irish citizenship laws, even after the referendum, are still relatively liberal. After all, in some countries, the children of non-national parents have to decide at 18 whether to assume

European nationalities. In Ireland, the child still gains citizenship if the parents have been 'legally resident' for three years. Yet if the amendment was so minor, why bother holding a referendum? The topics for other referenda in recent Irish history have been abortion; divorce; the peace process; and adherence to the Treaty of Nice. The potency of the referendum and amendment cannot be understood solely in relation to dry official regulations: they carry a political and cultural charge in their own context.

What I mean by this is that the resulting citizenship law restored primacy (not exclusivity) to the *ius sanguinis* route to Irishness and, in practice, only excludes people from particular parts of the world. The 'one grandparent' avenue to Irish citizenship still applies. This means that someone whose grandparent emigrated, and who may never have set foot in Ireland, is unproblematically granted citizenship, whereas a child whose parents may live, work and pay taxes in Ireland has citizenship withheld. Even if the parent(s) do not work, as is the case with asylum seekers (legally prevented from taking paid work), the same principle applies: the amendment reduces the rights of some Irish children and does not affect others.

Conclusion: 'race', asylum and the state in Ireland

The asylum issue in Ireland has been 'bureaucratised' in the Weberian sense of the term: the humanitarian dimensions of the problem have been minimised by the state in favour of a number of processes appealing to technical and legal instruments, so that it appears that these are the only compelling sources of parameters. Weber argued that bureaucracy could become 'amoral' in that it is set up to perform any rationalised task asked of it in the most efficient form possible, a point that Bauman (1989) applies to the Holocaust. State bureaucracies dealing with asylum tend organisationally towards this 'amoral', technocratic approach. Beyond the ministries dealing with the technical side of these matters, debates have grown up that place emphasis on differing readings of Irish diaspora history, running from empathetic to resistant, seeing the reflection of Irish experience either as deserving of empathy, or unwarranted and distorted.

Moreover, the threats embodied by 'asylum seekers', such as invasion of space, unfair access to resources, spread of disease, sexual morality, were so potently deployed that the majority of voters in the 2004 referendum declared in an exit poll of over 3,000 people conducted by RTE (the state broadcaster), that they had cast their 'Yes' vote (in favour of restrictions) because they felt negative towards immigrants: 36 per cent because the country was being 'exploited by immigrants', and a further 27 per cent because there were 'too many immigrants'. This was not on the technical grounds of the referendum but on a broader, affective basis. In this lies one of the key mechanisms of whiteness, draining individuals of their humanity, and making them invisible except as masses (see chapter 2). Yet this ostensible solidity of thought hides fragility: this form of whiteness is open to amendment primarily because it is so emotional and resistant to facts. The deportation and return of Nigerian schoolboy Olukunle Elukanlo in spring 2005 demonstrated that empathy can be achieved and allied to political action when a person becomes more important than the representation. A campaign to bring back Elukanlo was initiated by his schoolmates, and became national. The Minister of Justice reversed his decision and the boy returned to Ireland in April (Cullen 2005). In a poll taken that weekend, 46 per cent stated they now wished for the referendum decision to be reviewed (Harris 2005).

ASYLUM AND WHITENESS IN THE UK

Britain has debated its migration policies since the mid nineteenth century, when Irish immigration was identified as having a negative impact on employment and morals. However, more recently, the politicisation of immigration has really intensified since the waves of migration after World War II. One of the most striking things about the direction such debates have taken since the early 1990s is that a link has been established at state and popular levels between immigration, asylum and the idea that these phenomena are necessarily problematic. By far the most problematic of these is asylum. Whilst the granting of asylum is frequently depicted as an integral part of Britain's history, reflecting its tolerant character, the record of successive British governments is actually more fraught (Schuster 2002, Stevens 2004). Legislation ties nationality, immigration and asylum (Nationality, Immigration and Asylum Act 2002; Immigration Asylum and Nationality Act 2006), while the statuses of citizen, labour migrant and asylum seeker have become blurred. Moreover, media representation of asylum seekers frequently portrays them as criminals, security threats and a burden on the public purse to an extent that British nationals are not (Buchanan and Grillo 2004).

The relationship between politics and the media in terms of racialisation is a symbiotic one. Law (2002) reports that overall, the British press is a lot less racist than during the 1970s and 1980s, yet asylum has added an autonomous sphere to the political agenda, where 'race' and politics intersect. In the post 7/7 period, the focus has turned to Muslims. Buchanan and Grillo (2004: 41) argue that tabloid newspapers posit an asylum 'crisis' consisting of 'ever increasing numbers of asylum seekers arriving illicitly in the UK, abusing the benefit system, being involved in criminal or terrorist activities' and generally posing a threat to the British 'way of life'. They also point to confusion over the status of asylum seekers and refugees, with the terms 'illegal immigrant', 'asylum seeker', 'refugee' and 'migrant' being 'used as synonyms', as well as the use of stock images of male asylum seekers 'breaking into' the country (ibid.). What is important in the argument is that the norms against which asylum seekers are spuriously evaluated constitute a version of whiteness where it articulates with Britishness. The context is of invasion of the nation and threats to welfare and other resources to which nationals have preferential entitlement. This discourse contains a strand of naturalising difference, and to see this more closely we shall look at some empirical work on attitudes to asylum seekers in general carried out in Britain in the last few years.

The first is a literature review carried out for the Commission for Racial Equality (Finney and Peach 2004). They note that research into such attitudes has developed from the literature on racism and immigration done in the previous decades, and that work specific to asylum has mostly emerged since 2000. This should alert us to the political contingency of public perceptions: that was the year when the policy of 'dispersal' (distributing asylum seekers to provincial centres) was first implemented in Britain. This made the issue more immediate for people living away from London and the main ports of entry. Moreover, people's heightened sense of vulnerability to attack after the 9/11 and particularly the 7/7 bombings has served to sharpen defensive attitudes towards Others. From the work available to them, Finney and Peach (2004) observe that there are a number of widespread beliefs that inform public opinion on asylum seekers:

- Britain is a 'soft touch';
- there are too many asylum seekers;
- the majority of asylum seekers are not 'genuine';
- asylum seekers pose a threat to British culture (including religion, values, ethnicity and health);
- asylum seekers pose a threat to the British economy (through illegality, increased competition and an economic burden); and
- asylum seekers are treated well to the detriment of the existing population.

They conclude that these attitudes are fostered in a context where there is 'a lack of confidence in policy and governance on asylum issues', and that 'fears about asylum are closely associated with ideas of national identity and national security' (ibid.: 28).

These conclusions are certainly borne out in the studies of responses to the location of asylum-processing amenities in specific places in England that we shall examine in the next chapter (Grillo 2005, Hubbard 2005a, b, Modell 2004, D'Onofrio and Munk 2004). However, here I will concentrate on the work done by Miranda Lewis (Lewis 2005), which comprised focus-group interview and discussion-based research in four sites in Britain (Cardiff, Camden (a borough of London), Norwich and Weymouth) with a large sample in order to illustrate the way people make sense of asylum in contemporary Britain. I will then draw some conclusions on the ideological associations being made and argue how this exemplifies certain aspects of whiteness.

The research took place prior to the 7/7 bombings in 2005, and captures a trend towards more hostile attitudes towards immigrants and asylum seekers noted in polls from 2000 onwards (Lewis 2005: 2–3). She observes a number of problems arising from these surveys, one of which is that: 'The terms race, immigration and asylum are often used interchangeably both by the public and the people carrying out survey work' (ibid.: 4). Throughout the report, Lewis stresses and reiterates the confusion reigning over the status of various groups of people, and over authentic information: 'Very few participants were able to distinguish confidently between different categories of migrants. In some cases this meant any non-white person was classed as an asylum seeker. White European migrants were also often described as asylum seekers' (ibid.: 8). Yet whatever the degree of misunderstanding, one pattern emerges strongly, white British people frequently lump everyone who is not white together into what they feel is an inferior and threatening group:

> Some were deeply opposed to any asylum seekers coming into Britain, while others took a more moderate but still largely hostile view. In some cases this extended to any non-white or non-British community [. . .] no one raised issues about white immigration from countries such as Australia or the US.
>
> (ibid.: 7)

One subset of the research sample was BME (Black and Minority Ethnic), and the comparison of White UK to BME attitudes is revealing: 'People from BME communities were less likely to display very overt hostility about asylum seekers, and more likely to express sympathy than their white counterparts' (ibid.: 10). However, they did express concerns 'that the focus on asylum seekers and immigration made them more vulnerable, and felt that it had increased intolerance and racism' (ibid.: 11). This also manifests itself as resentment at some of the new arrivals, who are seen as in some way undoing the integration achieved by the longer-standing communities.

Among the most salient issues in relation to which resentment is expressed towards asylum seekers are access to benefits, housing and culture. As the report recognises, much information and personal experience comes in the form of rumours and second- or third-hand accounts. Overall, 'Asylum seekers are widely believed to receive better welfare benefits than the white British-born population and to access the welfare system with greater ease' (ibid.: 27). These alleged benefits include:

> driving lessons, free bus passes and swimming lessons. Again there was a tendency to assume that anyone from a minority ethnic background was an asylum seeker, reinforcing the belief that vast numbers of asylum seekers are tapping into the benefit system.
>
> (ibid.: 28)

Indeed, a wide range of deteriorating life experiences are associated with the presence of 'asylum seekers'. This confusion of people's immigration status, the causes and effects of problems, coalesce around what is perceived as the diminishing capacity of the health service. Additionally, labour migrants working in the public health service, and people perceived as putting undue pressure on provision, leapfrogging the British for entitlement, are viewed as different aspects of the same problem (ibid.: 28–29).

While housing is seen as a major issue by the majority (ibid.: 30–35) there is a class distinction among the respondents: 'While few from the ABC1 groups were concerned about social housing, several expressed fears about the impact of asylum seekers upon house prices', and about 'areas being brought down' (ibid.: 31). Working-class respondents perceived heightened competition with asylum seekers for public housing. The latter are seen as receiving unfair advantage in accessing housing, while locals spend years on waiting lists. In fact, asylum seekers are not housed in local authority social housing but in private rented accommodation either procured through the local authority (in collaboration with the National Asylum Support Service (NASS)) or via private-sector companies to whom such work is often outsourced in the UK. To an extent, local authorities seek to avoid aggravating these fears by deploying invisibility strategies. In Birmingham, the local council seeks to place asylum seekers in areas with already large BME populations 'in an attempt to reduce their visibility and perceived impact' (ibid.: 31). Dorset County Council (in whose jurisdiction is Weymouth) takes primarily Eastern European asylum seekers into its 99 per cent white population in an attempt to achieve a quiet life. Therefore local government colludes with the idea that anyone who is not phenotypically white will trigger a set of associations that result in action troublesome for the local authority.

Indeed, the basic point to come out of Lewis's research is that the white UK respondents make assumptions about the non-white people they see. Whether they are fellow Brits, tourists, labour migrants, students, asylum seekers or refugees, all can be tarred with the same brush. This finding not only underlines the argument that whiteness is the way that people make sense of social difference, but that the way 'race' is now discursively constructed in Britain represents a new moment in its history. The following comment, for example, could well have been uttered in the late 1950s: 'I know this sounds awful but why can't they conform to our ways? They stick together and bring down an area' (ibid.: 37). However, there was a period during which people would not have voiced this feeling *in this way* because of prevailing taboos about 'race'. Apart from ignoring the 1919 'race' riots, the respondent who argues that 'There never was a problem with race in Cardiff, but now there are far more of them: it's a different world' (ibid.: 40) is absolutely correct. The 'them' in the respondent's formulation serves as a lightning rod for pent-up frustrations about the perceived deterioration of life in contemporary Britain to be funnelled into a safe place. Asylum seekers are a distinct group about whom prejudice can be publicly expressed with little fear of sanction, even by relatively moderate people. Racism towards non-white British groups overflows into an ideological space where it is unsanctioned and no longer contained by the politically correct orthodoxies that the respondents claim prevent the disadvantaged 'us' from articulating 'traditional' views about 'them' (ibid.: 37).

The exaggeration of the numbers of minorities – and asylum seekers – seen in past polls (ibid.: 14–15) is a common enough story (Clarke and Garner 2005, Byrne 2006). People overestimate the number of minorities and asylum seekers in their areas, often by a large factor. This fear of invasion, usurpation and obliteration is both irrational and comprehensible. If many people now think everyone who is not white is probably an 'asylum seeker', it is not surprising that such numbers are vastly inflated. Again, this draws attention to the current historical moment. Before asylum seekers were headline news, what happened to these feelings?

So in this contemporary configuration, we see, in part, a return to the colour line: with everyone not white considered as a threat. Yet, in the fieldwork looked at in other chapters we see that it is not necessarily always the case that the line separates white from black: it may fall elsewhere. Many asylum seekers are white Europeans. What the particular discourse about asylum seekers shows is that there is something specific about this category of 'Other' which, *at this moment*, allows the colour line to be reinvigorated. It does not constitute continuity between the colour line of the 1950s and the early twenty-first century, but a profound rupture with what has developed in the intervening period. At both popular and policy levels, the distinctions between migrants and asylum seekers have been blurred: the state institutionally links asylum, immigration and citizenship, so can we really be surprised that so do the media and the public? Here nationality and whiteness intersect. Indeed, throughout this book I have been arguing that it always intersects with something: whiteness in isolation is a paper exercise, as are all one-dimensional models of identity. When people are talking about hierarchies of entitlement and justice, they set up a scenario in which nationality generates entitlement, and when it comes down to it, colour is the privileged sign of nationality: whiteness is a kind of flag. In their implicit discussions of entitlement, people are still envisaging a white Britain after more than fifty years of non-European labour immigration, and depressingly, after centuries of settlement of black and Asian people.[87] An opposition between white British and non-white Other is established. In this vision, a discourse of anxiety at the pace and content of social change is projected onto anyone suspected of being a 'non-national' – to use the telling Irish administrative term. Now, these non-nationals can be objectified as scroungers, criminals, threats, job-stealers. No-one is really 'deserving' except the omnipresent 'genuine asylum seekers' that most people are at pains to accommodate in their exclusionary standpoints without wondering how these claims to authenticity can be successfully arrived at.

Conclusion

The processes referred to in this chapter started before 9/11, but in the post–2001 period, and especially since the 2005 bombings, sharper focus has been bestowed upon Muslim threats to the West. The term 'refugee' no longer holds the same connotations either for policy makers or public as it did before 1990. Anxieties about the welfare state, house prices (in the owner–occupier cultures of the UK and Ireland particularly), changing employment conditions and perceptions of degradation (regardless of context) coalesce around the ideas of defending borders.

In this process, physical appearance again becomes the key distinguishing factor: differences of class, gender, region are forgotten, as security against the outside is emphasised as the overwhelming priority. In Europe, as in Australia, the bureaucratic response to immigration has been to erect taller and more effective fences, to attempt to position the racialised Others asking to be let in at greater distance from us. As bodies racialised as not white literally fall from the sky (Back 2003), out from underneath lorries (Lewis 2006), get washed up on Mediterranean beaches, or festooned on wire separating Ceuta and Melilla from Africa, the fences get placed further away. Australia's 'Pacific Solution' (Garner and Moran 2006) is the blueprint for the EU's plan to process asylum seekers in 'Third Countries' (i.e. Third World states on the periphery of Europe or at the source of large numbers of migrants) (Dietrich 2005). Even the granting of refugee status is now temporary in some places. The UK passed a law in August 2005 stating that once granted refugee status, an individual must have his/her case reviewed every five years with a view to return to the country of origin. The message could hardly be clearer: all migrants are a threat and must be dealt with at arm's length. The particular context of such policy initiatives is one in which the failure to achieve or bear whiteness marks the body as such a threat.

Different groups act on asylum seekers to produce identities. The state wins votes by appearing tough but reasonable defenders of the nation. The populist media keeps in touch with the people by critiquing the liberal laxity of the politically correct governing classes. Middle-class nimbys hang onto purity and the good life. Anti-racists struggle to posit a different version of the nation, and the working-class assailants who attack 'asylum seekers' may see themselves as defenders of the nation/neighbourhood against those funnelling resources away from their rightful targets. Yet where individuals are 'adopted' locally, a different set of strategies is enacted. Local campaigns to resist deportation attract personal support from people who are happy for ever more stringent regulations to be enacted. Both types of discourse thus co-exist: a white exclusive one, and a white inclusive one. Yet the former is currently the dominant discourse (complicated by the state's avowed multiculturalism).

The discourse of the asylum seeker/immigrant as a 'folk devil' (Cohen 2002) or fifth columnist (Lea and Lynn 2004) is a product of the process of building the European Union. To summarise, because internal borders have so diminished in importance due to the consequences of the Schengen Accords (1986) and the Treaty of Amsterdam (1997), the external ones have become commensurately more important, particularly when flows of migrants have increased overall since the 1980s. This discourse has taken deeper hold in some member states (e.g. the UK, the Republic of Ireland) than it has in others, where the trope of debate has always been immigration alone rather than asylum (e.g. France, Germany, Italy). By the first decade of the twenty-first century, this process has reached the point where the term 'asylum seeker' has swollen to accommodate a number of meanings and anxieties around social strains from other spheres. So few people have a grasp of the rather mundane facts about asylum (what an asylum seeker is, how many there are, what entitlements they have, what the restrictions on them are, etc.) that the discourse is not, strictly speaking, about asylum seekers at all. Rather it is about white Europeans reconfiguring their social and psychological boundaries to exclude groups of people from their national imaginaries, and thus from the resources available within those nations. The very different legal statuses inhabited by different groups of people (labour migrant on a work permit, asylum seeker, refugee, student, tourist, national) are dissolved in the act of redrawing the boundaries so that everyone on one side is white and unchallenged and everyone else is game for the attachment of familiar meanings (scrounger, illegal worker, feckless gambler, rapist, criminal, pimp, prostitute, etc.). This comforting whiteness can, in particular contexts, be subject to scrutiny, because local conditions highlight the diversity encompassed by the terms 'asylum seeker' and 'migrant worker'; many of them in Britain and Ireland are of Central and Eastern European origin.[88]

The issue of asylum illustrates that whiteness is open to activation in different ways. Asylum has been the catalyst for racialisation that has resulted in the blurring of categories so that 'not white' corresponds to asylum seeker, and threatening presence. Some more detailed examination of how these threats are imagined and represented follows in the next chapter.

9 Racial purity, integration and the idea of home

Material and emotional attachments of people to place are a staple of social science research. The language to describe such attachments is often drawn from nature. Allen White (2002: 1056) argues that:

> In the UK hydraulic metaphors imagine flows of migrants (water, blood, diseases) leaving and entering states (reservoirs, lake or the body) that are protected by international borders and immigration laws (dams or surgical instruments). Flows may be 'out of control' threatening the livelihoods of all citizens, thus 'floods' of refugees or asylum seekers threaten to 'swamp' the state.

Another set of metaphors about home uses 'roots': one puts down roots in a place or is uprooted from one. The image of normal growth and development in a specific location is disturbed by a number of factors that physically tear one away: economics, famine, war, oppression. People do settle, often for generations, in one place, and immobility is the default setting upon which communities are built. Yet it is equally true, as Goldberg argues, that the 'history of the human species, for all extents and purposes, can be told as the history of human migrations' (2000: 14). It is in the tension between these two almost banal truths, that ideas of home are constructed. The end of White's observation underscores such complexity: 'Representing the state and refugee movements in such a simplistic, but seductively holistic, way legitimates the replacement of polyvocal, complex and chaotic stories and realities of migrant life with a monochrome universe of truth' (White 2002: 1056).

Moreover, the relationships between individuals and peoples, between peoples and the lands they inhabit, are neither neutral nor natural, but are vehicles of social systems of inequality through which their actors interpret themselves as more or less belonging, more or less entitled to enjoy the fruits of belonging, however meagre and contingent those fruits may be. In this chapter, I shall focus on empirical fieldwork conducted in contemporary Britain, which will illuminate some of the changing stakes in what whiteness means and how it refers to itself at this precise juncture.

TOWN AND COUNTRY

We saw in chapter 8 that the racialisation of asylum had produced a configuration of whiteness that overrode that of previous ones, positing white people again as the sole repositories of Britishness and everyone else as potentially suspect. In this section we are going to look at the way this relationship of white people to particular places is expressed in both rural and urban settings in some recent fieldwork in England.

The countryside has long been constructed as a repository for pure English values, and a space of authenticity vis-à-vis the dangerous cosmopolitan urban centres. Work by Neal (2002), Garland and Chakraborti (2006), and Neal and Agyemang (2006), for example, shows how this functions in twenty-first-century Britain. In Rowe's (1998: 176–177) study of ideological interpretations of disorder in twentieth-century Britain, he compares rural calm with urban revolt by juxtaposing press coverage of rioting on a North London estate with former Home Secretary Lord Whitelaw's memoirs. Urban inhabitants, argues Rowe, are constructed as implicitly culturally alien and their presence degrades cities, exacerbating their distance from the putative bucolic norm.[89] At the very least, urban centres are seen as intrinsically multicultural spaces, places where anything to do with asylum would be better suited (Jay 1992). Places where, as one of David Modell's (2004) interviewees suggests, asylum seekers can 'mix with their own kind'. To distance the semi-rural, seaside village habitus from British urban centres, another of his subjects asserts that London probably has more in common with Baghdad than with Lee-on-Solent.

In two related articles, Phil Hubbard (2005a, b) argues that in the process of opposing the location of asylum seekers in particular spaces in England, rural landscape is racialised as white. Alongside protests over land use per se, he identifies elements of discourse produced in campaigns in rural Nottinghamshire and Oxfordshire that construct asylum seekers, regardless of their geographical origins, as an undifferentiated (overridingly male) criminal, sexually threatening and alien presence in the English countryside. Hubbard contends that there is a specific narrative of white rurality dependent on implicit norms of place, remote from chaotic and dangerous multicultural settings. One Oxfordshire complainant writes to the local planning authority: 'As a Bicester resident, I do not want to live in a multicultural community. Having lived in London and Surrey I have experienced the trouble this brings' (Hubbard 2005a: 14). Such logics are presented as rationalising the defence of beleaguered communities against inappropriate encroachment.

Indeed, elements of this discourse can also be identified in both urban and semi-rural settings (Grillo 2005, Clarke and Garner 2005, Modell 2004). Residents of such sites where asylum hostels and processing centres are planned assert that their type of living space precludes both the business function of dealing with asylum seekers and is inappropriate for those kind of people in any case.

In Portishead, near Bristol (a coastal town in South West England), where an office on a small business park was transformed into an asylum-screening centre in 2005 – not accommodation but for processing applications – the arguments are expressed in three registers (Garner, forthcoming). These are premised on assertions that both the town, and the area within the town in question, are residential, semi-rural, village-type locations. First, a de-racialised technocratic register, in which objections based on planning regulations are raised. There is concern over the change of use, poor access and transport, insufficient parking, and lack of amenities. Suggestions for more appropriate places to house such a facility (usually Bristol, but occasionally other urban centres in the region) are made.

Second, there is a more emotionally-charged resentment of the impacts such changes would have: the deterioration of living conditions, concern over property values and loss of trust in local and national officialdom. This concern is focused nationally on the Home Office's handling of the immigration issue, and locally on the County Council's long-term failure to provide sufficient infrastructure and what is viewed as lack of value for money in terms of local taxation.

Third, there is much speculation over the behaviour of the asylum seekers. Where an opinion is offered, this is expected to be universally detrimental to the lives of locals, involving as it does a variety of threats to Portishead's way of life (see below).

Yet virtually nowhere in the approximately 200 objections to planning application at Portishead are explicitly racialised comments.[90] The syntax of 'race-talk' has developed to a point where most people now go out of their way to disown racism. Just as Grillo's (2005) Saltdean OAPs officially rejected the hand of support offered by the British National Party, and ideologically distanced themselves from it, so people in Portishead explicitly deny their vantage point is a racist one in their letters. One woman cites her own 'Asian origins' as proof that her comments cannot be racist. She goes on to claim that 'the least we can expect is begging' from the asylum seekers. What emerges is a discourse of anxiety and frustration about a number of elements of contemporary life in Britain, one of which is the association of asylum with threat, danger and degradation. As one of the screening centre's opponents notes wryly:

> Whether we like it or not, 'Asylum' is a word guaranteed to raise more than a little controversy and anger. It is quite conceivable that prospective home buyers from outside the town will be reluctant to move to the town.

At the time of the campaigning, when most of these objections were written (March–April 2004), no specifics had been provided or sought in terms of the profile of the asylum seekers who would be using the centre, yet the construction of them is of a homogenous group of desperate people who wander recklessly alongside main roads, steal, beg, hang around threateningly, may be terrorists, and pose sexual threats to women and children. According to many of the letter-writers, the asylum seekers are often biding their time to disappear into the nation's motorway infrastructure and parallel economy. On the other hand, the community of residents constructed by the objectors is composed of law-abiding, quiet, unthreatening and reasonable people responding to the unfair imposition of a detrimental facility. As Potter and Wetherell (1992: 182) point out, in the liberal political discourse of Western democracy, compulsion is a negative, constituting an infringement of individual liberties. So we are less concerned here with whether or not the potential change of use of the building is actually an 'imposition', and more interested in the types of argument deployed to oppose it. In this case the common sense of liberal individualism provides the starting assumption for opposition. Property-ownership, combined with citizenship, bestows rights, and these include the right to resist compulsion. The authorities are thus depicted as unreasonable imposers of foreign bodies that do not bear rights (Agamben's 'homo sacer' or 'bare life', 1998) on national bodies that do.

The argument put forward by the Portishead objectors is to do with protecting a type of life, on a new-build estate on the outskirts of a small town in which the inhabitants are white and British. The last part of the sentence is not as insignificant as its position at the end of the sentence suggests. What this discourse achieves at one important level is the homogenisation of two heterogeneous populations: Portishead residents on one side and asylum seekers on the other. While the residents are brought together by realisation of a common Weberian 'class' interest around keeping their estate pure, it is they who hold the power in this situation to imagine and define the asylum seeker as a conglomeration of similar people whose innate characteristics will lead inevitably to behaviour that will defile the Vale estate.

The actual profile of asylum seekers shows they are primarily male, yet drawn from Europe, Asia, the Middle East and Africa (Heath *et al.* 2006). They are from a variety of social backgrounds, religions and age groups. Whatever you can say about asylum seekers, homogenous is not an accurate description.[91] The collective assumptions expressed in the Portishead round of opposition to planning permission is not solely driven by racism, yet 'race' is a key discourse underpinning the other anxieties and enabling them to coalesce. Indeed, the point is neither to brand the actors in this discourse as racist, or indeed as non-racist, although cases are made by protagonists on both sides of the issue (Aaranovitch 2004, Bright 2004), but to examine how discourses about 'race' are utilised in the everyday talk of local matters to create communities, both of defended white citizens and menacing asylum seekers.

The view of the nation (invaded by asylum seekers), the region (of which the centre is Bristol), sets up a racially weighted polarity consisting of multicultural Bristol *v.* the white hinterland. In their letters of objection, people state that they have chosen to live in Portishead because it is both quiet and up-and-coming, and on that particular estate because it is new and contains potentially more valuable housing. For the objectors, this tranquillity and investment is threatened by the asylum seekers, regardless of numbers, both because of the implications of their coming (knock-on effects) and their putative inherent qualities: desperation, incipient violence, trouble-making, etc. In such a context, the overwhelming whiteness of Portishead enables the development of a solidarity of interest against encroachment, one that is structured by values and their projected opposites.

Indeed, the theme of defence against invasion by immigrants/asylum seekers suffuses responses to asylum seekers. One interviewee in Modell's (2004) documentary on a South coast community split by the asylum issue expresses concerns about potential asylum-seeker accommodation in Lee-on-Solent (Hampshire). Recalling his time living in Reading, he states that 'our colonial friends' had moved into a set of streets, '. . . we moved out and I don't know how many roads they've taken over now'. He specifies that these people were Jamaicans: 'I've got nothing against them, not one little bit, 'cause there are some nice guys, but it lowers the price, the value of your property as soon as they move in'. The acute awareness of disadvantageous social change that is attached in narratives to the arrival and entrenchment of racialised minority groups here is a common story. In this narrative, the colonials 'colonize' an area of the town. Yet in Lee-on-Solent this ignores an intrinsic issue. The people destined for accommodation in the former barracks have no choice where they are housed. They are not private individuals accumulating capital for investment in a housing market, as were the Jamaicans in Reading referred to by the interviewee. They cannot therefore 'take over' any streets by buying property. The frequent conflation of labour migrant with asylum seeker here bestows the latter with fictitious agency and power: the potential to usurp residents, to threaten their entitlement to property.

Elsewhere, Katherine Tyler's studies of the Leicestershire village of 'Greenville' (2003, 2004, 2006) show that semi-rural space is defended using the development of middle-class values of belonging through adherence to ways of being and behaving, which are classed and raced. A self-employed interviewee, Mike, discusses a client who lives next door to one of the village's Asian families:

> I have got a customer up there and they are very nice houses . . . But he is very racist, very British Raj and he is an ex-air force navigator . . . 'Yes dear boy and old chum' [mockery of upper-class accent] and all this you see [. . .] He has got Indians living to the back and side of him . . . The house with the mosque thingy . . . So you can understand it from their point of view. They have worked hard all their lives to achieve whatever bracket of wealth or status, to enjoy their retirement in a quiet village, and all of a sudden you get three families moving into one house and try and run a business from it. Transporter vans coming and going and they probably have a couple of sewing machines running in the garage. Women doing a bit of machining and then multiples of kids running around the garden, as he is sitting out on a nice sunny day and it all drives you mad. It is very difficult for them.
>
> (Tyler 2003: 402–403)

Mike's speculations make his fantasies explicit, and aligns him as an ally of the Raj man: worship, business and noise will erupt. It is tempting to think of this as revealing the projection of some contemporary British fears: secular doubt in the face of faith where the latter is seen as communal, self-effacing and irrational; guilt over others' industriousness that threatens your supposition of laziness and incompetence; maybe combined with unfair competition (through unwaged family labour). Finally, there is the plague of large noisy families and expressive communities, the hint of high birth-rates and the ultimate assumption of power by the 'hordes'. In addition, this example from semi-rural Leicestershire shows that whiteness is classed, even when stressing its external border, and that the locations of the actors, at least in this hierarchical imaginary, stem at least partly from the reconfiguration of the coloniser–colonised relationship.

Ambivalence

While 'home' for many villagers (or people who do not live in villages but would like to) covered in the research referred to in this chapter is threatened by jarring otherness, there are a number of ways in which the co-incidence of home and matter-out-of-place is experienced. Our research project on white identities in provincial England undertaken by the author provides the material for the following sections (Clarke and Garner, forthcoming). Eric, one of our respondents in Bristol, is asked what picture the word 'immigrant' conjures up:

> Oh it conjures up negative images, I hate to say it, but it does. It conjures up East Europeans or Africans, Soweto, not Soweto, what do you call them, what's that place, there's a lot of them in Cardiff [Author's note: we think he means Somalia]. It conjures up bad images. It conjures up spongers, people living off us who are not destroying our way of life, but having an effect on the British side, I suppose [. . .] This is why we're partly being diluted. It's not being diluted by Indians or Pakistanis who've been here for 55 years or whatever. It's by people coming in, and I've noticed it, I go to London once a month, and I do find it, I'll be honest, mildly irritating because you hardly see what you would call a normal white British person on the street, because it is just full of foreigners, Foreigners in inverted commas, sorry . . .

Even this account includes ambivalence. Multicultural urban space is viewed as un-British in this narration, yet the exact positioning of the line separating the British from the foreigners is hesitatingly created. White Europeans and black Africans are mentioned as foreigners, yet Indians and Pakistanis (and presumably their descendants) who have settled in Britain since World War II are abstracted from the process of dilution. Yet at the end, the normal British person is unambiguously white. Dilution rather than destruction is the outcome, through parasitical behaviour. It is not clear how this presence and behaviour are linked so unequivocally in Eric's mind, but we can see this is an ideological effect. Particular types of bodies are understood as behaving in intrinsically negative ways, and again it is the trope of productivity that is dominant. Our respondents virtually always couched discussion of immigration in the basis that it must be productive and that economically-contributing individuals are more or less welcome.

It has been established then that in the eyes of non-migrants, residential space can be taken over and altered negatively, by or for migrants.[92] Another of our interviewees, Denise, talks of the areas in a northern English city where she grew up. The first has been altered by white people:

> When I grew up we all knew each other, the people that had their houses, their council houses, but they looked after them, they had pride in them, in the gardens, and there was respect. But I think over the years, when we had gone back, a lot of the people had been replaced with single parents . . . And, not, oh gosh, not that single parents, it's just the type of single parents, it's the one that they were almost school children themselves, so of course it changes because they're not the same, they don't have the same values or anything, so they were allowing their children to go and play out till all hours. It was just different. A lot of the people had moved on, been replaced and it just was, it wasn't very nice.

She goes on to talk of the area

> where my Dad and his wife lived, slowly over the years, there was more Indians and Pakistanis moving into the area, and you know, that was a bit strange [. . .] Once one family moved in, a house came up for sale, they bought the next house and the next house, and it went on from there, and it was like living in a foreign country.

So the two experiences, read together, are of conditions deteriorating and combinations of class and 'race' as explanatory factors. It is strikingly similar to the narrative about housing in Reading told to Modell (2004). The absence of a qualifying adjective suggests that the single parents in the former area are white. When an area becomes a byword in a city for minority residence, the two are often conflated so that racialisation subsumes the class dimension, that is, it is spoken of as a place for minorities rather than a working-class district, even though the latter might well be an equally accurate description. Few people talk of the compounding effect, but Gladys in Bristol does so. She is married to a man from an Asian country and she comments on a particular part of Bristol because of his invisibility in the streets there: 'there are huge divides, some of them are economic, some of them are cultural, and when the two combine it is quite a staggering difference'. The husband's transformation into someone who is at a certain level 'at home' in this part of the city, causes his wife to look at the place with a particular gaze in which her whiteness and invisibility elsewhere are highlighted, and where she reflects on what makes this space not home for her.

So there are a number of criss-crossing themes in people's references to space, 'race' and home that are informed by their vantage point as white British people with classed locations. Home is projected as an absence of otherness and the maintenance of particular values, often backward-looking, to recapture a moment in one's personal biography, as is the case with some of Byrne's white mothers (2006), Tyler's 'village people' (2006), and Modell's anti-asylum protesters (2004), when surroundings were uncomplicatedly devoid of otherness. Moreover, the 'golden age' phenomenon (Back 1996) relates not only to racial purity but social mores, cohesion and patterns of life that were less alienating. Indeed, it is important to think of whiteness and the lines between white and other identities being drawn as part of an ensemble of elements connected, especially for older people, with perceived reduction in the quality of life. The attachment of particular causes to particular effects might be debatable, but it is clear that for many people the numerous shifts in British life (rising costs of living, different working patterns, female employment levels, increasing feelings of vulnerability to crime, for example) are the changing demographic features of neighbourhoods.

Culture and 'race'

A striking feature of contemporary discourse about 'race', immigration and Britishness picked up in our work is the importance of cultural space as a contested resource. Many people see Britain as losing its identity (although a minority see change as a positive thing), and this is expressed through a variety of references to culture. One particular battleground is the way religion impacts on people's lives, not necessarily in the formal churchgoing context, but in terms of how Christmas is celebrated and referred to. One outstanding gripe from people is to do with the idea of Christmas being abolished in some way: school plays banned, words or phrases used to avoid saying 'Christmas', Christmas cards not being placed in public spaces, etc., are all examples people have commented on. Yet it is not at all clear where, when or even if such events took place, or who is actually offended by such expressions (although it frequently occurred in the context of discussion of Islam in Britain). They may well all refer to a reading of one or two incidents reported nationally. Burkeman's (2006) search for institutions 'stealing Christmas' in Britain in 2006 finds only unsubstantiated stories.

What then is the function of these stories and the comments they provoke? In the realm of tolerating diversity, one thing which is frequently pinpointed as a step too far is interference with Christmas, a festival that epitomises something British for our respondents. For some this might have more to do with symbols of Christianity, while for others it is more of a paradoxically secular festival in which they feel particularly invested. This type of discourse occurs in the context of white cultures in general being referred to by white respondents as intrinsically uninteresting (Frankenberg 1994, McKinney 2005) and the implication in some multicultural proclamations that British culture was, in journalist Julie Burchill's laconic term, a 'wasteland' before mass immigration (2001). Indeed, comments by then Cabinet minister Robin Cook (2001), who commented in a speech that the typical British meal in 2001 was chicken tikka masala, point towards the idea that, as many respondents intimated, British culture per se has benefited from external infusion and needed literally 'spicing up'. The question of culture has been central to racialisation since at least the English colonisation of Ireland, and provided the object of discourses in which it is argued that civilisation A is superior to civilisation B. Indeed culture has always been constitutive of the idea of 'race'. Robert Young contends that:

> Culture has always marked difference by producing the other; it has always been comparative, and racism has always been an integral part of it: the two are inextricably clustered together, feeding off and generating each other. Race has always been culturally constructed. Culture has always been racially constructed.
>
> (1995: 54)

So it is not surprising to find that in the early twenty-first century, in the long shadow of the Holocaust, where direct talk of racial inferiority is shocking, the sphere in which it is possible to talk openly about race is the cultural one. Much has been written about what are identified as 'new' forms of racism; from the 'new racism' based on socio-biology that informed the Thatcherite era in the UK (Barker 1981, 1990) to the 'neo-racism' suggested by Balibar (1991) as the dominant form in contemporary Europe, and 'color-blind racism' (Bonilla-Silva 2003) in the USA. What binds these concepts is their reliance of the normativity of culture as an experience that produces (in both Foucault and Balibar's senses) the people (as a national population): people who are culture-coded as either normal or Other. The history of post-war migration into Europe shows how culture has been deployed as an exclusionary device by the state, and on a popular level to distinguish between (assimilable) migrants, like 'us', and (unassimilable) ones who are not (Goodhart 2004).

The British State moved from a position of inviting workers from the colonies to Britain to rebuild the economy in the late 1940s, to one in which immigration controls were imposed on some Commonwealth nationals (of colour) and nationality was reconfigured as pertaining to bloodlines rather than residence throughout the 1960s. This was due to problems of assimilating what was referred to as 'coloured immigration' (Miles and Phizacklea 1984, Miles 1993). By 2005, the British government was recognising that EU expansion policy allowed Eastern Europe to supplant other places as sources of immigration (Home Office 2005).

THREE ENGLISH PEOPLE'S TAKES ON INTEGRATION

Although the term has been conceptualised as involving a two-way process of negotiation (Parekh 2000, Castles *et al.* 2002), integration is perceived by people in contemporary Britain as a synonym of assimilation. The idea of home as a place is constructed as much along the lines of people as of spaces, buildings, and adherence to particular values. Three examples from our fieldwork in England illustrate the dynamics of this home-building process, and how whiteness runs as a thread, sometimes in a surprising way, through the discourse (Clarke and Garner forthcoming).

Jack

The first is Jack, in his 50s. He lives in a residential area in a city in the South West of England, and has responded to a question earlier in the interview about what pleases and displeases him in Britain at the moment, by talking immediately about 'people coming from all over the world and living here'.

He feels that:

> to a certain extent that if people are going to be here, they should play by our rules rather than we should bend over backwards to let them play by their rules. I wouldn't expect to go to a foreign country and totally live out my culture if it wasn't the way people did things there.

Jack's is a common formulation of the problem of integration and cultural behaviour, a discursive 'commonplace' (Billig 1991), as well as a clinching argument. We might call it the 'when-in-Rome' view. Variations included references to not being allowed to build a church in Saudi Arabia, or styles of dress in Arab cultures. First, this sets out a general principle of equality that must be respected. Second, it posits an equivalence between the structural position of Third World migrants in Britain, and British migrants elsewhere, thus glossing over a central part of British experience. Colonialism involved making other people play by British rules. By arguing that the migrants whose culture is causing a problem are on a level playing field with the British, respondents are ideologically casting the past as finished business that no longer has an impact on the present. One element of white British identities is clearly some kind of fragmented and suppressed relationship with Empire. While few speak openly about its legacy as a source of pride, fewer still engage critically with this legacy and attempt to articulate how it may still structure contemporary experiences (Knowles 2005, 2004, 2003). The principal way in which recognition of Empire is recorded is paradoxically through its elision in the 'when-in-Rome' argument.

Jack's personal take is influenced by his strong secularism and antipathy towards religion, which he sees as a major source of conflict and tension in the world: he returns to this topic more than once in his interviews. Jack revisits it later when asked directly what his feelings about immigration are:

> I think the problems with it will be that unless people are integrated more into society, and by integrated, that means, we haven't just got to accept them, they've got to accept a degree of British-ness, then you're going to get hot spots where there's going to be resentment that people are taking their place in the hospital queue or their place in the school or their place in the whatever, because it is my country, what are you doing here. But if those people come in and are given a programme whereby they understand that, all right you can live here, but this is what we do, but you can't have them saying, well, we don't do it like that. Well, okay – go back (*laughing*). That's not quite right, again that's sounding not the way that I intend it to sound, but I feel we're going to have problems if we don't integrate fully.

Jack advances from describing the contours of a general problem to fleshing out his earlier comment. This time the problems coalesce around hierarchies of entitlement for services and resources such as schools and hospitals. The resentment about losing out in the struggle for these resources, he seems to be saying, is generated not only by foreignness per se, but by people not adjusting to particular types of cultural norm. Again, typically these norms are not specified, but could be the basis of a 'programme'. When talking generally, Jack is aware of an inconsistency between his idea of himself as liberal and rational, and the starkness of his opinions on this issue. He previously said he did not want to sound as though he was 'to the right of Attila the Hun', and here he backpedals again: 'That's not quite right, again that's sounding not the way that I intend it to sound . . .'. The distinction between how unknown groups of people and individuals known to the respondent are talked about mirrors the broader patterns in our research: immigration per se is seen as at least partly to do with structure, while integration is the realm of the individual. Some respondents have exemplary individuals in mind, as Jack does:

> I've got a couple of very good friends and one of them is going up to Liverpool on a stag weekend that he's organized because he's a passionate Everton fan. He's a second-generation Asian, but you just wouldn't know it because he's a Scouser.[93] And he waves the flag for England for the cricket, I play cricket with him. That's my kind of immigrant. If everybody was like that, there would be no problem, you know, but they aren't. They want to have, they want to import somehow too much, and it's not their culture, it's their religion, and that's the problem.

The contrast between Jack's friends and the non-integrating immigrants revolves around local and national sporting allegiances and outward adherence to British cultural practices like the stag night. He focuses on religion among the many possible cultural distinctions, which again is tied in with his antipathy towards it. Yet there is an interesting slippage here between statuses. The friend is a 'second-generation Asian' (i.e. born and bred in Liverpool), yet he is held up as a model immigrant. The man is clearly not an immigrant however, but a British national whose parents were immigrants. There is quite a difference in socialisation for someone who has grown up in the British culture and someone who comes to it as an adult (Bagguley and Hussain 2005). Moreover, the right of people to evaluate British culture and not adhere to parts of it is not considered.[94] The integration foregrounded here is closer to assimilation. This is the choice of the individual rather than the prescribed programme-led solution Jack has floated for new immigrants. However, while Jack wholeheartedly approves of this model behaviour, his opinion is not the only one prospective sports integrators will encounter. One of my own undergraduate students (a Brummie of Mauritian-Indian origin) reported that despite wearing an England shirt in Germany for the 2006 World Cup, he was called an 'Al-qaida bastard' by other England supporters on one occasion. His Birmingham accent and support for England were not enough for him, in this instance, to pass the test.

Denise

Another question we posed was 'When does an immigrant stop being an immigrant?' Denise, a mother of three in her 30s, living in the same town as Jack, speaks from a different ideological space. A devout Anglican, she is originally from a housing estate in the North and has lived abroad. Denise's second interview rested heavily on the idea that she perceived increasing pressure as being put on British tolerance of outsiders. Her answer to the question about when an immigrant stops being one is:

When they are, if they are nationalized. If they at least try and nationalize themselves to this country. My husband's cousin is Indian. Her family are Indian and have been here nearly 40 years, but they're very westernized. They don't, you know, they do wear their saris at special occasions and things, but they're not here demanding to bring a bit of India or, you know, to be Indian in this country. I think I wouldn't, you know . . . The children's godmother is from Jamaica, her, you know, her parents and all her family are from Jamaica, but they've been in England many years, and to me, they're just as English as I, well, Janine is just as English as I am because. Well, she was born here, but not because of that, because she's not, you know, they're just the same as me and anybody else. They're not trying to be different.

Q So is it to do with culture?

A I don't even mind their own . . . it is not even within their own culture, it's not even within their own . . . you know . . . to have their own culture, it's when they're almost forcing that.

Denise had been reluctant to be recorded in her first interview. This time she was more confident, and very emotional. She brought the interview back repeatedly to the question of the relative rights of British people and immigrants. Her close personal relationship with the daughter of immigrants opens up a space in which she is ambivalent about the necessity of whiteness and Britishness:

Q   Going back to the question of identity, how do you feel about being English? Or what does it mean to you?

A   I don't know really. I was going to say that white, but that is not strictly true, is it, because there's lots of non-white English people like my friend. But today I think it's more I would be saying that because I am a white English person, so I think that's why I would say now as opposed to a time ago where I wouldn't have even dreamt of saying that.

So black and Asian people can be on the British side of the dividing line if they adhere to a code of not trying to 'be different'. Denise's current heightened awareness of her whiteness is also inextricable from her nationality and her thoughts on what it means to be British in the face of unreasonable pressure. Her reference points are often religious, as in the following statement:

I've not come across anybody yet, *even in church*, who isn't feeling that we're sort of. . . . It isn't the, something else to do with it as well which is how we seem to be bending everything to accommodate the different, and the different religions as well. And I think that, you know, we should allow for different religions, but not when their religion takes precedence over ours, because we certainly can't go to a Muslim country and have the same rights. [My emphasis mimicking stress in voice]

While her starting point and appreciation of religious faith are virtually the opposite of secular Jack's, her understandings of the power balance is virtually identical: the use of the when-in-Rome argument underpins it. If anything, Denise's appreciation is that conditions are more unequal than in Jack's. The qualifier 'even in church' identifies a community whose opinion would otherwise be taken as the epitome of tolerance, having been moved to question the unfairness of a situation:

Whatever the reasons, they're in this country, and that's just the way it is, they shouldn't be so, oh I can't think of the word. I'm sure it'll come to me later. I feel really passionate about the whole thing on this now.

Denise has obvious difficulty throughout the second interview in calming herself when talking about this issue. She is sometimes so upset that she is lost for words. While talking about problems involved in a cultural disagreement at a factory (below), she even refers to the recording at one moment. Earlier in the interview she introduced a statement with 'this is going to sound really racist now':

> Some Muslims in the factory found it offensive that some women in the factory wear T-shirts, because they were exposed, but if they don't like it, even on your tape, go back to where it is not bloomin' offensive, to where it can't be offensive to you.

Denise's interviews demonstrate quite a complex set of associations about class and 'race', with childhood experiences, religious conviction and the experience of having lived abroad all playing a part. Her resistance to the idea of people not integrating almost prevents her speaking at some points, yet makes her confident enough at others to stop caring about whether she sounds racist. Her vision of beleaguered Britain in which the pendulum has swung too far towards accommodation of others is a hegemonic one encountered in a number of our interviewees, and those of Lewis (2005), for example. Yet the specifics of her responses mark them out as particularly powerful. Home (a habitus shaped by tolerance of cultural practices) for her is threatened primarily by the unreasonableness of Muslims, who are seen as taking advantage. Her line of Britishness clearly encloses Whites but runs zig-zag fashion through black and Asian communities depending on the degree to which individuals are 'forcing' their cultural will on the local norms.

Bill

The third example is drawn from an interview with Bill, a social worker in his 60s who is a member of an Anglican church on a large housing estate in the other city where we worked.

Of the four areas where we did fieldwork, this place, 'Broomfield', had the highest proportion of ethnic minority residents, around 7 per cent. Here he talks about three local residents.

Q   When does an immigrant stop being an immigrant?

A   I think if you've come from another country really, you are an immigrant, it's about when you stop thinking about. I don't know about . . . depending on . . . You see one of the reasons I think of Shafiq as being an immigrant is that, for all his kindness and his carefulness, you feel that he is still having to work very hard at negotiating across the boundaries. With Richard and Carolyn, you don't feel that, well, they do it without you noticing it.

Bill said he tried to talk to Richard about the cricket, and he wasn't interested unless the West Indians were playing.

> Now you could argue, couldn't you, that he would be supporting England if he was really English . . . I don't think that, you see. There is something about the way they (Richard and Carolyn) go on that makes me feel that they don't need to do that, they're comfortably part, they make great efforts to be. I mean, Carolyn is the sort of person who turns up with stuff when there's an event at the church; she has ways of making sure she has become part of the community. She's actually, somebody said, (*whispering*) I'm going to invite Carolyn to stand for the church council this year. Now they've been coming for two and a half years, I think. In Broomfield terms, most of these people have been coming for 30 years! So you kind of feel, you know, don't you, she's worked, she's being seen as part of the thing.

Bill's idea of integration displaces national sporting allegiance as a primary measure. This type of hypothetical test has been referred to since it was placed on the national agenda by former Conservative Cabinet Member (Lord) Norman Tebbit in the 1980s. Yet for Bill, this West Indian couple are integrated regardless. They have passed a far more stringent examination. The fact that Carolyn is on the cusp of a Church committee nomination is in local terms evidence of integration. This appears an ideal situation. The other person Bill referred to, Shafiq, is a convert to Catholicism, and English is not his first language. It might be suggested that the anglophone Christian West Indian couple in this example have a relative advantage over non-Christian non-anglophones. Yet this type of cultural capital has not always been useful. British black churches often opened in the 1950s and 1960s as a response to exclusion from mainstream churches by white British Christians. Moreover, the generation of Christian West Indians of the 1950s and 1960s were identified paradoxically as problematic immigrants by successive governments because they appeared 'culturally inassimilable'. Carolyn's feat of rapidly making herself part of such a community is, viewed from a historical perspective, no mean one.

Three views of integration

The route of individuals to integration appears to revolve around reaching a certain degree of intimacy: in each of the three cases this has been true in different ways. Yet the respondents have different gauges of what aspects of integration are more important. For Jack it was sporting allegiance and normative masculinity. Immigrants should not just be integrated nationally, but incorporated into the local rivalries and male-dominated culture of sports and stag nights. Denise's concerns are about the Christian-based culture of Britain being changed by assertive foreigners, primarily from the Indian sub-continent, who are taking advantage of Britain's tolerant disposition. Lastly, Bill sees sporting allegiance as relatively unimportant, and feels that integration is to do with a process of pro-actively contributing and becoming a part of a community. The conditions under which people integrate or not in these examples cannot serve as the basis of general claims. What they do illustrate however are manoeuvres frequent among our interviewees; the first is the identification of *individual* integration success stories. When this is done, it is often in contrast to examples of *collective* failure to integrate. The second is to implicitly highlight the values of Britishness held in esteem by the speaker: in pointing out how outsiders remain outside or become insiders, the key values that prevent or make this possible are identified also. The personal experiences of each respondent frame the narration; Jack's antipathy to religion, Denise's membership of the Church and upbringing in a multicultural setting, and Bill's lifelong involvement in community work. However, the 'nodal points' (Laclau and Mouffe 1985) at which their accounts coalesce are the individual nature of integration (hard work can procure this) and the understanding of integration as a one-way assimilative process. This fits neither with the idea of multiculturalism *as an exchange*, nor with culture as dynamic rather than static.

The wider context of these interviews is one of post-7/7 bombings, ongoing wars in Afghanistan and Iraq, the opposition to them in Britain, the prosecution of the war on terror and its associated ideological battles, and the resurgence of debates about British identity. As indicated in the previous chapter, these have a relationship with the previous fifteen years of turning asylum and immigration into a live political issue also. Key themes within that debate have been the place of Islam in Britain and the degree to which Britain can absorb immigrants of different types. Indeed, the idioms in which such debates can be phrased are altering from the multicultural (where a vague and unstable commitment to nominal equality of cultures within the national one is present) to the 'post-multicultural', for want of a better term. Here, cultures are viewed as intrinsically different and hierarchical. British culture, with minimal definition, is held up unconditionally as the one into which others (now especially Muslims) must assimilate. You could be forgiven for reacting to this with a yawn or a shoulder shrug. Haven't we seen all this before?

Wasn't this the norm when post-war migrants first arrived in large numbers in Britain? Yet the situation is emphatically dissimilar. What is important to think about is how Britain has passed through its formal multicultural phase into post-multiculturalism. How has discourse returned to a similar form of expression even though it has been through two decades of challenge and brief hegemony, at least in some circles? From the top, important political actors have been involved in this shift over the last two to three years,[95] and its manifestation is visible in fieldwork. Now, the dominant popular model of Britain's diverse culture seems to be one in which the traditional white Christian basis is under increasing threat from over-assertive minorities, supported by their political allies, the liberal and 'politically correct' local and national leadership. The anxiety expressed by white British respondents in the work referred to here can be read as a function of the undermining not of whiteness, but of a series of long-term changes to the employment market, the polarised distribution of wealth, the welfare state and the property market, among other things. Insecurities over these areas can be expressed in direct relation to these but also in closing ranks against those seen as dangerously different and not taking their place in the queue. This queuing, a paradigmatic British social practice, places the productive indigenous, white British at the front, and deliberately unproductive white British somewhere towards the back. When the queue appears to be operating in a different way, the emotional responses are anger, feelings of betrayal and the identification of particular bodies as agents of declining living standards. Those bodies are sometimes those of white Europeans, but much more frequently they are of non-white Others, from anywhere, with any status including British nationals. This is the point at which whiteness is the key dividing line between the relatively powerful and the powerless.

Conclusion

The idioms through which 'race' is discussed have been transformed since the 1950s. In Britain the parameters of what it is acceptable to talk about have passed through a period of notional multicultural equality into one of contestation, where minorities and their cultural difference are fair game for critique. This is particularly true for British Muslims.[96] It is clear from the way that our respondents discuss immigration that the problematic integration of difference looms large in their thinking. This problem often supposes a static, rather than dynamic, idea of culture, and a partial grasp of particular items as markers of culture: language, dress, selected religious ideas. Why can this be comprehended through racialisation rather than ethnicity, and why is it to do with whiteness?

First, the cultural characteristics of Others are projected as collective, unchanging and innate. Individuals whose behaviour does not conform to that of the non-integrating mass are not viewed as exceptions indicating that the monolithic view may be wrong (maybe there are plenty of Muslims who are 'integrated'), but as exceptions that prove the rule. In this way, the conflict can be depicted as one between tolerant hosts and ungrateful guests refusing to accommodate themselves (Gibson 2003). Under particular circumstances, some of which we have tried to pinpoint here, this discourse moves to a defensive pitch. The defence of home (safety, space and values) is expressed sometimes through raceless themes (overcrowding, misuse of planning, etc.), sometimes through raced (crime, insecurity, house prices, sex) themes, but the context is the key. Second, in the work here, white English communities represent themselves as law-abiding, decent, monogamous, reasonable people contrasted with Others, who are a priori criminal, rapacious, unreasonable and reluctant to contribute. I made it clear at the outset that whiteness is as much an interpretive framework as a collection of power relations. Using this framework, I would suggest that one of the ideological effects of whiteness is to induce a narcotic cohesion, a cohesion that suspends the constant and fluid fracturing of identity along class, gender and political lines, for example – enabling the imagined community of Britain to be drawn together, revealing who is the same as us (in the speaker's terms) and who is different. For some, the exact composition of that community is more inclusive than for others, yet the bonding agent is whiteness: expressed as a set of racialised (i.e. bound to bodies and seen as natural) cultural characteristics.

Conclusion
In defence of the whiteness problematic

RECAP, MODEL AND COMPARISON

Throughout the argument presented here I have maintained that whiteness is not only something that is the object of study, but also a way of approaching that object: a critical perspective.[97] Indeed, using the same term for both is potentially confusing, so I am going to refer to the perspective as the 'whiteness problematic', to cover the way of problematising social relations so that the racialisation process is at the heart of them, and that 'white' marks a powerful spot. So just as Mills advocates separating whiteness as identity from white supremacy as a system, my recommendation is to distinguish whiteness as an analytical framework used by researchers (the whiteness problematic) from whiteness as a set of social relationships.

Chapters 1–4 presented the various themes arising from the study of whiteness in US literature, and found some resonances with the work carried out in the UK. These are particularly noticeable in the ways in which whiteness is articulated through values. The values of white interviewees are expressed through their critique of those they impute to non-white colleagues, compatriots, and immigrants: racialisation without 'race'. The concept of whiteness exists only in relation to what it is not, which is evident from its origins in New World systems of forced labour, which came to operate a colour-coded social hierarchy linking status to colour.

The relationality of the racialisation process illustrates how racism cannot be understood merely by references to themes or tropes but only in historical, social, material and cultural contexts. An intrinsic part of this context is the structural or institutional aspect. The distinction between whiteness and 'white supremacy' (identity *v.* systemic domination), emphasised and developed by Mills (2004), is a valuable one, which postulates differing levels, or domains of action (structure and agency), which cannot function independently.

The fact of historical white political domination requires much recognition of nuance when qualitative fieldwork is conducted: not all white people have the same degree of power over all non-white people all the time, or in the same place. John Hartigan's (1999) white respondents in Briggs and Les Back's in South London (1996) are remote from sources of decision-making power, yet despite their class location, they are still able to claim or aspire to white identities that enable them to experience a minimum of privileges outside of their residential area. The privileges are more partial for them than for Tyler's wealthy English villagers (2006) or Pierce's corporate lawyers (2003), for example, yet this uneven distribution of privilege does not invalidate the problematic. The relationality of whiteness involves two simultaneous border maintenance processes: one between white and people of colour, and the other between white and not-quite-white (explored in chapters 4 and 6). All white subjects are located somewhere on this spectrum, which is an outcome of the ongoing classificatory process conceptualised as racialisation.

This drive towards classification stems from the Enlightenment project. Ordering the great chain of being, from *homo sapiens* downwards, and grading *homo sapiens*, which is the story of 'race' as an idea and racism as a set of practices, is anything but neutral. Whiteness is the point from which such classifications are carried out: a fulcrum of domination. It places itself on the positive side of all the binaries used to attach value and meaning to groups of people: cleanliness/dirt; purity/impurity; restraint/excess; backwardness/modernity.

In the process of racialised classification that whiteness commands, the untidy and contradictory relations between white people are suspended. Black men become a homicidal set of simulacra, Asians a 'horde', Jews an alien infestation, indigenous peoples indolent savages, and so it goes on. White people are positioned in this relationship as individuals, whereas those racialised as not white are rendered 'undifferentiated', both in the literal and the medical senses of the term, where homogeneity is a property of an undeveloped subject.

In this ideological and psychosocial manoeuvre, materially important status differences are thus abolished. Asylum seekers are conflated with labour migrants, people with refugee status, tourists, students, undocumented migrants and non-white nationals. As the people reproduces itself within the ideological constraints of the nation-state, the parameters of peoplehood are expressed through insecurities and aporia, by defining Others using an amalgam of culture and nature (chapters 8 and 9).

In this book, much weight has been afforded to empirical accounts as a way of balancing the overwhelmingly theoretical corpus. This has allowed the various national contexts, looked at in chapters 5–7, to illustrate the importance of looking beyond the US borders in order to fully understand whiteness. The legacy of slavery and the contemporary presence of affirmative action mark out US discourse from the emphasis on indigenous land rights, and the post-colonial immigration policy of Australia and Ireland, the post-colonial nation-building of Ireland and Ecuador, and the post-imperial crisis of multiculturalism currently experienced in the UK. Yet while there is ample space to address the variety of specific contexts, there are also significant resonances. The British fieldwork[98] demonstrates that we need to explain why white people are now expressing racially-mediated beleagueredness and injustice. How can people who live safe lives in properties they own come to organise a campaign to keep people, who have escaped persecution and own very little, out of a barracks in their town, and in doing so wave banners decrying their own relative lack of human rights?[99] For McKinney's students (2005), Weis and Fine's unemployed working men (1996), and in Frankenberg's (2001) report of the panels on whiteness at the American Sociology Association's 2000 conference, a very similar discourse is noted, albeit ideologically attached to affirmative action. This dominant version of developed-world whiteness seems to contain an uncomfortable mixture of arrogance and fear.

Chapters 5–7 also illuminate some geographical and historical avenues that are routinely omitted from the American discussions of whiteness:[100] Ecuador, the Irish in the Caribbean, the Portuguese diaspora, Gypsy-Travellers, alongside others, such as the 'inbetween peoples' thesis (and to a much lesser extent the 'are-Jews-white?' debate), which are often mistaken for constituting whiteness studies alone (*International Labor and Working Class History* 2001, Kolchin 2002, Kaufman 2006a, b). These differing contexts underscore the necessity for balancing the cultural with the material in analyses as well as illustrating the differing stakes of whiteness, and the myriad ways in which it sustains itself as a desirable location, even if this is only strategic.

All of the above suggests a rich set of possibilities in terms of how 'white' can be marked as raced. Maybe the variety indicates the foolhardiness of tabling models. However, the model I am now proposing is meant as a starting point.

Power exercised through terror (chapter 1) creates contingent hierarchies (chapter 4) that are based on values, norms, and cultural capital (chapter 3). A major expression of domination for the white subject is to misrecognise oneself as an un-raced individual, while others are undifferentiated racialised and invisible (chapter 2). The boundaries about who belongs and why are continually being redrawn so that the overriding lines include the majority of Whites (chapters 4–7). This is not only a phantasy about the unattainable cohesion of the nation, as Zizek (1989) argues, but also a reflection of material order. In other words, what is it about this moment that inflects whiteness in the ways we have discussed?

Certainly there has been an intensification of mobility and an increasingly complex network of migratory movements that far exceed the old post-colonial nexus. There are increasing not decreasing disparities of wealth, both between and within countries: while per capita income might rise, that of the top rises much more quickly, and welfare provision, even where it exists, is more precarious than a generation ago due to the privatisation of such services and the retreat of the state. From the bottom looking up, the new economic conjunction entails a combination of increasing affluence but relative degradation. This, I suggest, makes it more likely that people will be viewed as competitors – but differently so by different people. Although housing, benefits and resources are topics for complaint, the middle classes are more concerned by house prices and taxes, while the working classes focus more on access to social housing and the availability of jobs, for example. There is certainly a good deal of thinking upwards to be done by scholars on the basis of the increasing amount of qualitative studies of whiteness to have been published over the last decade, just as this work has been a necessary complement to the heavy theoretical bias of the corpus.

Whiteness and the 'murky waters' of history

In the Introduction and chapter 1, I acknowledged the work of the pioneering analysts of whiteness: those African-American radicals who began the task of reflecting critically on the power structures within which they worked. I also confessed my fundamentalism in this respect, and set out the objective of engaging critically with racial oppression as the required pay-off for venturing into this sub-field of the sociology of racism. One of the historical European figures I most admire, the French union leader Jean Jaurès, is quoted as saying: 'The river stays faithful to its origins when it flows toward the sea'.[101] I prefer this vision to the semantic neighbourhood of fundamentalism, and note that Frankenberg also uses a marine metaphor to express the idea that everyone is implicated in the racialisation process: '. . . we all immersed in the waters of history and those waters are pretty murky' (Frankenberg 2001: 74). On further reading I realise that her phrase also has echoes of reverse baptism: here we bathe and become impure? The historical dimension is so vital to the whiteness problematic that I want to use it to engage with a recent critique of whiteness. First though, I want to add the idea of history being relevant to the construction of knowledge, as Troy Duster (1990) points out. The development of science (eugenics in Duster's study) is contingent and political, he argues. Knowledge about genes is a product of social relationships, not a neutral process. The historical development of knowledge about and discourse on 'race', colonialism and its legacy are similarly products. If the historical forces at play in the present are left out of the equation, as most of the white interviewees in the fieldwork appear to do, then a particularly ghostly form of whiteness emerges, and one that enables people to see themselves as unfairly dealt with simply because they are white. The whiteness problematic involves historical method. The question is not whether to explore historical context, but where to stop, because the answer to this is crucial.

So when Eric Kaufman (2006a: 244) suggests, among other criticisms, that whiteness has played 'no role' in Tutsi–Hutu conflict in Rwanda and Burundi, for example, my response is that such a statement requires the suppression of a crucial strand of the problem of social relations, and one that the whiteness problematic would identify.[102] The Rwandan State was created by Belgian colonists, who also formally divided the population into Hutu and Tutsi. Never mind that people already identified themselves as Hutu or Tutsi before this: the point is that the European colonials drew the borders separating Central African nation-states, creating the Congo, Rwanda and Burundi, and *institutionalised* identity into culturally and politically unequal outcomes. The Belgians instigated documents stating the bearer's ethnic identity and made it compulsory to carry them. So, even if we ignore the role of the UN, the USA, France, Belgium and Great Britain as actors in the drama, whiteness had an important part to play in the genocide: it enabled the infrastructure of killing by 'interpellating'[103] Rwandans as 'Hutus' and 'Tutsis' in a particularly adversarial way within the institutional framework of a nation-state, with the stakes being the control of resources that this entails.

Evidence given by survivors to the International Criminal Tribunal for Rwanda frequently records the destruction of people's treacherous ID cards as a strategy for increasing their chances of getting past roadblocks, put there to sift out Tutsis and murder them. The deadly game of 'who's who' played out in Rwanda in 1994 was predicated on the spectre of European colonial power, what Mills would term the legacy of 'white supremacy'. Only white Europeans could wield this kind of classificatory and organisational power in Africa. This is not to deny the agency of the Africans involved in the killings but to highlight, as does Cheryl Harris (1993), the ongoing salience of the past.

Indeed, the case could be made that Rwanda illustrates some key features of whiteness: the political power of white Europeans over people of colour; the drive towards classification of people for reasons of governance; the choice of Tutsis as the favoured group more closely approaching the European norms (physical and cultural); the final wielding of power by the USA, the UK, France and, finally, the UN's choice not to intervene militarily against not particularly well-armed or well-organised militia, thus leaving hundreds of thousands to perish because their lives were of less value. Elements of this story are identified in the various chapters that comprise this book.

The problem of the twenty-first century . . .

Mike Hill's (2004) interpretation of the 2000 US Census is that the racial and ethnic categories deployed by the state have mushroomed to the point where progressive anti-racist movements are losing the capacity to argue that there is in fact a defining line between the powerful and powerless in terms of 'race'. The combination of colour-blind racism and minority ethnic classificatory entrepreneurialism has led to 120 possible racial and ethnic combinations in the 2000 Census.[104] While in the UK there is still a way to go before this level of complexity is achieved, the trend is towards more rather than fewer categories. As we tread the path of enshrining particular identities as formal, and therefore more valuable than others, certain things become more obscure. One of those is the line between 'white' and 'non-white' – I use these terms politically throughout, to talk of power relations and the outcome of them. Turning a heterogeneous world majority into a label of what they are not would be to acquiesce to exactly the logic I have been arguing against. Du Bois's prediction that the problem of the twentieth century would be that of the 'colour line' may well have resonance into the twenty-first, and for a different reason. Colour-blind orthodoxies, proliferating Census categories, classifications of movements as 'immigrant'- rather than 'race'-based, of communities as faith-based, seek to efface the racialisation of populations and the effects of power on racialised bodies. We correspondingly move away from seeing the 'colour line' as a point where culture starts to exceed the stakes of economics in the grid of hierarchies thrown up locally, nationally and internationally. What I mean by this is that the public and psychological wage that convinces the majority of white people to maintain an investment in the racial *status quo* rather than address their grievances upwards is topped up by the presentation of oppression and social unrest as not really to do with 'racism' anyway. Scholars are part of this movement. In the linguistic turn, as Robert

Young notes, 'race' becomes merely a trope, a 'narrative of specificity' (2001). In this way, we are abandoning our attempt to grasp the capacity of whiteness to reproduce its power of naming, reclassifying, returning the responsibility onto its racialised Others, etc. In short, the problem of the twenty-first century is to highlight the colour line, to retrieve it from postmodern relativity and neoliberal downsizing.

Using whiteness can be a structural tool of analysis, a way to interrogate situations by reference to a particular set of associations. Indeed, far from being a 'blunt instrument' (Kaufman 2006b), whiteness can illuminate connections: the process of racialisation and nation-making, identifications with international projects, how class and gender are inherently linked to racialisation. Yet to do so, it requires reorientation towards the material (not taken away from the cultural, but a balance), towards affairs outside the USA and towards empirical studies as well as theoretical or literary ones. You can probably reach the kind of conclusions this might lead you to using other methods and theories, so the claim is not of exclusivity. Instead I see using whiteness as a dot-connecting process that constantly confronts the researcher with his/her location in the 'murky waters'; with the interplay of 'race', gender and class; with the lines within the white group that speak of 'us' and 'them'. Ultimately it should help us to not let the big topics such as immigration, human trafficking and the Anglo-American neo-imperialist project float away like helium balloons from the grasp of sociologists, human geographers, historians, political scientists and activists who want to keep the various forms of racism involved in fuelling such projects at the heart of their analyses.

Notes

Introduction

1 If I am asked to develop a second edition of this text the priority will be to incorporate more material from scholars working on those countries.

2 Contrast for example 'Accuracy in America's assessment' (Farnes 1998) with Fears's (2003) *Washington Post* article. The quotation comes from Weinkopf (2003). A quick google search for 'whiteness studies' throws up numerous examples of hysterical blogs and caricatural reduction of the diversity of scholarship on whiteness to a few headlines involving 'race' treachery and making white students feel uncomfortable in class. Weinkopf even finishes by labelling whiteness studies actors as un-American because they over-racialise analyses.

3 Although see Miles and Phizacklea (1984).

4 The original quote in French is: 'L'impérialisme culturel repose sur le pouvoir d'universaliser les particularismes liés à une tradition historique singulière en les faisant méconnaître comme tels'. Author's translation into English.

5 The American journal *Race Traitor* expresses the objective of abolishing whiteness. Noel Ignatiev's (1997) paper is downloadable online at: *<http://racetraitor.org/abolishthepoint.pdf>*. For Henry Giroux's argument for radicalising whiteness, see Giroux (1997).

6 Gobineau (1853), Knox (1850), Chamberlain (1899).

7 The research on which some of this is based was carried out in the project: *Mobility and unsettlement: new identity construction in contemporary Britain* (ESRC grant RES-148–25–003) 2003–2007. Professor Simon Clarke was the joint Principal Investigator, and Rosie Gilmour the research assistant who did most of the interviews. This project is the source of the interview data used in chapter 9.

Chapter 1

8 Ida Wells-Barnett (1862–1931) was a crusading anti-lynching campaigner. Her best-known work was published in two pamphlets: *Southern Horrors: Lynch Law in All Its Phases* (1892) and *The Red Record: Tabulated Statistics and Alleged Causes of Lynching in the United States* (1895). Both are available online through Project Gutenberg: *<http://www.gutenberg.org/wiki/Main_Page>*.

9 It is tempting to see this as a concrete manifestation of Bob Marley's 'babylon system is the vampire' ('Babylon System', from *Survival*, 1980). Although

this simple equation in the US context is problematic, as the existence of an African-American middle class, Garvey's call for capitalist autonomy and Lamont's (2000) qualitative work testify. It might be a question less of either/ or material values than of a difference in emphasis.

10 The UMN/IRP 2002 one is accessible at (ER) 'Long Island Fair Housing: a state of inequity'. Online: <*http://www.eraseracismny.org/downloads/reports/ ERASE_HousingMonograph.pdf*>.

11 I am prepared to consider the argument that the way dominant groups racialise others is almost exactly the same in parts of the world where Asian, African, or Arab groups enjoy political hegemony over others. Yet this in no way annuls the argument about whiteness. Whiteness has a specific journey involving colonialism, exploration and self-endorsement in the Enlightenment. The institutions of Atlantic slavery and European imperialism set aside the legacy of whiteness from other relations.

12 The examples of the lynched Sicilians in 1891 and Leo Frank in 1915 are of borderline Whites who became 'black' through their status of lynched men. For these stories, see Jacobson (1998), and a short section on Frank in chapter 6.

13 The Southern Poverty Law Center's Intelligence Project (formerly known as 'Klanwatch') provides up-to-date information on such contemporary activities: Online: <*http://www.splcenter.org/intel/intpro.jsp*>.

14 This involves juxtaposing the Bureau of Justice homicide figures broken down by 'race' (of victim and of perpetrator) from 1976 to 2004 with the NAACP/CLP data on people executed broken down by 'race', 1976–2006. Obviously there is a small discrepancy in terms of years.

15 The original article is 85 pages long, but for the more fainthearted reader, abridged versions are available in Delgado and Stefancic (1997) and Roediger (1999).

16 *State of Western Australia v Ward* [2002] HCA 28 (8 August 2002). Referred to variously as *Ward* and *Mirriuwung Gajerrong*; *Members of the Yorta Yorta Aboriginal Community v Victoria* [2002] HCA 58 (12 December 2002).

Chapter 2

17 I find the treatment of *Night of the Living Dead* (Dir. George Romero 1969) in Dyer (1988) particularly interesting. Dyer explores othering mechanisms, the symbiotic relationships of the white subjects in their states of being; live, dead, living dead, etc., and how this represents the free market values and lack of spirituality, as he sees it, of collective whiteness.

18 An excerpt containing 50 items is downloadable online from: <*http://www. cwru.edu/president/aaction/UnpackingTheKnapsack.pdf*>. An alternative feminist version can be found in Frye (2001 [1982]).

19 Strong echoes of Dyer's argument are evident in sociological work (see also psycho-social work in this area by Seshadri-Crooks (2000), Clarke (2003)).

20 Following work by Andrew Herman (1999) on entrepreneurs and senior managers.

21 The students keep a diary for the course, which provides much of McKinney's material. The section in which whiteness as a liability is discussed is chapter 6.

22 She examines the role and effects of 'turning points' on students' experience in greater detail in McKinney (2006).

23 I am going to use this American term, as the book is aimed at both Europe (where it is not used) and North America. Similarly, I appreciate that the use of black (adjective), Black (substantive) is now more frequent in Europe than in North America. Those terms will be used as synonyms for African-American in relation to the USA.

24 See also the film 'Who Killed Vincent Chin?' (Dir. Tajima-Pena, R. and Choy, C., 1988).

25 This is not to say that relations between Asian and other minority groups have been without incident. This is particularly true around the question of economic resources, in majority African-American neighbourhoods where sometimes resentment is expressed towards local shopkeepers. This coalesced around the Latasha Harlins killing by a Korean shopkeeper in March 1991. During the L.A. riots in 1992, for example, Korean-owned groceries and other stores were targeted by predominantly black and Hispanic rioters.

26 See for example CBS documentary and supporting article: 'The Bridge to Gretna, 18 December 2005'. Online: <*http://www.cbsnews.com/stories/2005/12/ 15/60minutes/main1129440.shtml*>, and 'The hurricane that shamed America', broadcast in the UK on Channel 4 in its *Dispatches* series, October 2005 (2005). It is also clear that people from adjoining poor white neighbourhoods suffered, but their plight has not yet been researched or much publicised.

27 In the UK, the term Asian refers to people from the Indian sub-continent and their descendants rather than Chinese, Korean and Japanese in the USA, or Filipinos and Indonesians in the Australian context.

Chapter 3

28 This work began with Bourdieu and Passeron's (1964) study of French university students translated in 1979 as *The Inheritors*. It was developed later in *La Réproduction* (1970), and more fully in *La Distinction* (1979) and especially in the essay 'Forms of Capital' (Bourdieu 1986), an English version of which can be accessed online at: <*http://www.viet-studies.org/Bourdieu_capital.htm/*>. Accessed 3 January 2007.

29 Diane Reay (1998) amends the concept by contending that the value of obtaining a good education is shared by both working-class and middle-class parents (especially the mothers in her study, charged with the emotional labour of upbringing). The difference is in their abilities to bring about advantage for their children. If cultural capital is as important as Bourdieu suggests, it is worth thinking about how people from less culturally-affluent backgrounds who succeed in management, academia and elsewhere acquire it.

30 A similar set of resentments is expressed by interviewees in journalist Lesley White's long *Sunday Times* article on post-2001 riots Oldham (White 2002), where local Pakistani Muslims are seen as 'taking over' particular estates and council funding, largely by means of operationalising the values of previous generations of white working-class Oldhamites.

31 'Geordie' is a term for a native of Newcastle in the North East of England. It is abusively used by outsiders to cover natives of the North East region as a whole.

32 Thanks to Simon Clarke for this point.

33 See Squire (2005) for an analysis of New Labour's framing of these questions in the UK since 1997.

Chapter 4

34 Chapter 6 focuses on Gypsy-Travellers and Jews.

35 Scottish surgeon Knox's *The Races of Men* (1850), and French aristocrat Comte de Gobineau's *Essai sur l'inégalité des races humaines* (1853–1855), are key works in this regard.

36 For contemporary echoes of this theme, see Moran (2005).

37 See also the excellent Marriott and Matsumura (1999) for a collection of contemporary work on the poor in London and other British cities.

38 Online: <*http://www.victorianweb.org/history/race/rcov.html*>. Accessed 8 January 2007.

39 *Down in Tennessee*, 1864: 188–189.

40 Coalville is a small former mining town in Leicestershire, England.

Chapter 5

41 Versions of this section appear in Garner (2003) and (2007a).

42 According to Governor Stapleton's 1678 Census of the Leeward Islands (Nevis, Antigua, St Christopher, and Montserrat), the Irish made up 18.3 per cent of the overall population, i.e. 30 per cent of whites (45 per cent of the nearly 19,000 counted). They were most numerous in Montserrat (1,869 out of 3,674, i.e. 51 per cent), where they outnumbered the other white groups as well as the Blacks.

43 Some were also important actors in the Spanish Caribbean colonies, such as Cuba and Puerto Rico, just as they were later in South America as immigrants as well as missionaries from the earliest days. Dominant groups however could also float competing versions of whiteness, as David Lambert (2005a, b) illustrates in his studies of Barbados.

44 Only a couple of such revolts are supported by documentary evidence. An escape and subsequent attacks in Barbados in 1655 (Beckles 1990: 513, Allen 1994b: 230–231); and a more elaborate one of these, a plot in 1686, which ultimately resulted in no prosecutions of the Irish allegedly involved. In a context in which free Irishmen (who had served out their indentureship) could be whipped, fined and imprisoned even for publicly slurring the English Crown (Beckles 1990: 515), the fact that no charges were pressed against any Irishman in relation to a potentially large-scale revolt points to a lack of evidence that any were involved.

45 Willoughby to Privy Council, Dec. 16, 1667, C.O 1/21, no.162.

46 Willoughby to King, Sept. 16, 1667, Stowe MS 735, folio 19, British Library.

47 See Brereton (1998), Kuethe (1986), Quintanilla (2003), Garner (2003).

48 Cf. Beckles's work on gender and identity in Barbados (1995). The characteristics imputed to indentured white women in the early period were very similar to those attributed to black women working as enslaved labourers later. By the time that field work was exclusively a black domain, the notion of white woman had undergone a transformation into the bearer of morality and purity.

49 Guyana's coastal strip is reclaimed land (i.e. below sea level). An elaborate system of canals and dykes makes it habitable and cultivatable, and requires constant upkeep. Hence the importance of irrigation.

50 *The Colonist*, 16/4/1856. The riots lasted six days in February 1856, causing an estimated $G 267,209 worth of damage.

51 *Parliamentary Papers, 1847/8* 23, part 2 (p.206).

52 *The Colonist*, 22/6/1856.

53 The introductory essay by Appelbaum *et al.* (2003b) is an excellent overview for readers interested in looking at the broader canvas.

54 Cf. Cecily Forde-Jones's (1998) study of poor white women in Barbados, where moral character/respectability is the criteria for receiving parish support.

55 Also silence about star footballer Juan Sebastian Veron's similar origins (Farred 2004).

Chapter 6

56 Cf. Jacobson's (1998) chapter on 'race relations' in the US context.

57 One of the anti-semitic cartoons referred to by Dermot Keogh (1998: 58) depicts Irish Jews with ringlets, large noses and thick lips. Suzanna Chan (2005) begins her discussion of Irish whiteness with one of them.

58 See 'Patrin' website for links: *<http://www.geocities.com/Patrin/holcaust.htm>*. Accessed 8 January 2007.

59 As well as the excellent overviews by Kenrick and Puxon (1972) and Mayall (1988), the reader is directed to the University of Minnesota's Center for Holocaust and Genocide Studies webpages dealing with the persecution of gypsies at: *<http://www.chgs.umn.edu/HistoriesNarrativesDocumen/RomaSintiGypsies_/GypsiesAPersecutedRace/gypsiesapersecutedrace.html>*. Accessed 8 January 2007. The University of Hertfordshire (UK) also has a Romani Studies series: *<http://perseus.herts.ac.uk/uhinfo/university-of-hertfordshire-press/romani-studies/introduction-to-romani-studies.cfm)>*. Accessed 8 January 2007.

60 It is illegal to discriminate against a person due to membership of the Traveller community in both the Equal Employment Acts, 1998–2004, and the Equal Status Acts, 2000–2004.

61 The website of Pavee Point, the Irish Travellers' umbrella group, can be accessed online at: <http://www.paveepoint.ie/>. Accessed 8 January 2007.

62 44 per cent of Travellers reported living in fear of attack and persecution on the roadside (*Citizen Traveller* 2000).

63 Online at: *<http://www.opsi.gov.uk/acts/acts1994/Ukpga_19940033_en_1.htm>*.

64 In the early 1980s, I was told approvingly by a local community leader about a large lay-by in Norfolk (a mainly rural county in the East of England) used frequently by Travellers during the summer months. In order to prevent such use, a local farmer had tipped a large quantity of manure onto the site during a period when it was vacant between stays. The Travellers did not return that summer. Residual matter is thus deployed in this instance as a means of out-polluting the polluters. Such an action in another context would surely be considered illegal, and a health and safety matter. Yet it was supported locally because it prevented greater social pollution.

65 BBC News, 11 March 2005. *The Sun*'s 'Stamp on the Camps' front page campaign came in for particular criticism.

66 Evidence given to the ODPM Report in 2004 suggested that 80–90 per cent of Traveller applications for development are refused, compared to 10–20 per cent of applications from the settled community, ODPM 2004: 5, 49.

67 MORI/Stonewall poll, May/June 2002.

68 Martin was found guilty of killing Fred Barras, a youth whom Martin found burgling his property in 2000. Controversy raged around the incident because

Martin was depicted as the victim, and another man involved in the attempted crime had been wounded and then sued Martin. In-depth coverage can be found at the *Guardian*'s dedicated webpage. Online: <*http://www. guardian.co.uk/martin/0,,214318,00.html*>. Accessed 8 January 2007.

69 See also other *Occidental Quarterly* issues: 3(2) summer 2003, 3(3) Fall 2003, and 4(2) summer 2004.

70 See also the emerging agenda of questioning British Muslims' loyalty to Britain in the wake of the 7/7 bombings.

Chapter 7

71 Based on an amalgamation of a number of publications; Garner (2003, 2007a, b, c).

72 In 1843, O'Connell made a speech in reply to the Cincinatti Repeal Association's letter to him. Tens of thousands of signatures for the petition against slavery had been gathered in Ireland. See Allen (1994a: 172–176) for fuller treatment of this.

73 Within the USA as a whole, the number of Irish immigrants had more or less doubled every five years over the 1821–1850 period.

74 Appel's article also covers class occupations in a very thorough survey.

75 Much subtler treatment of this can be found in Jacobson (1995).

76 I use this term to reflect the institutional dominance and role played in policy-making by the Catholic Church from the inception of the State until the 1990s. See Powell (1992), Kiely (1999).

77 Robbie McVeigh (1998a) uses this as the title of his contribution to Paul Hainsworth's edited collection of essays on Northern Ireland.

78 There is a summary of such work in Garner (2003: 59–66).

79 I point the reader towards the resistance to the idea of the UK–Catholic Irish becoming unproblematically white that is the subject of work by Hickman (1998), Walter (1998), Mac an Ghaill (2001), Hickman *et al.* (2005).

Chapter 8

80 All statistics can easily be accessed through the UNHCR website: <*http:// www.unhcr.org/cgi-bin/texis/vtx/statistics*>. The document explaining 'protracted situations' is <*http://www.unhcr.org/cgi-bin/texis/vtx/statistics/opendoc. pdf?tbl=STATISTICS&id=40ed5b384*>.

81 This excludes Palestinian refugees, of whom there are around four million, because they fall under the responsibility of the United Nations Relief and Works Agency for Palestine Refugees in the Near East (UNRWA). Who is counted, by whom, and under what category they fall, are politically contingent processes.

82 Figures for 2005: 6.7 per cent in the Americas; sub-Saharan Africa, 30.6 per cent; Central Asia, South-West Asia, North Africa and Middle East, 29.4 per cent; Asia and Pacific, 10.3 per cent.

83 The parliamentarians mentioned here are backbenchers, but members of the governing parties: Fianna Fáil and the Progressive Democrats have governed in coalition since June 1997.

84 Particularly radio station 96FM, and local free newspaper, *Inside Cork*, which ran a series of 'exposés' on the conditions for asylum seekers, e.g. 'Shock

Government Disclosure on Asylum Welfare benefits: Irish significantly worse off', *Inside Cork* front page headline, 31 January 2002.

85 As of end 2005, the ratio stood at 6.5:1.

86 European Court of Justice. *Chen judgement* (Case C-200/02: *http://curia.eu.int/jurisp/cgi-bin/form.pl?lang=en*) October, 2004.

87 Remember the late Peter Fryer's (1984: 1) striking opening sentence: 'There were Africans in Britain before the English came here'.

88 The enlargement of the European Union to include Central and Eastern European states in 2004 means that in some countries, people such as Czechs, Poles and Latvians, among others, who would previously had to have work permits are no longer subject to passport control since they are EU Nationals rather than 'Third Country Nationals' (TCNs).

Chapter 9

89 Much could be made of the mass of hierarchical social relations binding city and country, which are glossed over in this ideological manoeuvre. See, for example, Raymond Williams (1973).

90 Two people sent cuttings from tabloid newspapers, with handwritten messages, but these were exceptions.

91 This homogenising practice is to an extent replicated in academia. Lisa Malkki (1995) critiques the tendency in 'refugee studies' to turn 'refugee' into an identity that trumps others.

92 As I write this, in Autumn 2006, the story of the arson of a Muslim dairy in Windsor, near London, is in the media. The owner had sought planning permission for a prayer room, and locals had opposed this on the grounds that there were not enough Muslims locally to justify this. See Barnett (2006).

93 The term 'Scouser' refers to a native of Liverpool. The city of Liverpool has two football teams, Liverpool and Everton, with a rivalry going back to the late nineteenth century, when Everton was a Protestant- and Liverpool a Catholic-supported and run team.

94 The extent of exactly this process is the subject of discussion in critical examinations of multiculturalism such as those put forward by Parekh (2000) and Modood (2005).

95 Such as the former Chair of the Commission for Racial Equality, Trevor Phillips, Home Secretary, John Reid, former Home Secretary, Jack Straw, Home Office Minister, Ruth Kelly, Chancellor, Gordon Brown and PM, Tony Blair's interventions on Britishness. See CRE (2005), Kearney (2005).

96 As I write, in autumn 2006, British Foreign Secretary (and former Home Secretary) Jack Straw raises the idea that wearing the veil is a practice that enforces separation, and is read by many people as threatening and frustrating. This goes immediately to the top of the media agenda, and coalesces around the case of a school teacher, Aysha Azmi, sacked by her local authority for refusing to remove her veil in class in front of male colleagues.

Conclusion

97 It is one of Frankenberg's eight elements of a definition of whiteness (2001: 76) and she uses the term 'standpoint'.

98 And some of the Australian work that we have not had space to cover (Moran

2005). I am certain that such fieldwork in Ireland would elicit similarly-shaped narratives of beleagueredness.

99   Which is the case in Modell's 'Keep Them Out', filmed in a small town on the South coast of England in the 2002–2003 period.

100 While my interest in the Caribbean is all my own, I acknowledge becoming interested in Latin America through Bonnett's (2000) case study in his introductory text and remarks in his (2003) review of Back and Ware (2001).

101 The French quote is: 'C'est en allant vers la mer que le fleuve reste fidèle à sa source'.

102 Moreover, the stark choice of 'race' or ethnicity presented in this section (Kaufman 2006a: 244–246) is based on the idea that 'race' refers strictly to phenotypical difference, a concept not infrequently held, and which is erroneously grounded in the idea that the nineteenth-century paradigm of body-fixated race science is the mainstream defining form of racism. In this book it is argued that culture has always been intrinsically related to 'race', so I do recognise the distinction between 'race' referring primarily to physical difference, and ethnicity referring to 'culture'.

103 'Interpellation' is the Marxist theorist Louis Althusser's term to describe a mechanism whereby the human subject is 'constituted', or hailed (constructed) by pre-given structures. In this instance I am indicating that the social identity invoked by the label 'Hutu' and 'Tutsi' *under colonial rule* corresponds to a particular set of positions constructed by the Belgian authorities, with Tutsi generally favoured economically and politically over Hutus, but subordinate to the Europeans.

104 'For Census 2000, 63 possible combinations of the six basic racial categories exist, including six categories for those who report exactly one race, and 57 categories for those who report two or more races'. Online: <*http://www. census.gov/population/www/socdemo/race/racefactcb.html*>. Accessed 9 January 2007.

Bibliography

Aaranovitch, D. (2004) 'They blame the buses. I blame the bigots', *Guardian*, 27 April.

Adams, M. and Burke, P. J. (2006) 'Recollections of September 11 in three English villages: identifications and self-narrations', *Journal of Ethnic and Migration Studies* 32(6): 983–1003.

Adamson, A. (1972) *Sugar Without Slaves*, New Haven: Yale University Press.

African Refugee Network (1999) *African Refugees: a needs analysis*, Dublin: ARN.

Agamben, G. (1998) *Homo Sacer: sovereign power and bare life*, Palo Alto: Stanford University Press.

Ahmed, S. (2004) 'Declarations of whiteness: the non-performativity of anti-racism', *borderlands* ejournal 3(2). Online: *<http://www.borderlandsejournal. adelaide.edu.au/issues/vol3no2.html>*

Akenson, D. (1997) *If the Irish Ran the World: Montserrat, 1630–1730*, Montreal: McGill/Queen's University Press.

Allen, K. (2000) *The Celtic Tiger: the myth of social partnership*, Manchester: Manchester University Press.

Allen, T. (1994a) *The Invention of the White Race (Vol. 1)*, New York: Verso.

—— (1994b) *The Invention of the White Race (Vol. 2)*, New York: Verso.

Almaguer, T. (1994) *Racial Fault Lines: the origins of white supremacy in California*, Berkeley: University of California Press.

Amnesty International/FAQs (2001) *The Views of Black and Ethnic Minorities*, Dublin: AI.

Andersen, M. (2003) 'Whitewashing race', in Doane and Bonilla-Silva (eds), pp. 22–34.

Anderson, W. (2005) *The Cultivation of Whiteness: science, health and racial destiny in Australia*, Melbourne: Melbourne University Press.

Anderson-Levy, L. (2005) 'Place-(ing) Race, Race-(ing) Place: the place of citizenship in the (re)production of whiteness in Jamaica'. Paper given at Caribbean Studies Association Annual Meeting, Santo Domingo, May 2005.

Annual Review of Population Law (1989) 'Fajujonu v. Minister for Justice' 16:1688, December 1989.

Anzaldúa, G. and Moraga, C. (eds) (1983) *This Bridge Called My Back: writings by radical women of color*, New York: Kitchen Table/Women of Color.

Appel, J. (1971) 'From shanties to lace curtains: the Irish image in Puck, 1876–1910', *Comparative Studies in Society and History* 13(4): 365–375.

Appelbaum, N. (2003) *Muddied Waters: race, region, and local history in Colombia, 1846–1948*, Durham, NC: Duke University Press.

Appelbaum, N., MacPherson, A. and Rosemblatt, K. (2003a) *Race and Nation in Modern Latin America*, Chapel Hill, NC: University of North Carolina Press.

—— (2003b) 'Introduction: racial nations', in Appelbaum *et al.*, pp. 1–31.

Arnesen, E. (2001) 'Whiteness and the historians' imagination', *international Labor and Working Class History* 60: 3–32.

Back, L. (1996) *New Ethnicities and Urban Culture: social identity and racism in the lives of young people*, London: UCL Press.

—— (2003) 'Falling from the sky', *Patterns of Prejudice* 37(3): 341–353.

Back, L. and Ware, V. (2001) *Out of Whiteness: color, politics and culture*, Chicago: University of Chicago Press.

Bagguley, P. and Hussain, Y. (2005) 'Citizenship, ethnicity and identity: British Pakistanis after the 2001 "Riots"', *Sociology* 39(3): 407–425.

Baker, D. (2006) 'Funny ha ha', *Catalyst* 8 December. Online: <*http://www.catalystmagazine.org/Default.aspx.LocID-0hgnew0o4.RefLocID-0hg01b001006009.Lang-EN.htm*>.

Baldwin, J. (1955) *Notes on a Native Son*, Boston: Beacon Books.

—— (1984) 'On being White and other lies', *Essence*.

—— (1985a) 'Color', in *The Price of the Ticket*, London: Michael Joseph, pp. 312–318.

—— (1985b) 'The American Dream and the American Negro', in *Price of the Ticket*, pp. 403–407.

—— (1985c) 'White man's guilt', in *Price of the Ticket*, pp. 409–414.

Balibar, E. (1991) 'Is there a neo-racism?', in E. Balibar and I. Wallerstein, *Race, Class, Nation: ambiguous identities*, New York: Verso, pp. 17–28.

Bancroft, A. (2005) *Roma and Gypsy-Travellers in Europe: modernity, race, space and exclusion*, Aldershot: Ashgate.

Banton, M. (1967) *Race Relations*, London: Tavistock.

Barany, Z. (2001) *The East European Gypsies: regime change, marginality, and ethnopolitics*, Cambridge: Cambridge University Press.

Barker, M. (1981) *The New Racism*, London: Junction Books.

—— (1990) 'Biology and the new racism', in D. Goldberg (ed.) *Anatomy of Racism*, Minneapolis: University of Minnesota Press, pp. 18–37.

Barnett, L. (2006) 'Fire-bombing of Muslim dairy highlights tensions in Windsor', *Times Online*, 5 October. Online: <http://www.timesonline.co.uk/article/0,,2-2390168,00.html>.

Barot, R. and Bird, J. (2001) 'Racialization: the genealogy and critique of a concept', *Ethnic and Racial Studies* 24(4): 601–618.

Barrett, J. and Roediger, D. (1997) 'Inbetween peoples: race, nationality and the "New Immigrant" working class', *Journal of American Ethnic History*, Spring: 3–44.

—— (2004) 'Making new immigrants inbetween: Irish hosts and white pan-ethnicity, 1890–1930', in N. Foner and G. Frederickson (eds) *Not Just Black and White: immigration and race, then and now*, New York: Russell Sage Foundation Press, pp. 167–196.

—— (2005) 'The Irish and the "Americanization" of the "New Immigrants" in the streets and in the churches of the urban United States, 1900–1930', *Journal of American Ethnic History* 24(4): 4–33.

Barry, J., Herrity, B. and Solan, S. (1989) *The Travellers' Health Status Study*, Dublin: Health Research Board.

Bashford, A. (2000) ' "Is White Australia possible?" Race, colonialism and tropical medicine', *Ethnic and Racial Studies* 23(2): 248–271.

Baudrillard, J. (1984) *Simulacres et Simulation*, Paris: Galilée.

Bauman, Z. (1989) *Modernity and the Holocaust*, Cambridge: Polity Press.

—— (1998) *Modernity and Ambivalence*, Cambridge: Polity Press.

Beckles, H. (1990) 'A riotous and unruly lot': Irish indentured servants and free-men in the English West Indies, 1644–1713', *William and Mary Quarterly* 47(1): 503–522.

—— (1995) 'Sex and gender in the historiography of Caribbean slavery', in V. Shepherd, B. Brereton and B. Bailey (eds) *Engendering History: Caribbean women in a historical perspective*, Kingston, Jamaica: Ian Randle Press, pp. 125–140.

Belchem, J. (2005) 'Comment: Whiteness and the Liverpool-Irish', *Journal of British Studies* 44: 146–152.

Bernstein, I. (1990) *The New York Draft Riots of 1863: their significance for American society in the Civil War period*, New York: Oxford University Press.

Bettie, J. (2000) 'Women without class: Chicas, Cholas, Trash, and the presence/absence of class identity', *Signs* 26(1): 1–35.

Billig, M. (1991) *Ideology, Rhetoric and Opinion*, London: Sage.

Bonilla-Silva, E. (2003) ' "New Racism", color-blind racism and the future of whiteness in the USA', in Doane and Bonilla-Silva (eds), pp. 271–284.

Bonnett, A. (2000) *White Identities: an historical and international introduction*, London: Longman.

—— (2003) Book Review: 'Out of Whiteness', Back and Ware, *Sociology* 37(3): 623–624.

Booth, C. (1902) *Labour and Life of the People of London*, London: Macmillan.

Bordieu, P. (1979) *La distinction: critique sociale du jugement*, Paris: Éditions de Minuit.

—— (1984) *Distinction: a social critique of the judgement of taste*, Cambridge, MA: Harvard University Press.

—— (1986) 'The (three) forms of capital', in J.G. Richardson (ed.) *Handbook of Theory and Research in the Sociology of Education*, New York: Greenwood Press, pp. 241–258.

Bourdieu P. and Passeron, J.-C. (1964) *Les Héritiers: Les étudiants et la culture*, Paris: Editions de Minuit.

—— (1970) *La Reproduction: éléments pour une théorie du système d'enseignement*, Paris: Editions de Minuit.

—— (1977) *Outline of a Theory of Practice*, Cambridge: Cambridge University Press.

Bourdieu P. and Passeron, J.-C. (1979) *The Inheritors: French students and their relation to culture*, Chicago, Ill.: University of Chicago Press.

Bourdieu, P. and Wacquant, L. (1998) 'Sur les ruses de la raison impérialiste', *Actes de la Recherche en Sciences Sociales*, no.121–122: 109–118.

Brander Rasmussen, B., Nexica, I.B., Klinenberg, E. and Wray, M. (eds) (2001) *The Making and Unmaking of Whiteness*, Durham, NC: Duke University Press.

Brereton, B. (1998) 'The White elite of Trinidad, 1838–1950', in H. Johnson and K. Watson (eds) *The White Minority in the Caribbean*, Kingston/London: Ian Randle Press/James Currey, pp. 32–70.

Bridges, A. (1984) *A City in the Republic: antebellum New York and the origins of machine politics*, Ithaca, NY: Cornell University Press.

Bright, M. (2004) 'Asylum seekers? Not here, not even for a few minutes', *Observer*, 25 April.

Brodkin, K. (1994) 'How did Jews become White folks?', in S. Gregory and R. Sanjck (eds) *Race*, New Brunswick, NJ: Rutgers University Press.

—— (1998) *How Jews became White Folks: and what that says about race in America*, New Brunswick, NJ: Rutgers University Press.

Bruce, S. (2000) *Fundamentalism*, Cambridge: Polity Press.

Buchanan, S. and Grillo, B. (2004) 'What's the story? Reporting on asylum in the British media', *Forced Migration Review* 19(1): 41–43.

Burchill, J. (2001) 'A nasty taste in the mouth', *Guardian*, 5 May.

Burkeman, O. (2006) 'The phoney war on Christmas', *Guardian*, 8 December.

Burleigh, M. (2000) *The Third Reich: a new history*, London: Pan.

Byrne, B. (2006) *White Lives: the interplay of 'race', class and gender in everyday life*, London: Routledge.

Carmichael, S. and Hamilton, C. (1967) *Black Power: the politics of liberation*, New York: Random House.

Carroll, D. (1995) *French Literary Fascism: nationalism, anti-semitism, and the ideology of culture*, Princeton, NJ: Princeton University Press.

Castles, S., Korac, M., Vasta, E. and Vertovec, S. (2002) 'Integration: mapping the field', Home Office Online Report 29/03. Online: <*http://www.blink.org.uk/docs/ mapping_the_field.pdf*>

Central Statistics Office (CSO) (1998) *The Demographic Situation of the Traveller Community in April 1996*, Cork: CSO.

Centre for Contemporary Cultural Studies (CCCS) (1982) *The Empire Strikes Back: race and racism in 70s' Britain*, London: Hutchinson.

Chamberlain, H.S. (1899) *The Foundations of the Nineteenth Century*, Munich: Bruckmann.

Chan, S. (2005) 'Some notes on deconstructing Ireland's Whiteness: immigrants, emigrants and the perils of jazz', *Variant* 22. Online: <*http://www.variant. randomstate.org/22texts/Whiteness.html*>

(charles), H. (1992) 'Whiteness – the relevance of politically colouring the "Non" ', in H. Hinds, A. Phoenix and J. Stacey (eds) *Working out New Directions for Women's Studies*, London: Taylor and Francis, pp. 29–36.

Citizen Traveller (2000) *A Survey of Travellers*, Dublin: Citizen Traveller.

Clarke, S. (2003) *Social Theory, Psychoanalysis and Racism*, London: Palgrave.

Clarke, S. and Garner, S. (2005) 'Fieldnote: psychoanalysis, identity and asylum', *Psychoanalysis, Culture and Society* 10: 197–206.

—— (forthcoming) *White Identities,* London: Pluto.

Clementi, C. (1937) *A Constitutional History of British Guiana,* London: Macmillan.

Cohen, D. (2002) 'Who was who? Race and Jews in turn-of-the-century Britain', *Journal of British Studies* 41(4): 460–483.

Cohen, S. (2002) *Folk Devils and Moral Panics,* 3rd edn, New York: Routledge.

Collins, M. (2004) *The Likes of Us: a biography of the white working-class,* London: Granta.

Colloredo-Mansfeld, R. (1998) ' "Dirty Indians", radical *Indigenas,* and the political economy of social difference in modern Ecuador', *Bulletin of Latin American Research* 17(2): 185–205.

Commission for Racial Equality (CRE) (2005) *Citizenship and Belonging: what is Britishness?,* London: CRE.

Cook, R. (2001) 'Speech to Social Market Foundation', *Guardian,* 19 April.

Corcoran, M. (1997) 'Clandestine destinies: the informal economic sector and Irish immigrant incorporation', in J. Mac Laughlin (ed.) *Location and Dislocation in Contemporary Irish Society,* Cork: Cork University Press, pp. 236–252.

Coulter, C. (2002) 'Minister with a mission to push through reform of the system', *Irish Times,* 13 July.

Cox, O.C. (1948) *Caste, Class and Race,* New York: Doubleday.

Craton, M. (1997) *Empire, Enslavement and Freedom in the Caribbean,* Kingston/London: Ian Randle Press/James Currey.

Cresswell, T. (1996) *In Place, Out of Place: geography, ideology and transgression,* Minneapolis: University of Minnesota Press.

Cullen, P. (1997) 'The 1997 Border Campaign', in J. Mac Laughlin and E. Crowley (eds) *Under the Belly of the Tiger: class, race, culture and identity in the global Ireland,* Dublin: Irish Reporter Publications, pp. 101–107.

—— (2005) 'How pupil power brings McDowell to book', *Irish Times,* 26 March.

Cusack, J. (1997) 'Officers accused of targeting black passengers', *Irish Times,* 18 October.

Cutler, D., Glaeser, E and Vigdor, J. (1999) 'The rise and decline of the American ghetto', *Journal of Political Economy* 107(3): 455–506.

Daniels, J. (1997) *White Lies: race, class, gender, and sexuality in white supremacist discourse,* New York: Routledge.

Dávila, J. (2003) *Diploma of Whiteness: race and social policy in Brazil, 1917–1945,* Durham, NC: Duke University Press.

Davis, M. (1992) *City of Quartz: excavating the future in Los Angeles,* New York: Vintage.

Dei, G. (1999) 'The denial of difference: reframing anti-racist praxis', *Race, Ethnicity and Education* 2(1): 17–38.

—— (2000) 'Towards an anti-racism discursive framework', in G. Dei and A. Calliste (eds) *Power, Knowledge and Anti-Racism Education: a critical reader,* Halifax, NS: Fernwood, pp. 23–40.

De la Cadena, M. (1998) 'Silent racism and intellectual superiority in Peru', *Bulletin of Latin American Research* 17(2): 143–164.

De la Torre, C. (1999) 'Everyday forms of racism in contemporary Ecuador: the experiences of middle-class Indians', *Ethnic and Racial Studies* 22(1): 91–112.

Delgado, R. and Stefancic, J. (eds) (1997) *Critical White Studies: looking behind the mirror*, Philadelphia: Temple University Press.

Department of Justice, Equality and Law Reform (Ireland) (2000) *The First Progress Report of the Committee to Monitor and Co-ordinate the Implementation of the Recommendations of the Task Force on the Travelling Community*, Dublin: Government Publications.

Dieter, R. (1998) *The Death Penalty in Black and White: who lives, who dies, who decides*, Death Penalty Information Center. Online: <*http://www.deathpenaltyinfo.org/article.php?scid=45&did=539*>. Accessed 16 July 2006.

Dietrich, H. (2005) 'The desert front – EU refugee camps in North Africa?', *Statewatch News*, March 2005. Online: <*http://www.libertysecurity.org/article415.html*>. Accessed 8 January.

Doane, A. and Bonilla-Silva, E. (eds) (2003) *White Out: the continuing significance of racism*, New York: Routledge.

D'Onofrio, L. and Munk, K. (2004) *Understanding the stranger. Final report*, London: ICAR. [Online: <*http://www.icar.org.uk/pdf/uts003.pdf*>]

Donohue, M. (1997) 'Callely targets "rogue" asylum seekers', *Irish Times*, 26 November.

Douglas, M. (1966) *Purity and Danger: an analysis of concepts of pollution and taboo*, London: Routledge.

Du Bois, W.E.B. (1996 [1903]) *The Souls of Black Folk*, New York: Penguin.

—— (1998 [1935]) *Black Reconstruction in the United States, 1860–1880*, New York: Free Press.

—— (1999 [1920]) *Dark Water: voices from within the veil*, Mineola, NY: Dover Publications.

Duster, T. (1990) *Backdoor to Eugenics*, New York: Routledge.

Dyer, R. (1988) 'White', *Screen* 29(4): 44–64.

—— (1997) *White*, London: Routledge.

Ellison, R. (1952) *Invisible Man*, New York: Random House.

Engels, F. (1969 [1844]) *The Condition of the Working Class in England: from personal observation and authentic sources*, St Albans: Panther.

Equality Authority (Ireland) (2006) *Annual Report 2005*, Dublin: Equality Authority.

European Commission (1998) *Eurobarometer 1997*, Brussels: EC.

—— (2001) *Eurobarometer 2000*, Brussels: EC.

Eze, E. (1997) *Race and the Enlightenment: a Reader*, Boston: Blackwell.

Fanning, B. (2002) *Racism and Social Change in the Republic of Ireland*, Manchester: Manchester University Press.

Fanon, F. (1967) *Black Skin, White Masks*, New York: Grove Press.

Farnes, D. (1998) 'Frivolous courses pervasive at top American colleges' (Accuracy in Academia). Online: <*http://www.academia.org/campus_reports/1998/september_1998_1.html*>.

Farough, S. (2004) 'The social geographies of White masculinities', *Critical Sociology* 30(2): 241–264.

Farred, G. (2004) 'Fiaca and Veron-ismo: race and silence in Argentine football', *Leisure Studies* 23(1): 47–61.

Fears, D. (2003) 'Hue and cry over whiteness studies: an academic field's take on race stirs interest and anger', *Washington Post*, 22 June.

Fekete, L. (2002) 'Minister defends deportation drive', *IRR News*, 1 September.

Feldman, D. (1994) *Englishmen and Jews: social relations and political culture, 1840–1914*, New Haven: Yale University Press.

Field, B. (2001) 'Whiteness, racism, and identity', *International Labor and Working Class History* 60: 48–56.

Fine, M., Powell, L., Weis, M. and Mun Wong, L. (eds) (1996) *Off White: readings on race, power and society*, New York: Routledge.

Finney, N. and Peach, E. (2004) *Attitudes Toward Asylum Seekers, Refugees and Other Immigrants: a literature review for the CRE*, London: ICAR.

Foner, P. (ed.) (1999) *Frederick Douglass: selected speeches and writing*, Chicago: Lawrence Hill Books.

Foote, N. (2006) 'Race, state and nation in early twentieth century Ecuador', *Nations and Nationalism* 12(2): 261–278.

Forde-Jones, C. (1998) 'Mapping racial boundaries: gender, race, and poor relief in Barbadian Plantation Society', *Journal of Women's History* 10(3): 9–31.

Fox, D.F. (1917) 'The negro vote in old New York', *Political Science Quarterly* 32: 252–275.

Fox, J. and Zawitz, M. (2004) 'Homicide trends in the United States', US Department of Justice, Bureau of Justice Statistics. Online: *http://www.ojp.usdoj.gov/bjs/homicide/homtrnd.htm/*. Accessed 31 October 2006.

Frankenberg, R. (1994) *White Women, Race Matters*, Madison: University of Wisconsin Press.

—— (ed.) (1997) *Displacing Whiteness: essays in social and cultural criticism*, Durham, NC: Duke University Press.

—— (2001) 'The mirage of an unmarked Whiteness', in Brander Rasmussen *et al.*, pp. 72–96.

Frederickson, G. (1988) *The Arrogance of Race: historical perspectives on slavery, racism and social inequality*, Hanover, NH: Wesleyan University Press.

Frye, M. (1983) 'On being White: toward a feminist understanding of race and race supremacy', in *The Politics of Reality: essays in feminist theory*, Freedom, CA: Crossing Press, pp. 110–127.

—— (1992) 'White woman feminist, 1983–92', in *Wilful Virgin: essays in feminism, 1976–1992*, Berkeley, CA: Crossing Press, pp. 147–169.

—— (2001) 'White woman feminist, 1983–92', in B. Boxill (ed.) *Race and Racism*, Oxford: Oxford University Press, pp. 83–100.

Fryer, P. (1984) *Staying Power: the history of black people in Britain*, London: Pluto.

Gainer, B. (1972) *The Alien Invasion: the origins of the 1905 Aliens Act*, London: Heinemann.

Garland, J. and Chakraborti, N. (2006) ' "Race", space and place: examining identity and cultures of exclusion in rural England', *Ethnicities* 6(2): 159–177.

Garner, S. (2003) *Racism in the Irish Experience*, London: Pluto.

Garner, S. (2006) 'The uses of whiteness: what sociologists working on Europe can learn from North American work on whiteness', *Sociology* 40(2): 257–275.

—— (2007a) 'Atlantic crossing: whiteness as a Trans-Atlantic experience', *Atlantic Studies* 4(1): 117–132.

—— (2007b) 'Ireland and immigration: explaining the absence of the far right', *Patterns of Prejudice* 41(2): 109–130.

—— (2007c) 'Babies, blood and entitlement: gendered citizenship and asylum in the Republic of Ireland', *Parliamentary Affairs* 60(3).

—— (forthcoming) 'Opposition to asylum in provincial England: the Portishead case'.

Garner, S. and Moran, A. (2006) 'Asylum and the nation-state: putting the "order" back into "borders" in Australia and the Republic of Ireland', in R. Lentin and A. Lentin (eds) *Race and State*, Newcastle: Cambridge Scholars' Press, pp. 103–120.

Gibbons, M. (2004) 'White Trash: a class relevant scapegoat for the cultural elite', *Journal of Mundane Behaviour* 5(1). Online: <http://mundanebehavior.org/index2.htm/>. Accessed on 22 November 2006.

Gibson, S. (2003) 'Accommodating strangers: British hospitality and the asylum hotel debate', *Journal for Cultural Research* 7(4): 367–386.

Gilman, S. (1991) *The Jew's Body*, New York: Routledge.

Gilroy, P. (2004) *After Empire: melancholia or convivial culture?*, London: Routledge.

Giroux, H. (1997) 'White noise: racial politics and the pedagogy of Whiteness', in H. Giroux, *Channel Surfing: race talk and the destruction of today's youth*, New York: St Martin's Press, pp. 89–136.

—— (1998) 'White noise: toward a pedagogy of whiteness', in K. Myrsiades and L. Myrsiades (eds) *Race-ing Representation*, Boulder, CO: Rowman and Littlefield, pp. 42–76.

Gobineau, A. (1853–55) *Essai sur l'inégalité des races humaines*, Paris.

Goldberg, D. (1990) *Anatomy of Racism*, Minneapolis: University of Minnesota Press.

—— (2000) *The Racial State*, Boston: Blackwell.

Goodhart, D. (2004) 'Too diverse', *Prospect*, February.

Gotham, K. (2000) 'Urban space, restrictive covenants and the origins of racial residential segregation in a US city, 1900–50', *International Journal of Urban and Regional Research* 24(3): 616–633.

Gould, S. (1997 [1992]) *The Mismeasure of Man*, 3rd edn, London: Penguin.

Grant, M. (1916) *The Passing of the Great Race: the racial basis of European history*, New York: Charles Scribner.

Griffin, G. (1998) 'Speaking of whiteness: disrupting white innocence', *Journal of the Mid-West Modern Language Association* 31(3): 3–14.

Grillo, R. (2005) ' "Saltdean can't cope": protests against asylum seekers in an English seaside suburb', *Ethnic and Racial Studies* 28(2): 235–260.

Grün, R. (1998) 'Becoming White: Jews and Armenians in the Brazilian ethnic mosaic', *Anthropological Journal on European Cultures* 7(2): 107–130.

Guerin, P. (2002) 'Racism and the media in Ireland: setting the anti-immigration agenda', in Lentin and McVeigh (eds), pp. 91–101.

Guglielmo, J. and Salerno, S. (2003) *Are Italians White? How race is made in America*, New York: Routledge.

Guglielmo, T. (2003) 'Rethinking Whiteness historiography: the case of Italians in Chicago, 1890–1945', in Doane and Bonilla-Silva (eds), pp. 49–61.

Gwaltney, J. (1980) *Drylongso: a self-portrait of Black America*, New York: Vintage.

Hage, G. (2000) *White Nation: fantasies of white supremacy in a multicultural society*, London and New York: Routledge.

Halfacree, K. (1996) 'Out of place in the country: travellers and the "rural idyll" ', *Antipode* 28(1): 42–72.

Hall, C. (1992) *White, Male and Middle Class: explorations in feminism and history*, Cambridge: Cambridge University Press.

Hall, S., Critcher, C., Clarke, J., Jefferson, A. and Robert, B. (1978) *Policing the Crisis Mugging, the State and Law and Order*, London: Palgrave.

Halter, Marilyn (1993) *Between Race and Ethnicity: Cape Verdean American immigrants, 1860–1965*, Chicago: University of Illinois Press.

Hanchard, M. (1998) *Orpheus and Power: the Movimento Negro of Rio de Janeiro and São Paulo, Brazil, 1945–1988*, Princeton, NJ: Princeton University Press.

—— (ed.) (1999) *Racial Politics in Contemporary Brazil*, Durham, NC: Duke University Press.

Haney-López, I. (1996) *White by Law: the legal construction of race*, New York: New York University Press.

Harris, A. (2005) 'Consider migrants' personal situation says poll', *Sunday Independent*, 3 April.

Harris, C. (1993) 'Whiteness as property', *Harvard Law Review* 106(8): 1707–1791.

Harris, T. (1999) 'White men as performers in the lynching ritual', in Roediger, *Black on White*, pp. 299–304.

Hartigan, J. (1997a) 'Locating White Detroit', in Frankenberg (ed.), pp. 180–213.

—— (1997b) 'Name calling: objectifying "Poor Whites" and "White Trash" in Detroit', in Wray and Newitz (eds), pp. 41–56.

—— (1999) *Racial Situations: class predicaments of whiteness in Detroit*, Princeton, NJ: Princeton University Press.

—— (2005) *Odd Tribes: toward a cultural analysis of white people*, Durham, NC: Duke University Press.

Haughey, N. (2003) 'Residents of limbo', *Irish Times Weekend*, 7 June.

Hawes, D. (1996) *The Gypsy and the State: the ethnic cleansing of British society*, Bristol: Policy Press.

Haylett , C. (2001) 'Illegitimate subjects?: abject Whites, neo-liberal modernisation and middle class multiculturalism', *Environment and Planning D: Society and Space* 19(3): 351–370.

Hayward, K. and Yar, M. (2005) 'The "chav" phenomenon: consumption, media and the construction of a new underclass', *Crime, Media and Society* 2(1): 9–28.

Heath, T., Jeffries, R. and Pearce, S. (2006) *Asylum Statistics United Kingdom 2005: Home Office Statistical Bulletin*, London: Home Office, 10.

Helleiner, J. (2000) *Irish Travellers: racism and the politics of culture*, Toronto: University of Toronto Press.

Henwood, D. (1997) 'Trash-o-nomics', in Wray and Newitz (eds), pp. 177–191.

Herman, A. (1999) *The Better Angels of Capitalism*, Boulder, CO: Westview Press.

Hewitt, R. (2005) *White Backlash and the Politics of Multiculturalism*, Cambridge: Cambridge University Press.

Hickman, M. (1998) 'Reconstructing deconstructing "race": British political discourses about the Irish in Britain', *Ethnic and Racial Studies* 21(2): 288–307.

Hickman, M., Morgan, S., Walter, B. and Bradley, J. (2005) 'The limitations of whiteness and the boundaries of Englishness: second-generation Irish identifications and positionings in multiethnic Britain', *Ethnicities* 5(2): 160–182.

Hill, M. (2004) *After Whiteness: unmaking an American majority*, New York: NYU Press.

Hill-Collins, P. (1990) *Black Feminist Thought*, New York: Routledge.

Hoggart, R. (1957) *The Uses of Literacy: aspects of working-class life with special reference to publications and entertainments*, London: Chatto and Windus.

Hoggett, P. (1992) 'A place for experience: a psychoanalytic perspective on boundary, identity and culture', *Environment and Planning D: Society and Space* 10: 345–356.

Hoggett, P., Jeffers, S. and Harrison, L. (1996) 'Race, ethnicity and community in three localities', *New Community* 22(10): 111–125.

Holmes, C. (1979) *Anti-semitism in Britain, 1876–1939*, London: Holmes and Meier.

Holloway, S. (2003) 'Outsiders in rural society? Constructions of rurality and nature – society relations in the racialisation of English Gypsy-Travellers, 1869–1934', *Environment and Planning D: Space and Society* 21: 695–715.

—— (2005) 'Articulating otherness? White rural residents talk about Gypsy-Travellers', *Transactions* 30: 351–367.

Home Office (2005) *Making Migration Work for Britain: five-year strategy for asylum and immigration*, Norwich: HMSO.

hooks, b. (1992) 'Representing whiteness in the black imagination', in *Black Looks: race and representation*, Boston: South End Press.

—— (2000) *Where We Stand: class matters*, New York: Routledge.

Horsman, R. (1981) *Race and Manifest Destiny: the origins of American Anglo-Saxonism*, Cambridge: Cambridge University Press.

Howard, P. (2004) 'White privilege: for or against', *Race, Gender and Class* 11(4): 63–79.

Hubbard, P. (2005a) 'Accommodating otherness: anti-asylum centre protest and the maintenance of white privilege', *Transactions of the Institute of British Geographers* 30: 52–65.

—— (2005b) ' "Inappropriate and incongruous": opposition to asylum centres in the English countryside', *Journal of Rural Studies* 21: 3–17.

Hughes, L. (1947) *The Ways of White Folks*, New York: Alfred A. Knopf.

Ignatiev, N. (1996) *How the Irish Became White*, New York: Routledge.

—— (1997) 'The point is not to interpret Whiteness but to abolish it'. Online: <http://racetraitor.org/abolishthepoint.html>. Accessed 8 January 2007.

International Labor and Working Class History No. 60 Fall 2001, 'Scholarly controversy: whiteness and the historians' imagination'.

Irish Independent (1998) 'Pub loses licence for racist ban on woman', 23 October.

Irish Times (1998) 'Dealing with immigration', 17 January.

Irish Times/MRBI (2000) *Political Issues*, April.

Jacobson, M. (1995) *Special Sorrows: the diasporic imagination of Irish, Polish and Jewish immigrants in the United States*, Cambridge, MA: Harvard University Press.

—— (1998) *Whiteness of a Different Color: European immigrants and the alchemy of race*, Cambridge, MA: Harvard University Press.

—— (2006) *Roots Too: White ethnic revival in post-Civil Rights America*, Cambridge, MA: Harvard University Press.

Jay, E. (1992) *'Keep them in Birmingham': challenging racism in South West England*, London: CRE.

Johnson, H. and Shapiro, T. (2003) 'Good neighborhoods, good schools: race and the "good choices" of White families', in Doane and Bonilla-Silva (eds), pp. 173–188.

Jones, D.M. (1997) 'Darkness made visible: law, metaphor and the racial self', in Delgado and Stefancic (eds), pp. 66–78.

Jones, J. (2004) 'The impairment of empathy in goodwill Whites for African Americans', in Yancy (ed.), pp. 65–86.

Jordan, W. (1968) *White over Black: American attitudes toward the Negro, 1550–1812*, Chapel Hill: University of North Carolina Press.

Joseph, G. (2000) 'Taking race seriously: Whiteness in Argentina's national and transnational imaginary', *Identity* 7(3): 333–371.

Katz, M. (1989) *The Undeserving Poor: from war on poverty to war on welfare*, New York: Pantheon Books.

—— (1998) *In the Shadow of the Poorhouse: a social history of welfare in America*, New York: Basic Books.

Kaufman, E. (2006a) 'The dominant ethnic moment: towards the abolition of "Whiteness"?', *Ethnicities* 6: 231–253.

—— (2006b) 'Whiteness – too blunt an instrument?: a reply to David Roediger', *Ethnicities* 6: 263–266.

Kaur, R. (2003) 'Westenders: Whiteness, women and sexuality in Southall', in J. Andall (ed.) *Gender and Migration in Contemporary Europe*, Oxford: Berg, pp. 199–222.

Kearney, M. (2005) 'Brown seeks out "British values" ', BBC News, 14 March. Online: <*http://news.bbc.co.uk/2/hi/programmes/newsnight/4347369.stm*>. Accessed 8 January 2007.

Kefalas, M. (2003) *Working-class Heroes: protecting home, community and nation in a Chicago neighborhood*, Berkeley: UCLA Press.

Kelleher, O. (2003) 'Nigerian woman may sue State over five nights in jail', *Irish Times*, 8 February.

Kendall, F. (2006) *Understanding White Privilege: creating pathways to authentic relationships across race*, New York: Routledge.

Kenrick, D. and Puxon, G. (1972) *The Destiny of Europe's Gypsies*, Oxford: Heinemann Educational for Sussex University Press.

Keogh, D. (1998) *Jews in Twentieth-Century Ireland: refugees, anti-semitism and the Holocaust*, Cork: Cork University Press.

Kershen, A. (2005) 'The 1905 Aliens Act', *History Today* 55(3): 13–19.

Kiely, G. (ed.) (1999) *Irish Social Policy in Context*, Dublin: University College of Dublin Press.

Kirby, P. (2002) *The Celtic Tiger in Distress: growth with inequality on Ireland*, London: Palgrave.

Knowles, C. (2003) *Race and Social Analysis*, London: Sage.

—— (2004) 'Living with ghosts: an exploration of white Britishness in post-colonial Hong Kong', Paper presented to the American Sociological Association Annual Conference, 22 November.

—— (2005) 'Making Whiteness: British lifestyle migrants in Hong Kong', in C. Alexander and C. Knowles (eds) *Making Race Matter*, Basingstoke: Palgrave, pp. 90–110.

Knox, R. (1850) *The Races of Men: a philosophical inquiry into the influence of race over destinies of nations*.

Kolchin, P. (2002) 'Whiteness studies: the new history of race in America', *Journal of American History* 89: 154–173.

Konetzke, R. (1958–62) *Colección de documentos para la historia de la formación social de hispanoamérica, 1493–1810*, Madrid: Consejo Superior de investigaciónes científicas, 5 vols.

Kuethe, Allen (1986) *Cuba, 1753–1815: Crown, Military and Society*, Knoxville: University of Tennessee Press.

Kushner, T. (2005) 'Racialization and "White European" immigration to Britain', in K. Murji and J. Solomos (eds) *Racialization: studies in theory and practice*, Oxford: Oxford University Press, pp. 207–225.

Laclau, E. and Mouffe, C. (1985) *Hegemony and Socialist Strategy Towards a Radical Democratic Politics*, London: Verso.

Lambert, D. (2005a) 'Producing/contesting whiteness: rebellion, antislavery and enslavement in Barbados, 1816', *Geoforum* 36: 29–43.

—— (2005b) *White Creole Culture, Politics and Identity During the Age of Abolition*, Cambridge: Cambridge University Press

Lamont, M. (2000) *The Dignity of Working Men*, Cambridge, MA: Harvard University Press.

Lamont, M. and Lareau, A. (1998) 'Cultural capital: allusions, gaps and glissandos in recent, theoretical developments', *Sociological Theory* 6: 153–168.

Law, I. (2002) *Race in the News*, London: Palgrave.

Lea, S. and Lynn, N. (2004) 'A phantom menace and the new apartheid: the social construction of asylum seekers in the United Kingdom', *Discourse and Society* 14(4): 425–452.

Lentin, R. (2001) 'Responding to the racialization of Irishness: disavowed multiculturalism and its discontents', *Sociological Research Online* 5(4).

—— (2003) 'Pregnant silence: (en)gendering Ireland's asylum space', *Patterns of Prejudice* 37(3): 301–322.

—— (2004) 'From racial state to racist state: Ireland on the eve of the citizenship referendum', *Variant* 2(20): 7–8.

—— (2006) 'From racial state to racist state? Racism and immigration in twenty first century Ireland', in A. Lentin and R. Lentin (eds) *Race and State*, Cambridge: Cambridge Scholars' Press, pp. 187–206.

Lentin, R. and McVeigh, R. (eds) (2002) *Racism and Anti-racism in Ireland*, Belfast: Beyond the Pale.

—— (2006) *After Optimism? Ireland, racism and globalisation*, Dublin: Metro Eireann.

Lerner, M. (1993) 'Jews are not White', *Village Voice* (38), 18 May, pp. 33–34.

Lewis, M. (2005) *Asylum: understanding public attitudes*, London: Institute for Public Policy Research.

Lewis, P. (2006) 'Hanoi to Haddon services – life and death of a stowaway', *Guardian*, 27 May.

Lipsitz, G. (1995) 'The possessive investment in Whiteness: racialized social democracy and the "White" problem in American studies', *American Quarterly* 47(3): 369–387.

—— (1998) *The Possessive Investment in Whiteness: how white people profit from identity politics*, Philadelphia: Temple University Press.

Lloyd, D. (1999) *Ireland After History*, Cork: Cork University Press.

Lobe *v.* Minister of Justice, Equality and Law Reform (2003) *IESC 3* (23 January 2003). Online: <http://www.bailii.org/ie/cases/IESC/2003/3.html>.

Loyal, S. (2003) 'Welcome to the Celtic Tiger: racism, immigration and the state', in C. Coulter and S. Coleman (eds) *The End of Irish History? Critical reflections on the Celtic Tiger*, Manchester: Manchester University Press, pp. 74–94.

Luibhéid, E (1997) 'Irish immigrants in the United States' racial system', in J. Mac Laughlin (ed.), pp. 253–273.

—— (2004) 'Childbearing against the state? Asylum seeker women in the Irish Republic', *Women's Studies International Forum* 27: 335–349.

Lukács, G. (1971) *History and Class Consciousness*, Boston: MIT Press.

Mac an Ghaill, M. (2001) 'British critical theorists: the production of the conceptual invisibility of the Irish diaspora', *Social Identities* 7(2): 178–202.

Mac Einri, P. (2006) ' "A slice of Africa": whose side were we on? Ireland and the anticolonial struggle', in A. Lentin and R. Lentin (eds) *Race and State*, Cambridge: Cambridge Scholars' Press, pp. 255–273.

McDonald, K. (2004) 'Understanding Jewish influence', *Occidental Quarterly*, Washington: Summit Publishers.

McGréil, M. (1996) *Prejudice in Ireland Revisited*, St Patrick's College: NUI Maynooth.

McIntosh, P. (1988) 'White privilege and male privilege: a personal account of coming to see correspondences through work in Women's Studies', Working Paper 189, Wellesley College.

McKenna, G. (1999) 'New row over refugees deepens Cabinet rift', *Irish Independent*, 15 November.

McKinney, K. (2005) *Being White: stories of race and racism*, New York: Routledge.

—— (2006) ' "I really felt White": turning points in whiteness through interracial contact', *Social Identities* 12(2): 167–185.

Mac Laughlin, J. (1995) *Travellers and Ireland: Whose country? Whose history?* Cork: Cork University Press.

—— (ed.) (1997) *Location and Dislocation in Contemporary Irish Society*, Cork: Cork University Press.

McVeigh, R. (1992) 'The specificities of Irish racism', *Race and Class* 33(4): 31–45.

—— (1998a) ' "There's no racism because there's no Black people here": racism and antiracism in Northern Ireland', in P. Hainsworth (ed.) *Divided Society: ethnic minorities and racism in Northern Ireland*, London: Pluto, pp. 11–32.

McVeigh, R. (1998b) 'Irish Travellers and the logic of genocide', in M. Peillon and E. Slater (eds) *Encounters: a sociological chronicle of Ireland, 1995–96*, Dublin: Institute of Public Administration, pp. 155–162.

Maglen, K. (2005) 'Importing trachoma: the introduction into Britain of American ideas of an "immigrant disease", 1892–1906', *Immigrants and Minorities* 23(1): 80–99.

Malkki, L. (1995) 'Refugees and exile: from "Refugee Studies" to the national order of things', *Annual Review of Anthropology* 24: 495–523.

Man, A. (1951) 'Labor competition and the New York Draft Riots of 1863', *The Journal of Negro History* 36(4): 375–405.

Marriott, J. and Matsumura, E. (eds) (1999) *The Metropolitan Poor: semifactual accounts, 1795–1910*, London: Pickering and Chatto.

Marx, A. (1998) *Making Race and Nation: a comparison of South Africa, the United States and Brazil*, Cambridge: Cambridge University Press.

Massey, D. and Denton, N. (1988) 'The dimensions of residential segregation', *Social Forces* 67(2): 281–315.

—— (1994) *American Apartheid: segregation and the making of the underclass*, Cambridge, MA: Harvard University Press.

Mayall, D. (1988) *Gypsy-Travellers in Nineteenth-century Society*, New York: Cambridge University Press.

Mayhew, H. (1967 [1861]) *London Labour and the London Poor: A cyclopaedia of the condition and earnings of those that will work, those that cannot work, and those that will not work*, New York: A.M. Kelley.

Miles, R. (1982) *Racism and Migrant Labour*, London: Routledge.

—— (1989) *Racism*, London: Routledge.

—— (1993) *Racism after 'Race Relations'*, London: Routledge.

Miles, R. and Phizacklea, A. (1984) *White Man's Country: racism in British politics*, London: Pluto.

Miller, D. (1987) *Material Culture and Mass Consumption*, Oxford: Blackwell.

Miller, K. (1969) 'Green over Black: the origins of Irish-American racism, 1800–1863', MA dissertation paper, University of California-Berkeley.

—— (1985) *Emigrants and Exiles: Ireland and the Irish Exodus to North America*, New York: Oxford University Press.

Mills, C.W. (1997) *The Racial Contract*, Ithaca, NY: Cornell University Press.

—— (1998) *Blackness Visible: essays on philosophy and race*, Ithaca, NY: Cornell University Press.

—— (2003a) 'White supremacy as a sociopolitical system: a philosophical perspective', in Doane and Bonilla-Silva (eds), pp. 35–48.

—— (2003b) *From Class to Race: essays in White Marxism and Black radicalism*, Oxford: Rowman and Littlefield.

—— (2004) 'Racial exploitation and the wages of Whiteness', in Yancy (ed.), pp. 25–54.

Modell, D. (dir.) (2004) *'Keep Them Out'*, Channel 4, 6 May.

Modood, T. (2005) *Multicultural Politics: racism, ethnicity and Muslims in Britain*, Edinburgh: Edinburgh University Press.

Moore, B. (1975) 'The social impact of Portuguese immigration into British

Guiana after emancipation', *Boletin de estudios latinamericanos y del caribe* (19): 3–18.

Moraga, C. (1983) 'La Güera', in G. Anzaldúa and C. Moraga (eds) *This Bridge Called my Back: writings by radical women of color*, New York: Kitchen Table/ Women of Color, pp. 24–33.

Moran, A. (2005) *Australia: nation, belonging and globalization*, London: Routledge.

Moreton-Robinson, A. (2005a) 'The house that Jack built: Britishness and White possession', *ACRAWSA Journal* 1: 21–29.

—— (2005b) 'The possessive logic of patriarchal white sovereignty: the High Court and the Yorta Yorta decision'. Online: <*http://www.borderlandsejournal. adelaide.edu.au/vol3no2_2004/moreton_possessive.htm*>.

Morris, E. (2005) 'From "middle class" to "trailer trash": teachers' perceptions of White students in a predominantly minority school', *Sociology of Education* 78: 99–121.

Morrison, T. (1987) *Beloved*, New York: Alfred Knopf.

—— (1993) *Playing in the Dark: whiteness and the literary imagination*, New York: Vintage.

Morton, S. (1839) *Crania Americana: a comparative view of the skulls of various aboriginal natives of North and South America, to which is prefixed an essay on the variety of human species*, Philadelphia: J. Dobson.

Mullen, P. (2001) 'Different words and words of difference', *Focus* 64: 28.

Murphy, S. (2001) 'From a Black Irishwoman's perspective', *Focus* 64: 19–20.

NAACP/CLP (2006) 'Death Row USA: Summer 2006', Online: <*http://www.death-penaltyinfo.org/DRUSA%20Summer%202006.pdf*>

Naipaul, V.S. (1969) *The Middle Passage*, London: Penguin.

Nath, D. (1950) *The History of Indians in British Guiana*, London: self-published.

Nayak, A. (2003) 'Ivory lives: economic restructuring and the making of White-ness in a post-industrial Youth Community', *European Journal of Cultural Studies* 6(3): 305–325.

NCCRI/Equality Authority (2003) 'Case study: media coverage of refugee and asylum seekers, Raxen 3', Dublin: NCCRI/Equality Authority.

Neal, S. (2002) 'Rural landscapes, representations and racism: examining multi-cultural citizenship and policy-making in the English countryside', *Ethnic and Racial Studies* 25(3): 442–461.

Neal, S. and Agyemang, J. (eds) (2006) *The New Countryside? Ethnicity, nation and exclusion in contemporary rural Britain*, Bristol: Policy Press.

Nic Suibhne, M. (1998) 'Fortress Ireland', *Guardian Weekend*, 3 October.

Ní Shuínéar, S. (1994) 'Irish Travellers, ethnicity and the origins question', in M. McCann, S. Ó Síocháin and J. Ruane (eds) *Irish Travellers: culture and ethnicity*, Belfast: Queens University Press, pp. 54–77.

—— (2002) 'Othering the Irish (Travellers)', in Lentin and McVeigh (eds), pp. 177–192.

Office of the Deputy Prime Minister (ODPM) (2004) *Gypsy and Traveller Sites, Vol. 1: Thirteenth Report of session 2003–04*, London: HMSO.

Okely, J. (1983) *The Traveller Gypsies*, Cambridge: Cambridge University Press.

Oliver, M. and Shapiro, T. (1997) *Black Wealth/White Wealth: a new perspective on racial inequality*, New York: Routledge.

Omi, M. and Winant, H. (1994) *Racial Formation in the USA: from the 1960s to the 1980s*, New York: Routledge.

Parekh, B. (2000) *Rethinking Multiculturalism: cultural diversity and political theory*, London: Macmillan.

Parkin, C. (2000) 'Court orders release of detained businessmen held in jail after airport immigration mix up', *Irish Examiner*, 28 November.

Paulin, T. (2000) 'Frozen out by the Irish', *Guardian*, 29 August.

Paynter, R. (2001) 'The cult of Whiteness in Western New England', in C. Orser (ed.) *Race and the Archaeology of Identity*, Salt Lake City: University of Utah Press, pp. 125–142.

Pearson, N. (2003) 'The High Court's abandonment of "the time-honoured methodology of the Common Law" in its interpretation of native title', in *Mirriuwung Gajerrong* and *Yorta Yorta' Australian Indigenous Law Reporter*, 15. Online: *<http://www.austlii.edu.au/au/journals/AILR/2003/15.html>*.

Phillips, D. (2001) 'Community citizenship and community social quality: the British Jewish community at the turn of the twentieth century', *European Journal of Social Quality* (3)1/2: 26–47.

Phoenix, A. (1996) ' "I'm white – so what?" The construction of whiteness for young Londoners', in Fine *et al.* (eds), pp. 187–197.

Pierce, J. (2003) ' "Racing for innocence": Whiteness, corporate culture and the backlash against affirmative action', in Doane and Bonilla-Silva (eds), pp. 199–214.

Pilgrim House Foundation (1998) *Asylum Seekers and Prejudice Study*, Inch, Co. Wexford: Pilgrim House.

—— (1999) *Characteristics and Experience of Asylum Seekers in Ireland*, Inch, Co.Wexford: Pilgrim House.

Potter, J. and Wetherell, M. (1992) *Mapping the Language of Racism: discourse and the legitimation of exploitation*, London: Harvester.

Powell, F. (1992) *The Politics of Irish Social Policy 1600–1900*, New York: Edwin Mellen Press.

Premdas, R. (1995) *Ethnic Conflict and Development: the case of Guyana*, Avebury, Aldershot: UNRISD.

Public Affairs News (2000) 'Refugees', Policy "Shambles" ', February, p. 8.

Queenan, J. (2007) 'A whiter shade of guile', *Guardian*, 5 January.

Quintanilla, M. (2003) 'Planters on the West Indian frontier: British settlement of the ceded islands, 1763–1779'. Paper presented at the Irish Society of Geographers' annual conference, 2 May.

Radcliffe, S. and Westwood, S. (1996) *Remaking the Nation: place, identity and politics in Latin America*, London: Routledge.

Rafter, N. (1988) *White Trash: The Eugenic Family Studies, 1899–1919*, Boston, MA: Northeastern University Press.

Rahier, J.M. (1998) 'Blackness, the racial/spatial order, migrations and Miss Ecuador 1995–96', *American Anthropologist* 100(2): 421–430.

Reay, D. (1998) 'Engendering social reproduction: mothers in the educational marketplace', *British Journal of Sociology of Education* 19(2): 195–209.

Reay, D., James, D., Crozier, G., etc. (forthcoming, *Sociology*).

Robinson, C. (1982) *Black Marxism: the making of the Black radical tradition*, Chapel Hill, NC: University of North Carolina Press.

Rodriguez, J. (2006) *Civilizing Argentina: science, medicine, and the modern state*, Chapel Hill, NC: University of North Carolina Press.

Roediger, D. (1991)*The Wages of Whiteness: race and the making of the American working class*, London: Verso.

—— (1999) *Black on White: black writers on what it means to be white*, New York: Schocken.

Rolston, W. (2003) 'Frederick Douglass: a black abolitionist in Ireland', *History Today* 53(6): 45–51.

Rowe, M. (1998) *The Racialisation of Disorder*, Aldershot: Ashgate.

Saxton, A. (1990) *The Rise and Fall of the White Republic: class politics and mass culture in nineteenth century America*, New York: Verso.

Schlesinger, A. (1988 [1945]) *The Age of Jackson*, Boston: Little, Brown.

Schubert, G. (1981) 'To be Black is offensive: racist attitudes in San Lorenzo', in N. Whitten (ed.) *Cultural Transformations in Modern Ecuador*, Chicago: University of Illinois Press, pp. 563–588.

Schuster, L. (2002) 'Asylum and the lessons of history', *Race and Class* 44(2): 40–56.

Segrest, M. (1994) *Memoir of a Race Traitor*, Boston: South End Press.

Seshadri-Crooks, K. (2000) *Desiring Whiteness: a Lacanian analysis of race*, London: Routledge.

Shaw, W. (2006) 'Decolonising geographies of Whiteness', *Antipode* 38(4): 851–869.

Sheriff, R. (2001) *Dreaming Equality: color, race and racism in urban Brazil*, New Jersey: Rutgers University Press.

Shiells, G. (2006) 'A different shade of White', *National Library of Australia News*, August. Online: <*http://www.nla.gov.au/pub/nlanews/2006/aug06/article4.html*>. Accessed on 8 January 2007.

Sibley, D. (1995) *Geographies of Exclusion: society and difference in the West*, London: Routledge.

Sigona, N. (2005) 'Locating "The Gypsy Problem" – the Roma in Italy: stereotyping, labelling and "Nomad Camps" ', *Journal of Ethnic and Migration Studies* 31(4): 741–756.

Silke, J. (1976) 'The Irish abroad, 1534–1691', in T.W Moody *et al.* (eds) *A New History of Ireland*, vol. 3, pp. 591–633.

Skeggs, B. (1995) 'Women's studies in Britain in the 1990s – entitlement cultures and institutional constraints', *Women's Studies International Forum* 18(4): 475–485.

—— (1997) *Formations of Class and Gender: becoming respectable*, London: Routledge.

Skidmore, T. (1993) 'Bi-racial U.S.A. vs. multi-racial Brazil: is the contrast still valid?', *Journal of Latin American Studies* 25(2): 373–386.

Small, S. (1994) *Racialised Barriers: the Black experience in the United States and England in the 1980s*, London: Routledge.

Smith, R. (1999) *Civic Ideals: conflicting visions of citizenship in U.S. history*, New Haven: Yale University Press.

Smyth, K. (2002) 'Asylum seekers plagued by legally questionable ID arrests', *Irish Examiner*, 4 January.

Solomos, J. and Murji, K. (eds) (2005) *Racialization: studies in theory and practice*, Oxford: Oxford University Press.

Squire, V. (2005) ' "Integration with diversity in modern Britain": New Labour on nationality, immigration and asylum', *Journal of Political Ideologies* 10(1): 51–74.

Stepan, N. (1991) *The Hour of Eugenics: race, gender, and nation in Latin America*, Ithaca, NY: Cornell University Press.

Stern, A.M. (2003) 'From Mestizophilia to biotypology: racialization and science in Mexico, 1920–1960', in Appelbaum *et al.*, pp. 187–206.

Stevens, D. (2004) *UK Asylum Law and Policy: historical and contemporary perspectives*, London: Sweet and Maxwell.

Stoddard, W. (1922) *Revolt Against Civilization*, New York: Scribner.

Stutzman, R. (1981) 'El Mestizaje. An all inclusive ideology', in N. Whitten (ed.) *Cultural Transformations in Modern Ecuador*, Chicago: University of Illinois Press, pp. 45–94.

Sweeney, F. (2001) ' "The republic of letters": Frederick Douglass, Ireland, and the Irish narratives', *Eire-Ireland*, Spring–Summer.

Tavan, G. (2005) *The Long Slow Death of White Australia*, Carlton, VA: Scribe.

Taylor, G. (2005) *Buying Whiteness: race, culture, and identity from Columbus to hip hop*, London: Palgrave.

Thorsen, K. (dir.) (1990) *James Baldwin: the price of the ticket*, California Newsreel Films.

Tinker, H. (1974) *A New System of Slavery*, Oxford: Oxford University Press.

Trelease, A. (1971) *White Terror: the Ku Klux Klan conspiracy and Southern reconstruction*, New York: Harper and Row.

Twinam, A. (2004) 'Purchasing whiteness: some revisionist thoughts'. Paper presented at Vacara (Virginia-Carolinas-Georgia Colonialists group), Vanderbilt University, Nashville, TN, April 2–3.

—— (2005) 'Racial passing: informal and official "Whiteness" in Colonial Spanish America', in J. Smolenski and T. Humphrey (eds) *New World Orders Violence, Sanction, and Authority in the Colonial Americas*, Philadelphia: University of Pennsylvania Press, pp. 249–272.

—— (2006) 'Purchasing Whiteness: conversations on the essence of pardo-ness and Mulatto-ness at the end of Empire'. Paper presented at Lockmiller seminar, Emory University, 29 March.

Tyler, K. (2003) 'The racialised and classed constitution of village life', *Ethnos* 68(3): 391–412.

—— (2004) 'Reflexivity, tradition and racism in a former mining town', *Ethnic and Racial Studies* 27(2): 290–302.

—— (2006) 'Village people: race, class, nation and community spirit', in Neal and Agyemang (eds), pp. 129–148.

UNHCR (2006) *Global Refugee Trends 2005*, Geneva: UNHCR.

Vanderbeck, R. (2003) 'Youth, racism and place in the Tony Martin affair', *Antipode* 35(2): 363–384.

Vera, H. and Gordon, A. (2003a) *Screen Saviours: Hollywood fictions of whiteness*, Lanham, MD: Rowman and Littlefield.

—— (2003b) 'The beautiful American: sincere fictions of the White Messiah in Hollywood movies', in Doane and Bonilla-Silva (eds), pp. 113–125.

Verdicchio, P. (1997) *Bound by Distance: rethinking nationalism through the Italian diaspora*, Madison, NJ: Fairleigh Dickinson University Press.

Wade, P. (1997) *Race and Ethnicity in Latin America*, London: Pluto.

—— (2001) 'Racial identity and nationalism: a theoretical view from Latin America', *Ethnic and Racial Studies* 24(5): 845–865.

Wagner, M. (1977) 'Rum policy and the Portuguese, or the maintenance of élite supremacy in post-emancipation British Guiana', *Canadian Review of Sociology and Anthropology* 14(4): 406–416.

Walter, B. (1998) *Outsiders Inside: whiteness, place and Irish women*, London: Routledge.

Ware, V. (1992) *Beyond the Pale: White women, racism and history*, London: Verso.

Watt, P. (1998) 'Going out of town: youth, "race", and place in the South East of England', *Environment and Planning D: Society and Space* 16: 687–703.

Watt, P. and Stenson, K. (1998) 'The street: "It's a bit dodgy around there": safety, danger, ethnicity and young people's use of public space', in T. Skelton and G. Valentine (eds) *Cool Places: geographies of youth cultures*, London: Routledge, pp. 249–266.

Weinkopf, C. (2003) 'Whiteness studies', *FrontPage Magazine*. Online: <*http://www.frontpagemag.com/Articles/ReadArticle.asp?ID618565*>. Accessed 3 January 2007.

Weinstein, B. (2003) 'Racializing regional difference: São Paulo versus Brazil, 1932', in Appelbaum *et al.*, pp. 237–262.

Weis, M. and Fine, M. (1996) 'Narrating the 1980s and 1990s: voices of poor and working-class White and African-American men', *Anthropology and Education Quarterly* 27(4): 493–516.

Weis, M., Proweller, A. and Centrie, C. (1996) 'Re-examining "a moment in history": loss of privilege inside White working-class masculinity in the 1990s', in M. Fine, L. Powell, M. Weis and L. Mun Wong (eds) *Off White: readings on race, power and society*, New York: Routledge, pp. 210–226.

Wells, S. and Watson, K. (2005) 'A politics of resentment: shopkeepers in a London neighbourhood', *Ethnic and Racial Studies* 28(2): 261–277.

White, A. (2002) 'Geographies of asylum, legal knowledge and legal practices', *Political Geography* 21(8): 1055–1073.

White, L. (2002) 'This ghetto is the home of a racial minority in Oldham: its residents are White people', *Sunday Times Magazine*, 13 January, pp. 46–54.

Wildman, S. (1997) 'Reflections on Whiteness: the case of Latinos(as)', in Delgado and Stefancic (eds), pp. 323–326.

Williams, R. (1973) *The Town and the Country*, Oxford: Oxford University Press.

Winant, H. (1994) *Racial Conditions: politics, theory, comparisons*, Minneapolis: University of Minnesota Press.

—— (1997) 'Behind blue eyes: Whiteness and contemporary U.S. racial politics', *New Left Review* 225: 73–88.

—— (2001) 'White racial projects', in Brander Rasmussen *et al.*, pp. 97–112.

Winddance Twine, F. (1998) *Racism in a Racial Democracy: the maintenance of white supremacy in Brazil*, New Brunswick, NJ: Rutgers University Press.

Wistrich, R. (1992) *Antisemitism: the longest hatred*, New York: Pantheon Books.

Wray, M. (2006) *Not Quite White: White trash and the boundaries of Whiteness*, Durham, NC: Duke University Press.

Wray, M. and Newitz, A. (eds) (1997) *White Trash: race and class in America*, New York: Routledge.

Wright, R. (1957) *White Man, Listen!*, Garden City, NY: Doubleday.

—— (1992 [1940]) *Native Son*, New York: Harper and Row.

Yancy, G. (ed.) (2004) *What White Looks Like: African-American philosophers on the Whiteness question*, New York: Routledge.

York, B. (1990) *Empire and Race: the Maltese in Australia, 1881–1949*, Kensington, NSW: University of New South Wales Press.

—— (n.d) 'Maltese "prohibited immigrants" '. Online: <*www.maltamigration.com/history/maltese-australian/prohibited1.shtml?s615220567C-7D6905110654 615A92.shtml?s*>. Accessed 5 September 2006.

Young, R.J.C. (1995) *Colonial Desire: hybridity in theory, culture and race*, London: Routledge.

—— (2001) 'The linguistic turn, materialism and race: toward an aesthetics of crisis', *Callaloo* 24(1): 334–345.

Zaretsky, R. (1996) 'Fascism: the wrong idea in Virginia', *Quarterly Review* 72(1). Online: <*http://www.vqronline.org/articles/1996/winter/zaretsky-fascism-wrong-idea/*>. Accessed 12 September 2006.

Zizek, S. (1989) *The Sublime Object of Ideology*, London: Verso.

Index